Management and Organisation

2nd edition

BANKERS WORKBOOK SERIES

LIZ CROFT BA, MBA, ACIS

Revised with additional material by
Brian Stone BA, Dip BAdmin, Dip CAM, FCIB, FRSA

First published in 1991
Reprinted 1992
2nd edition 1994
3rd edition 1996

BANKERS BOOKS LIMITED
c/o The Chartered Institute of Bankers
10 Lombard Street
London EC3V 9AS

CIB Publications are published by The Chartered Institute of Bankers, a non-profit making registered educational charity, and are distributed exclusively by Bankers Books Limited which is a wholly owned subsidiary of The Chartered Institute of Bankers.

ISBN 0–85297–412–4

Contents

vii

Introduction

The Concept of the Course

This is a practical workbook written for students studying for banking and finance qualifications and also for practitioners in the financial services who are looking for a practical refresher.

Each unit is divided into sections and contains:

- Learning objectives;
- Clear, concise topic-by-topic coverage;
- Examples and learning activities to reinforce learning, confirm understanding and stimulate thought;
- Often, past examination questions to try for practice;
- Self-assessment questions to test your knowledge, understanding and skills.

Learning activities

Learning activities are provided throughout. These come in a variety of forms. For example, they:

- Test your ability to recall information, your ability to analyse material, or assess whether you have appreciated the full significance of a piece of information.
- Require discussion with colleagues, friends or fellow students.
- Require you to do some research.

Virtually all require you to record something in writing and you should keep your notes/answers for later reference.

Where the activity comprises a series of short questions, a reference is given to the precise part of the preceding text where you can find the answer. For others, where appropriate, a suggested answer/response/solution is given, but often in abbreviated form to help you avoid the temptation of merely reading the 'answer'! You will find our suggestions in the Appendix.

At the end of each unit there are self-assessment questions. These usually comprise a number of short answer questions and multiple-choice questions and, often, a full specimen examination question. The answers to all of these questions are also to be found in the Appendix.

Syllabus

The key sections of the Management and Organisation syllabus are:

- Management and Organisation in Context

- Managing People in Groups
- People in Organisations
- Management Theories, Processes and Practices
- Organisational Systems

Your contribution

Although this workbook is designed to stand alone, as with most topics, certain aspects of this subject are constantly changing. Therefore it is very important that you keep up-to-date with these key areas.

We anticipate that you will study this course for one academic year, reading through and studying approximately two units every three weeks. However, note that as topics vary in size and as knowledge tends not to fall into uniform chunks, some units are unavoidably longer than others.

The masculine pronoun 'he' has been used in this workbook to encompass both genders and to avoid the awkwardness of the constant repetition of 'he and/or she'.

Study Guide

Below we offer advice and ideas on studying, revising and approaching examinations.

Studying

As with any examination, there is no substitute for preparation based on an organised and disciplined study plan. You should devise an approach which will enable you to complete this workbook and still leave time for revision of this and any other subject you are taking at the same time. Many candidates find that about six weeks is about the right period of time to leave for revision, enough time to get through the revision material, but not so long that it is no longer fresh in your mind by the time you reach the examination.

This means that you should plan how to get to the last chapter by, say, the end of March for a May sitting or the end of August for an October sitting. This includes not only reading the text, but making notes, working through the student activities and answering any illustrative examination questions which are included.

We offer the following as a starting point for approaching your study.

- *Plan time each week* to study a part of this workbook. Make sure that it is 'quality' study time: let everyone know that you are studying and that you should not be disturbed. If you are at home, unplug your telephone or switch the answerphone on; if you are in the office, put you telephone on 'divert'.

- Set a *clearly defined objective* for each study period. You may simply wish to read through a unit for the first time or perhaps you may want to make some notes on a unit you have already read a couple of times. Don't forget the student activities, self-assessment questions and any examination questions.

- *Review your study plan.* Devise a study checklist and/or timetable so that you can schedule and monitor your progress. Don't panic if you fall behind, but do think how you will make up for lost time.

- Look for *relevant examples* of what you have covered in the 'real' world. If you work for a financial organisation, this should provide them. If you don't, then think about your experiences as an individual bank or building society customer or perhaps about your employer's position as a corporate customer of a bank. Keep an eye on the quality press for reports about banks and building societies and their activities.

Revising

The period which you have earmarked for revision is a very important. Now it is even more important that you plan *time each week for study* and that you set *clear objectives* for each revision session. So ...

- *Make use of a timetable.*

- *Use time sensibly.* How much revision time do you have? Remember that you still need to eat, sleep and fit in some leisure time!

- *How will you allocate the available time between subjects?* What are your weaker subjects? You will need to focus on some topics more than others. You will also need to plan your revision around your learning style. By now, you should know whether, for example, early morning, early evening or late evening is best.

- *Take regular breaks.* Most people find they can absorb more if they attempt to revise for long uninterrupted periods of time. Award yourself a five minute break every hour or so. Go for a stroll or make a cup of coffee, but don't turn the television on!

- *Believe in yourself.* Are you cultivating the right attitude of mind? There is absolutely no reason why you should not pass the exam if you adopt the correct approach. Be confident, you have passed exams before so you can pass this one.

The examination

Passing examinations is half about having the required knowledge, understanding and skills, and half about doing yourself justice in the examination. You must have the right *technique*.

The day of the exam

- Set at least one alarm (or get an alarm call) for a morning exam.

- Have something to eat but don't eat too much; you may feel sleepy if your system is digesting a large meal.

- Don't forget pens, pencils, rulers, erasers and anything else you will need.

- Avoid discussion about the exam with other candidates outside the exam hall.

Tackling the examination paper

First, make sure that you satisfy the examiner's requirements

- *Read the instructions on the front of the exam paper carefully.* Check that the exam format hasn't changed. It is surprising how often examiners' reports remark on the number of students who attempt too few – or too many – questions, or who attempt the wrong number of questions from different parts of the paper. Make sure that you are planning to answer the right number of questions.

- *Read all the questions on the exam paper before you start writing.* Look at the weighting of marks to each part of the question. If part (a) offers only four marks and you can't answer the 12 marks part (b), then don't choose the question.

- *Don't produce irrelevant answers.* Make sure you answer the question set, and not the question you would have preferred to have been set.

- *Produce an answer in the correct format.* The examiner will state the format in which the question should be answered, for example in a report or memorandum. If a question asks for a diagram or an example, give one. If a question does not specifically asks for a diagram or example, but it seems appropriate, give one.

Second, observe the following simple rules to ensure that your script is acceptable to the examiner.

- *Present a tidy paper.* You are a professional and it should always show in the presentation of your work. Candidates may be penalised for poor presentation and so you must make sure that you write legibly, label diagrams clearly and lay out your work professionally. Assistant examiners each have dozens of papers to mark; a badly written scrawl is unlikely to receive the same attention as a neat and well laid out paper.

- *State the obvious.* Many candidates look for complexity which is not required and consequently overlook the obvious. Make basic statements first. Plan your answer and ask yourself whether you have answered the main parts of the question.

- *Use examples.* This will help to demonstrate to the examiner that you keep up-to-date with the subject. There are lots of useful examples scattered through this workbook and you can read about others if you dip into the quality press or take notice of what is happening in your working environment.

Finally, Make sure that you give yourself the opportunity to do yourself justice.

- *Select questions carefully.* Read through the paper once, then quickly jot down any key points against each question in a second read through. Reject those questions against which you have jotted down very little. Select those where you could latch on to 'what the question is about' – but remember to check carefully that you have got the right end of the stick before putting pen to paper.

- *Plan your attack carefully.* Consider the order in which you are going to tackle questions. It is a good idea to start with your best question to boost your morale and get some easy marks 'in the bag'.

- *Read the question carefully and plan your answer.* Read through the question again very carefully when you come to answer it.

- *Gain the easy marks.* Include the obvious if it answers the question and do not spend unnecessary time producing the perfect answer. As we suggested above, there is nothing wrong with stating the obvious.

- *Avoid getting bogged down in small parts of questions.* If you find a part of a question difficult, get on with the rest of the question. If you are having problems with something the chances are that everyone else is too.

- *Don't leave the exam early.* If you finish early, use your spare time to check and recheck your script.

Don't worry if you feel you have performed badly in the exam. It is likely that the other candidates will have found the exam difficult too. As soon as you get up and leave the exam hall, forget the exam and think about the next – or, if it is the last one, celebrate!

Don't discuss an exam with other candidates. This is particularly the case if you still have other exams to sit. Put it out of your mind until the day of the results. Forget about exams and relax.

Unit 1

The Concept and Nature of Organisations

Objectives

After studying this unit, you should be able to:

- **be able to define the word 'organisation';**

- **know what distinguishes an organisation from other human groups;**

- **appreciate the ways in which organisations affect our daily lives;**

- **explain how the study of organisations has been approached;**

- **begin to look at other issues which arise from thinking broadly about organisations.**

---

1   Introduction

1.1   Organisations are such a pervasive feature of our society that it is possible to take their presence for granted. They are apparent in our social, political and work environments and it appears to be virtually impossible to live in our society and not be influenced by them. Most of us are born in an organisation (a hospital), go to nursery, then school and finally work, all as part of an organisation. Western society is heavily dependent on activities organised by groups of people for their existence; for example, food and its preparation, health care, and education. As a society we appear to be limited not by individual intelligence or skills, but rather by our ability to work together in an organisation. The dominant role of organisations in our society has ensured that the study of organisations and of people in organisations has become an important area in its own right.

Student Activity 1

Think of some of the organisations already mentioned in the text, and the organisation for which you work. In a few words, try your own definition of the word 'organisation', thinking of all the things all organisations – not just profit-making ones – have in common.

Consider our comments when you have done this. (You will find our comments on the Student Activities in the Appendix.)

Keep all your responses to Student Activities, amended where appropriate, with this workbook or in your study file.

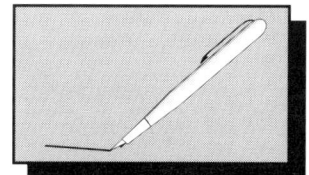

2 Definition of organisations

2.1   Before progressing further, it would be helpful to examine in more detail what we mean by the term 'organisations'. Many different suggestions can be provided.

2.2   Katz and Kahn state: 'An organisation is a social device for efficiently accomplishing through group means some stated purpose.'

2.3   Mullins says: 'There are however three common features in any organisation, people, objectives and structure. It is the interaction of people in order to achieve objectives that forms the basis of an organisation.'

2.4   Schein defines organisations as: 'The planned co-ordination of the activities of a number of people for the achievement of some common explicit purpose or goal, through the division of labour and function and through a hierarchy of authority and responsibility.'

Common features of the definitions

Social

2.5   Organisations are by necessity collections of individuals who interact with one another because of being members of a particular group. However, this feature could apply just as well to members of a family. Other features must also be present.

Performance

2.6   The performance of an organisation as a whole determines its survival and the performance required has to be clearly defined. If an organisation consistently fails to meet this standard, then it is likely that over a period of time it will not survive. Continued membership of an organisation by an individual also normally depends on an acceptable level of performance being achieved by that individual. To achieve this acceptable standard of performance, effort has to be co-ordinated and therefore controlled by someone. This necessitates the establishment of a structure for the organisation. This structure should have a clearly defined hierarchy of positions each with a greater or lesser degree of authority and power giving different levels of management. Each individual member of the group has a part to play in the achievement of these goals and so effort must be co-ordinated and the work divided amongst the individuals.

2.7   Today, there are two common interpretations of the word organisation. One is a reference to the *corporate body*, the other to the *way work is distributed in a group*. This word organisation is a key one for the syllabus, providing a link between its various parts. In the *first section* of the workbook we focus on the *organisation as a corporate entity*; in the *second* on the *self-organisation of managers* with project planning, etc, and in the *third* the *organisation of people and work groups*.

Student Activity 2

From the time you woke this morning, organisations have affected you in many ways: a radio alarm clock probably made by a Japanese company possibly played you music produced by a record company broadcast by the BBC before you were even properly awake.

Continue this exercise by listing at least 10 more organisations which will have affected you before you finished breakfast.

3   Organisational studies

3.1   The study of organisations as business units could be said to have begun in the 19th century when the Industrial Revolution saw the development of large-scale business units. These studies and later writings on organisations had as their basis the view that if certain principles of management or organisation were put into effect, then management would be more successful in ensuring the goals of that organisation were achieved in an effective manner. The aim of organisational studies today is still effectiveness and efficiency in the use of resources to achieve goals.

Classical and scientific management school

3.2   The first comprehensive group of thinkers and writers on organisations and management is termed the classical and scientific management school. The scientific management school believed an organisation should be an alliance of management and workers to increase efficiency and productivity and therefore profitability. One of its major writers was Taylor (1856–1915). He believed management should make a contribution to efficiency by applying certain scientific techniques and principles. Attention must be given to employees' attitudes (this is developed further in the next group of theorists, the human relations writers).

3.3   The classical school also had as one of its major writers Henri Fayol (1841–1925). He set out certain principles for structuring an organisation and other principles which management should follow to give maximum efficiency. From about the 1930s a group of theories were developed that emphasised the importance of human relations in organisations. Elton Mayo is seen as perhaps the first researcher in this school. His experiments at the Western Electric Company in Ohio took place between 1924 and 1932.

Scientific management and human relations school

3.4   The scientific management and human relations school were interested in increasing productivity in the workplace but their opinions about how to motivate people were quite different. Taylor emphasised the economic motive in work (pay) and Mayo the emotional and non-rational feelings in improving efficiency (feeling part of a group at work, etc).

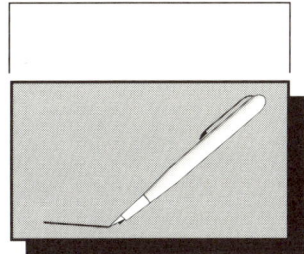

Student Activity 3

Name two industrial techniques, such as time-and motion studies, which follow Taylor in relating work to efficiency or to pay.

The 'systems' approach

3.5 The third approach to the study of organisations is termed the 'systems' approach. This emphasises the interdependence of the component parts of the organisation and encourages managers to learn from the experience of researchers in other disciplines. The importance of the environmental influence on a system is acknowledged. An important development of the systems school has been the socio-technical systems school. This presents the view that the behaviour of individuals in an organisation is significantly affected by the technology used.

Current approaches to the study of organisations

3.6 The three basic approaches to the study of organisations have been described; i.e. the scientific management school (classical), the human relations and the systems approaches. All these approaches will be explored in more detail in Unit 10. You should be aware that each approach constitutes a different attitude to organisations and how they function. In fact Koontz, O'Donnell and Weihrich cite 11 current approaches to the study of organisations. Each one is still being developed and could form the basis for future studies and the development of theory. You do not need to know the details of each different approach but you should have an idea of the range of approaches.

Empirical, or case approach

3.7 Management is studied from past experience in individual case histories. Generalisations are then drawn from the individual cases. Often the cases are used to support theoretical ideas.

Interpersonal behaviour approach

3.8 This is the study of human interactions within the organisation and is based on the belief that a knowledge of interpersonal relations will help managers to motivate their subordinates to do their work better. However, based on individual behaviour, it cannot provide general comment.

Mathematical or 'management science' approach

3.9 This approach takes the view that management is a task which can be aided by mathematical formulae and models, e.g. operational research, simulation. This approach is concerned with techniques that can aid management in solving their problems.

Contingency or situational approach

3.10 Developed by Lawrence and Lorsch (1967), this is described in greater detail in Unit 10.

The managerial roles approach

3.11 This approach observes what managers actually do and from this draws conclusions about what their jobs (or roles) are. Mintzberg moved away from the traditional view that the functions of management are planning, organising, co-ordinating and controlling, and suggested that management fills 10 roles, within three broad categories:

- Interpersonal roles:
  - the role as figurehead (to perform ceremonial and social duties as the organisation's representative);
  - the role as leader;
  - the role of liaison, especially with people outside the organisation.
- Informational roles:
  - receiving information about performance of the organisation's operations;
  - passing on information (to subordinates, etc);
  - transmitting information outside the organisation.
- Decision roles:
  - taking entrepreneurial decisions;
  - handling disturbances;
  - allocating resources to get jobs done;
  - negotiating (with persons or groups of people).

3.12   This approach is described in Unit 10 when we examine the role of the manager.

3.13   All these approaches summarised above are used in this course and feature in the examination.

4   The nature of organisations

4.1   Although there are many different approaches to the study of organisations, writers appear to agree that organisations have certain common features, i.e. they produce goods and services through collective effort.

4.2   The study of organisations raises many interesting issues:

- The environmental influences on the organisation;
- The competition they face, customer and employee expectations;
- The management of change in the organisation;
- How conflict in the organisation may be resolved;
- The culture and structure of the organisation;
- Communication in the organisation; and
- The role of individuals and groups in the organisation.

4.3   All these topics will be studied in greater detail in the workbook and the range of approaches and solutions to the problems explored.

Student Activity 4

For examination purposes, you would be well advised to choose a definition of an organisation written by a respected author. Some are quoted in this unit. Choose one from this selection, or from your outside studies, and be sure you can reproduce and discuss it. Learn it, and write a few sentences stating why you consider it a good definition.

Summary

Having studied this Unit carefully you should now:

● **be 'in possession' of a respected writer's definition of an 'organisation';**

● **be able to define the word 'organisation' yourself;**

● **know what distinguishes an organisation from other human groups;**

● **be able to discuss the myriad ways in which organisations affect our daily lives;**

● **have a basis for your further study of organisations;**

● **have understood that this study leads in many different directions.**

Self-assessment questions

1. What have you found that writers and researchers believe to be the main features of an organisation?

2. Which of the following are not an organisation, and why not?

   (a) Manchester City Football Club;

   (b) a bus queue;

   (c) your local hospital;

   (d) your employers;

   (e) the spectators at Wimbledon;

   (f) Granada TV Company.

3. In what way is your family an organisation?

4. Name a type of organisation which could easily be found over 1,000 years ago.

5. What are the three major approaches to the study of organisations? How do they largely differ?

6. List one organisation with which your organisation has some contact, under each of these headings:

   (a) suppliers;

   (b) governmental agencies;

   (c) customers;

   (d) industry bodies;

   (e) competitors.

7. 'Organisation' is derived from the Greek work 'organon' meaning 'tool'. Why do you think this is?

8. Why has there been no mention of 'profit' in this unit?

9. What were Mintzberg's three major categories of managerial role?

10. Suggest a way in which your organisation does not behave like an organisation, as it has been discussed in this Unit.

(The answers to these self-assessment questions, and those in the other units, are given in the Appendix.)

Unit 2

The Organisation and the Environment

Objective

After studying this unit, you should be able to:

- **have the basis for an environmental analysis of an organisation;**

- **know what major factors influence an organisation from outside;**

- **understand an organisation's social responsibility;**

- **be clear about internal as well as external environments.**

1 Introduction

1.1 Any business organisation exists in local, national and international contexts in which it finds its customers and from which it purchases its equipment, raw materials, recruits its staff and draws most of its ideas and knowledge. The environment is constantly changing and exerting influences of various types on the organisation. Some are beneficial, some detrimental. It is part of the skill of senior management in the organisation to be able to take advantage of the beneficial factors and counteract the harmful ones. This involves managing the change that is happening (explored in Units 3 and 22).

1.2 When discussing these environmental factors or influences they can for convenience be grouped under seven major headings:

L: Legal

E: Ethical

P: Political

E: Economic

S: Social

T: Technological

Co: Competition

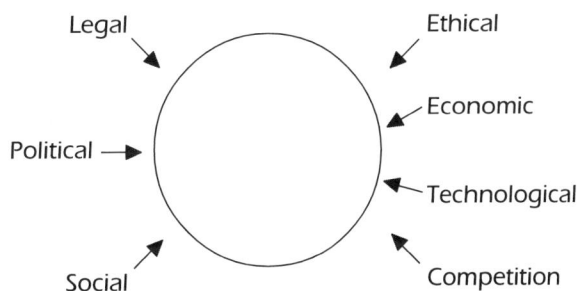

1.3 Every business is likely to be seriously affected by changes occurring in these areas and we look at each factor and the sort of changes they can create.

Think of one factor from any of the above areas (legal, ethical, political, economic, social, technological, competitive) which has created the need for your organisation to change. Write down this factor and briefly describe the change that has occurred.

How long did the change take?

Was it successful?

2   Legal factors

2.1   Examples of legal influences on organisations include acts which regulate their activities, e.g. the Employment Acts, which dictate conditions of work for employees, and the Financial Services Act. Financial service organisations are also affected by consumer legislation and rating agencies, who ascribe an index to a bank which reflects its business portfolio. This can have a dramatic effect on business consumer groups and how they regard the organisation.

3   Ethical factors

3.1   This area is closely linked with political factors as the political parties are responsible for introducing legislation. Ethical issues and how a business responds to its customers, shareholders, employees and suppliers, is increasingly important. This factor has close links with social responsibility and it is proposed to consider ethical issues under the social factors of LEPEST & Co.

4   Political factors

4.1   The political influences on organisations and in particular on financial enterprises include such issues as the international relations between powers. The relations between countries has an effect on investment and trade, e.g. unrest in China and South America caused a drop in trade and investment in these countries. The attitude of different individual countries towards investment by foreign powers also has an effect and can inhibit the growth of multi-nationals. When banks lend money to countries, there is some assessment of country risk and these factors can be relevant in determining strategy and lending policy.

4.2   The policies of the government or local authority may also influence organisations. An example of this is the privatisation or otherwise of various political parties. The policies of regeneration, in particular areas of high unemployment also have an influence on other organisations in the area.

4.3   Other political influences are:

- Government policies to control interest or exchange rate.
- Alignment of rules such as employees' rights under the Maastricht Treaty.
- Rationalisation of the European Stock Exchange.

- Privatisation – some of the public are now shareholders for the first time: British Gas, British Telecom, etc.

- The Single European Market – for financial organisations this means:

  - An end to protection from competition from abroad, both for banks and their customers.

  - The organisation and its customers have extended business opportunities.

4.4 For those companies considering global operations, a number of decisions have to be made, e.g. whether to:

- Export an entire home base operation (or part of it);

- Merge with or acquire a foreign company;

- Have some form of joint venture with a foreign financial institution.

4.5 If a company decides to operate abroad, then they have to decide whether to operate as a multinational corporation (one central control operating in many countries) or a conglomerate (the operation in that one country is controlled from a base in that country) with less emphasis on central control from a home base.

Student Activity 2

Find out about and write a brief statement about the standard policies of the Conservative and Labour parties.

Compare your statement with ours. To what extent do you consider your statement was influenced by your own political sympathies?

4.6 Other factors are:

- Restrictions on mergers.

- The Sexual and Racial Discrimination Acts were passed in 1975 and 1976 respectively. Many financial institutions are taking steps to ensure good career progression for women in line with the Opportunity 2000 initiative. Attention has also been paid to the under-representation of minority groups in the workplace, e.g. Lloyds TSB have taken steps actively to encourage employment of minority groups such as ethnic minorities and the disabled.

- Laws governing the management of pension funds and some tightening of the industry's controlling bodies. The responsibilities of the Banking Ombudsman have been increased to include the bank's relationship with small businesses.

Student Activity 3

Look again at the above paragraph. Is your organisation one which exists for *maximum shareholders' profits*, and never mind the social contribution, or for *maximum social contribution*, without too much regard for the shareholders? Write a paragraph on this matter, explaining and defending your views, with examples if possible.

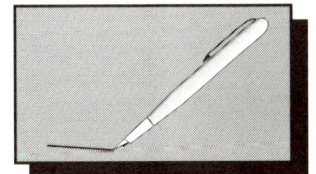

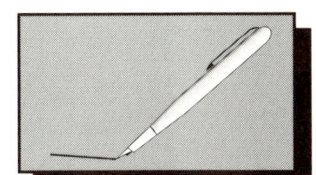

5 Economic factors

5.1   These include influences on the organisation such as the current state of a business's markets (is it a boom period for lending or investment?), the availability of foreign exchange, the purchasing power of the population and the state of trade in the world.

5.2   Economic changes seen in this country have seen the decline of manufacturing industries and the growth of services. Differences in the distribution of wealth between the north and south of the country have grown. Banks have offered additional benefits to attract employees south. Within the last two decades the UK has also seen the effects of high inflation (at one stage more than 19%), which erodes savings and pensions, and economic recession which creates unemployment. Now there is a reservoir of manufacturing skills which are unused and individuals need retraining. However, the adjustment is difficult to make and can occur only over a long period of time.

5.3   Other examples of economic factors are:

- The emergence of giant multinational firms;
- Growth in white collar jobs;
- Fierce competition for UK banks from foreign banks setting up here in business, building societies extending their services, and building societies converting to banks.

5.4   As the range of services and size of financial organisations increase, there has been a tendency to specialisation and decentralisation leading to quicker decisions.

5.5   Of late there has been recession in the financial services industry. There have been major redundancies and many cost cutting measures, e.g. centralised processing, satellite branches, cheaper out-of-town sites, and greater use of information technology.

Student Activity 4

Most organisations such as your own will take some socially responsible actions. Find out from your HR Department or your PR department examples of such actions taken by your organisation with regard to each of these groups, and write a paragraph about each, not more than five lines:

- Your customers;
- The staff;
- The local community;
- The nation.

6 Social factors

6.1   Social factors may also directly influence the activities of banks. Social factors could be said to include the climate in which the firm has to operate, e.g.

the prestige of financial activities in a country, the religious, cultural and racial influences exerted on finance, the changing patterns in population distribution, alterations in customer attitudes and the efficiency of public administration and their supporting services.

6.2 Other examples of social factors are:

- Customers are now better educated and tend to be more demanding, and there has been the experience of social mobility (an increase in expectations and standards of living among staff and customers). There has been an increase in criticism. This has happened despite the introduction in the late 1980s of programmes designed to offer a high level of customer service. Part of the problem could be attributed to the recession, which has meant the banks have been involved in numerous business failures. This generated bad publicity. Customers have become more sophisticated and this has led to a greater number of complaints. The appointment of an ombudsman was seen by some customers as an invitation to complain.

- Population changes, e.g. there is unlikely to be a repeat of the baby boom of the 1960s, meaning fewer school leavers and fewer people available for work. This is referred to as 'the demographic time bomb', although recession and technology innovation and application has prevented a labour shortage.

- Many women now work and many wish to pursue a career over the extent of their working lives. People have smaller families and more women want to return to work after raising a family. There are longer maternity leave schemes available for senior staff, so moncy invested in training and ability are not wasted.

- A decline in hierarchical authority in organisations has led to more involvement by employees.

- Changing social values and attitudes have led to new demands on business and its activities. Business is now seen as being accountable for its actions: social responsibility.

7 The responsibility of the organisation to society

7.1 It has long been accepted that business organisations have interactions with several different sectors of society.

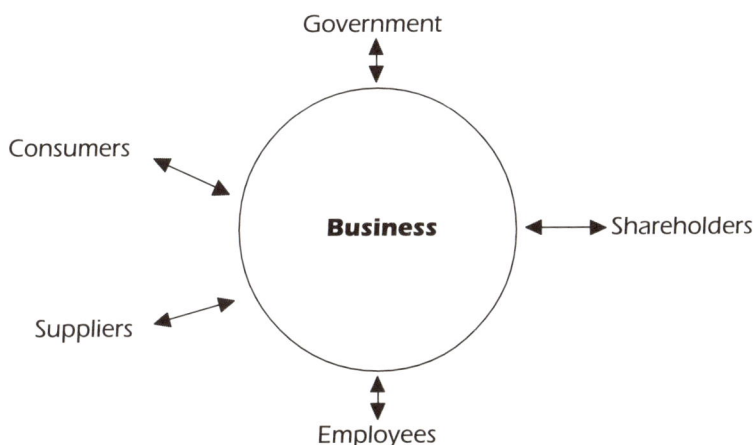

7.2 The view as to what exactly a business's obligations are to these different sectors of society varies considerably. Some believe a business's duty lies with shareholders (profit maximisation), whilst others believe a business exists solely for the benefit of society (maximum social contribution). Although the objective of business is commercial, its achievement depends on how employees and customers are treated and how wider society views that business. These are *ethical* issues.

7.3 The diagram below depicts different views social responsibility, from moderate to the extreme.

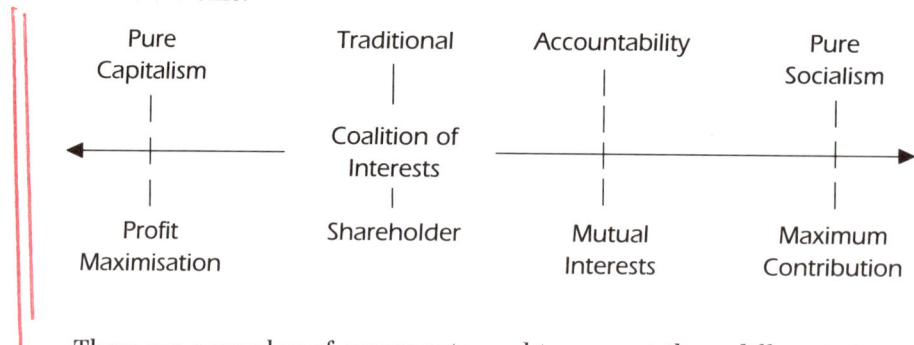

There are a number of arguments used to support these different views.

Classical/traditional view

7.4 *Caveat emptor:* let the buyer beware. The buyer's protection results from the seller's desire to survive in a competitive market. Buyers have personal morals but business relies on the dynamics of a free competitive market to protect society. This argument could be summarised under the following points:

- Employers should have the freedom to act and not be restricted by societal obligations. It would destroy our economy if it were otherwise.

- Directors act on behalf of shareholders. The company's money belongs to the shareholders and cannot be distributed freely by the directors.

- Firms with costly social benefit programmes have higher costs and so are less competitive.

- Business already does enough for society in providing employment, goods, services and income through corporation tax.

- Social responsibility programmes for business would mean extending their influence further and this is not necessarily a good thing.

- Social responsibility is and should remain a government activity.

7.5 Although this view was prevalent in the 19th century, many economists, e.g. Milton Friedman, and business people still support this view today.

The accountability view

7.6 This viewpoint argues that businesses receive their charter from society and they are therefore accountable to society for their behaviour. A business has an obligation not only to shareholders but also to consumers, employees, and society generally. Davis and Blomstrom state: 'Business is a social institution ... The direction of business is important to public welfare and business should perform a social function.'

7.7   The arguments in favour of this school can be summarised thus:

- A free enterprise economic system no longer exists, therefore business can be subject to restrictions without affecting the enterprise system.

- Businesses do have socio-human power and should therefore learn to use it carefully.

- Society and shareholders want business to act in a responsible way. Business today is subject to less competition and so can devote more time and energy to social responsibility programmes.

8   The change in attitudes towards social responsibility

8.1   Reasons put forward for this change in attitudes include:

- Businesses are now administered and run by professional managers and as such they can be difficult to gain a response from and deal with.

- It is no longer the surrounding community that appears to benefit directly from the activities of a business. Many firms are multinationals and the owners are receiving profits in a distant country.

- Better education and public awareness has led to an increase in consciousness about these issues. There are groups specifically created to promote public awareness, e.g. Greenpeace, etc. They have influenced governments and companies into taking direct action.

- Although competition between firms still exists, larger firms tend to dominate markets through mergers and takeovers and therefore have more time and energy to devote to issues of social responsibility.

9   Ethical issues

9.1   Failure to act in an ethically correct way could mean that a business is at risk. The risk involved in unethical action can be high and not only financial. There is also the loss of reputation, management time and energy (by dealing with a crisis instead of keeping strategy on course) and the loss of employee morale, and customer and shareholder trust.

9.2   Many organisations try to behave in an ethically correct manner by publishing 'codes of behaviour', designed with the co-operation of staff, to illustrate how employees should behave when faced with an ethical dilemma. It needs commitment by senior management if this attitude is to pervade all the organisation and its systems. For example, an employee is expected to follow all security procedures, but is also expected to provide a high level of customer service. Sometimes the employee may need to sidestep procedures to provide this.

10   Groups to whom a firm has a responsibility

10.1   If a firm accepts the principle of societal obligations, then there are a number of groups to whom they have a responsibility:

- Shareholders
- Employees
- Consumers
- Suppliers
- Community.

Shareholders

10.2   In the form of:

- Fair return on risk of investment.

Employees

10.3   In the form of:

- Job design
- Pay
- Fringe benefits
- Working conditions
- Health and safety
- Training and career development
- Equal opportunities
- Provision of information
- Bargaining and grievance procedures.

Consumers

10.4   In the form of:

- Pricing levels
- Quality
- Advertising
- Product/service development
- Information
- Safety.

Suppliers

10.5   In the form of:

- Fair negotiation
- Payment within agreed time
- Relevant information.

Community

10.6   In the form of:

- Pollution
- Creation and maintenance of employment
- Community activities
- Using the skills of employees to develop charitable goods or services.

10.7   Whilst changes in business's attitudes and actions required by a socially responsible stance seem to generate adverse cost benefit results, many organisations operating what is seen to be strong socially responsible programmes claim that in the long-term benefits can outweigh costs. For example, Sir Marcus Sieff (past chairman of Marks and Spencer plc) said, 'It is my experience that everything we have done in this field because we thought we had a moral obligation has turned out within a few years to be good business as well.'

11 Conflict between stakeholder groups

11.1 Even if a business decides to act in a socially responsible manner, it is not always easy to balance the demands of different groups, e.g. the demands of the customer for longer opening hours versus the needs of staff for reasonable working hours; the fear of employees and customers about AIDS versus the need to treat suffering individuals fairly; the cost of providing childcare services against the needs of mothers returning to work; the potential failure of a corporate or personal borrower versus the needs of the shareholders to minimise loss. The issues here are far from clear-cut and organisations find themselves facing difficult decisions.

Student Activity 5

Give four other examples of how conflict can arise between the different groups when an organisation tries to introduce socially responsible programmes.

11.2 It could be argued that, ethical issues apart, the degree of social responsibility shown is the result of:

- Influence of government legislation in force;
- Cost of any programme of social responsibility;
- The degree of competition experienced by the firm.

11.3 Firms can be categorised according to their response to social responsibility.

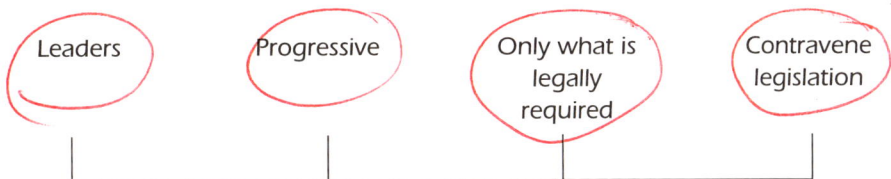

Leaders — Progressive — Only what is legally required — Contravene legislation

Most businesses regard acts of social responsibility as desirable. They raise morale, improve customer and public relations and in some cases gain tax allowances, e.g. meal services for employees. However, any firm interested in social responsibility also has to assess its obligations to the shareholder and profitability.

12 Technological factors

12.1 There is no doubt that technology has had a major impact on banking in the last two decades. Organisations wishing to remain competitive must invest large sums of money in research, design and development.

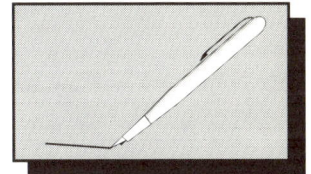

17

12.2 Technology has also played a part in altering job design, taking over routine activities and increasing the demand for specialist staff. It reduces the need for multiple levels of management and can aid communication so the head office can keep in touch with its units, even on an international basis. Technology can also increase the range of services on offer, and productivity, thereby reducing the numbers of staff needed. (Unit 7 looks at information technology and its role in banking in greater detail.)

13 Competition

13.1 UK banks face increased competition from a number of sources. As a result of the economic, technological and political climate, foreign banks have set up in business here, and building societies and retail organisations have extended the range of financial services they offer. Banks have taken action to maintain their position in what is now a highly competitive market. There are three main competitors facing those operating in the financial services industry.

● Those existing players who provide similar services and can launch, in response to a new product, an imitation just days later.

● Niche players who provide a restricted range of services and can act as strong competitors in those specialist areas.

● Non-financial companies who have diversified and offer restricted financial services, e.g. unit trusts, personal loans, credit cards, etc.

13.2 The UK banks have responded by:

● Extending into the overseas market, particularly Europe;

● Offering a wider range of investment services;

● Offering share dealing services;

● Developing mortgage lending business;

● Developing accountancy services;

● Developing insurance services;

● Developing a special services network for 'wholesale' banking customers separate to retail banking;

● Marketing and providing services geared to different customer needs: pensioners, women, students, etc.

● Using more sophisticated customer information services;

● Making premises more user-friendly.

13.3 The amount of competition has also led to stringent efforts to control costs, thereby trying to maximise profitability and competitive pricing. It has also led to changes in structure, for example the retail/corporate split, the geographic or relationship/transaction split. (The topic of competition for banks is now of such importance that Unit 3 of this text is devoted to a detailed examination of the strategies banks have developed to deal with the competition they face.)

14 The organisation and its internal environment

14.1 It is possible to use the LEPEST & Co model (legal, ethical, political, economic, social, technological and competitive influences) to examine the reaction of the organisation to its internal environment. In the same way as management must take advantage of the beneficial factors and counteract the harmful ones from the external environment, so management must also actively influence and direct the effect of internal factors (see also Unit 17).

Legal factors

14.2　The internal written systems (head office instructions) are a type of legislation that employees have to follow. There are also unwritten rules of behaviour, conduct and procedure. For instance, how employees should dress. It is these types of rules that create the atmosphere of the organisation.

Ethical factors

14.3　These include employers' dealings with employees and codes of conduct and internal employee policies.

Political factors

14.4　The internal political influences on organisations include such issues as the power, status and position of departments and individuals.

14.5　You need to be aware of the politics of the organisation to get things done. Approach those people with the power to act. A complaint by a customer addressed to the right person will get a much quicker response than one sent to the wrong individual, who then has to redirect it.

Economic factors

14.6　These factors include how resources are allocated and which departments or sections receive priority. They also include internal economic affairs like appraisal systems and performance-related pay. Other economic aspects are the costs of expansion, the savings associated with contraction, or the economies of restructuring the organisation.

Social factors

14.7　These include the attitudes of employees and how they are changing. That is, whether lifelong loyalty to one employer is still perceived as the expectation. There is now more mid-career assessment and changing employment trends with mid-career recruitment.

Technology

14.8　The internal technological factors include such things as the new technological processes, the management of change they involve and the increasing use of technology as a substitution for human resources.

Competitive

14.9　The internal competitive influences include competition for resources between people and departments to get things done and competition between individuals in establishing career paths.

Summary

Having studied this unit carefully you should now:

- **be able to apply a scheme for an environmental analysis of an organisation;**

- **know what major factors influence an organisation from outside;**

- **have a clearer idea of political influences on business;**

- **understand your organisation's social responsibility to a variety of bodies;**

- **be able to discuss internal as well as external environments.**

Self-assessment questions

1. What are the two opposing views on the social responsibility of business organisations?

2. Which view did Milton Friedman support?

3. If the number of school-leavers is falling what changes would you expect to see in recruitment?

4. What stakeholder responsibilities do banks have to consider?

5. Consider how financial organisations have accounted for and taken action to satisfy 'green issues', and give at least one example of internal and one of public action taken by such organisations.

6. How do we classify environmental influences on organisations?

7. What do we mean by the term 'social responsibility'?

8. Why is it important to consider the environmental influences on business?

9. Where might you find a public statement including your organisation's social responsibility, as they see it?

10. Give an example, not in the text, of the influence of the internal environment on your department, under the headings:

    (a) ethical factors;

    (b) economic factors;

    (c) technological factors.

Unit 3

Corporate Appraisal and the Achievement of Goals

Objectives

After studying this unit, you should be able to:

- **perform an external appraisal of on organisation;**

- **construct a SWOT analysis;**

- **understand the levels of corporate objective setting and planning;**

- **appreciate the relationship of evaluation to planning.**

---

1 Organisational goals and objectives

1.1 The activities of any business organisation are normally directed toward goals. These goals provide a focusing point for the activities of the organisation, although the overall objectives will be further divided and subdivided again to provide sectional or departmental, and individual goals or targets. In this unit the nature of these goals and how the activities of individuals within the organisation may be directed toward them, will be discussed.

1.2 The key functions of a banking organisation could be said to be the receipt and transmission of funds, plus the supply of finance and associated services. The goals of the organisation will determine the ways and extent to which finance and services are supplied and activities directed and controlled.

Why are goals important for the organisation?

1.3 The main reasons are that goals:

- Provide a standard of performance. Activities can be directed towards them and progress measured against them.

- Give guidelines for decision making and provide justification for whatever action is to be taken.

- Help to influence the structure of the organisation and the methods used to achieve them.

- Provide some indication as to the nature of the organisation and its priorities.

- Provide a basis for strategy.

Student Activity 1

Find a statement of the objectives or targets of your branch or section. If you cannot find one, make some suppositions about what they might be. Summarise them in a paragraph of not more than 10 lines of notes. Having done this, consider our suggestions

2 The stages involved in corporate appraisal

2.1 If the setting and achievement of objectives for the organisation is to be successful, a series of stages needs to be adhered to in developing and implementing these goals. This is known as corporate appraisal or strategic management. The objectives are usually established for a three to ten year period and this process of deciding upon and applying objectives can be set out in a diagrammatic form (see 3.2.2).

Stage 1 Preliminary objectives

2.2 These objectives may be established by an organisation continually reviewing its progress and achievement. For instance, an organisation may have previously established a growth rate of 6%, and if it is clear this rate of 6% will not be achieved, then the organisation may decide to lower it to a more realistic rate of 4% or take steps to increase the current growth rate.

2.3 Sometimes an event can cause an organisation to take stock of its current objectives and activities, e.g. a threatened takeover.

Stage 2 External appraisal

2.4 This has to take account of LEPEST & Co: the legal, ethical, political, economic, social, technological and competitive influences faced by the firm (see Unit 2). The financial organisation is especially interested in competition because this indicates where innovation is likely to be successful and where to place resources in order to achieve corporate objectives. Failure to secure money from depositors because of unsatisfactory or inadequate services, or failure to secure staff of the right calibre, will result in failure to compete and may herald the decline of the firm.

Stage 3 The SWOT analysis

2.5 Organisations can be analysed in general terms by conducting a SWOT analysis, which means observing closely its Strengths, Weaknesses, Opportunities and Threats. In fact you would start with the Os and the Ts; but it is important to note that the words opportunity and threat, strength and weakness, are not used here in the usual sense.

- An opportunity is not something the organisation can do to better itself, but something happening in the organisation's environment which is favourable to the organisation.

- A *threat* is not what someone is doing to harm the organisation, but *something happening in the organisation's environment which is unfavourable to the organisation.*

- A *strength* is not just a strong feature, but *something within the control of the organisation which gives it an advantage over competitors.*

- A *weakness* is not just a weak feature, but *something within the control of the organisation which gives competitors an advantage over it.*

2.6   For example, take Marks and Spencer: it is not, in our sense, an opportunity that they might like to sell mountain bicycles, but it is an opportunity if there more employment in managerial roles, because they could sell more suits. It is not a threat that competitors sell suits – they do that by definition; but it might be a threat if a new environmental movement against wool products were to gain ground. Their having a lot of stores is not, in our sense, a strength – so do BHS and Next; but having the best site in many cities is a strength, because it is a competitive strength. Finally, that they do not sell mountain bikes is not a weakness, un*less* all their managerial customers decided to cycle to work and all their competitors sold matching bike-and-suit sets!

2.7   In other words, a strength must either be there to take an advantage of an opportunity or to protect against a threat; and a weakness is not a weakness unless there is an associated threat or the inability to take advantage of an opportunity, in the sense of T and O suggested above.

Stage 4 External/internal appraisal

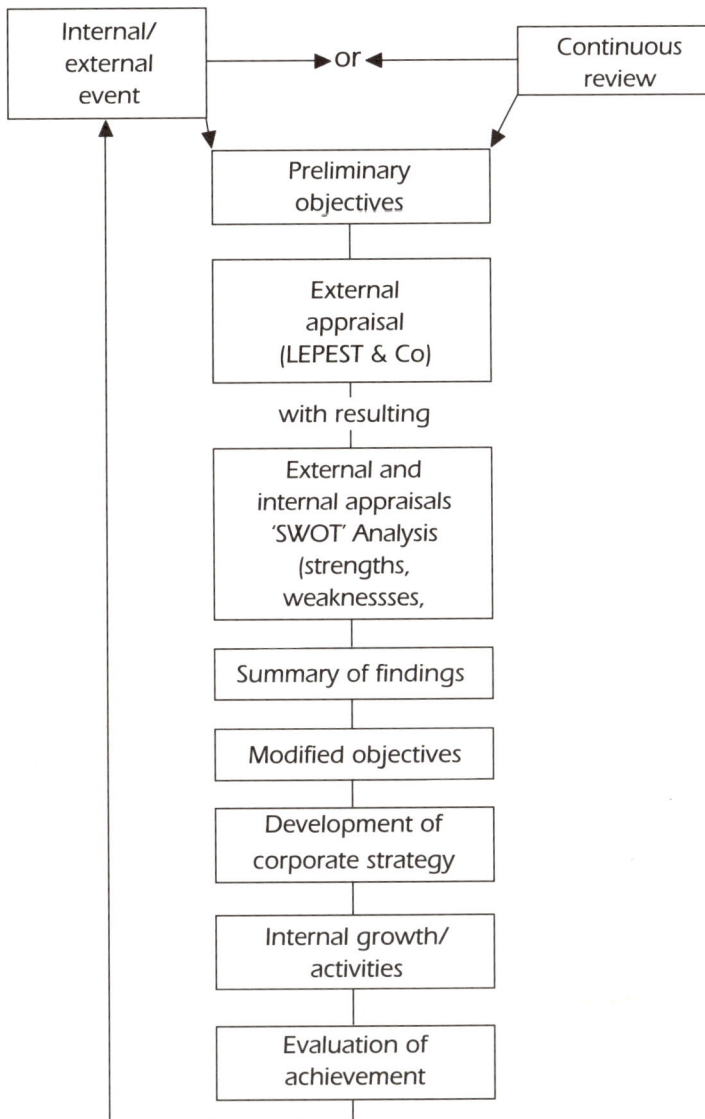

2.8   In order to know what services to provide, a customer analysis should be completed. A bank needs to know its customers (the individuals and corporates), why they open accounts, how they judge services, etc. A bank also needs to provide a competitor analysis so it can plan its strategy by identifying services and market segments where the bank is strong. The financial organisation also needs to know its supplier, an essential element in its quality of service. The bank could be badly affected by poor security, takeovers, strikes and shortages in its suppliers. It is also useful to know the local community, anticipating changes in the population, industrial scene and changing attitudes.

Student Activity 2

Perform the simplest of SWOT analyses on your organisation: name one *Opportunity*, favourable circumstance in the environment, one *Threat*, unfavourable circumstance, one *Strength*, competitive internal advantage, and one *Weakness*, internal disadvantage by comparison with competitors.

Stage 5 External/internal analysis

2.9   The external/internal analysis involves an examination of the bank's *Strengths*, *Weaknesses*, *Opportunities* and *Threats* (hence it is referred to as a SWOT analysis). Anticipation of future events is a necessary part of this process. Some changes, for instance structural, can take five to 10 years to complete.

2.10   There needs to be an examination of where the bank is now. Braddick in *Management for Bankers* suggests it should be completed in terms of:

- *Markets and services*. Are they in a growth period or have they reached a plateau or in decline? Which products should be maintained or abandoned?

- *Financial resources*. How is investment faring? Can the company raise money if needed?

- *Operations*. Are operations effective in terms of resourcing time, cost and accuracy?

- *Technology*. Are they keeping abreast of competitors' developments?

- *Management and staff*. Are employees motivated? How effective is the leadership? What potential is there?

- *Organisational structure*. Are there any communication or conflict problems which might indicate a need for structural change?

- *Information*. Is information received accurately and speedily transmitted?

2.11   The internal analysis enables the organisation to see where it wants to go in the future as opposed to where it is now.

2.12   In the light of the external/internal analysis of the bank, certain conclusions are likely to be drawn about the future direction of the bank. In order for planning to be successful the co-operation and commitment of the staff is needed. This can be achieved through involvement at all levels and stages.

```
                        Markets and services
   Competition           Financial resources      Legal
                            Operations
   Technological            Technology             Economic
                         Management and
        Social                staff               Political
                          organisational
                             structure            Ethical
                            Information
```

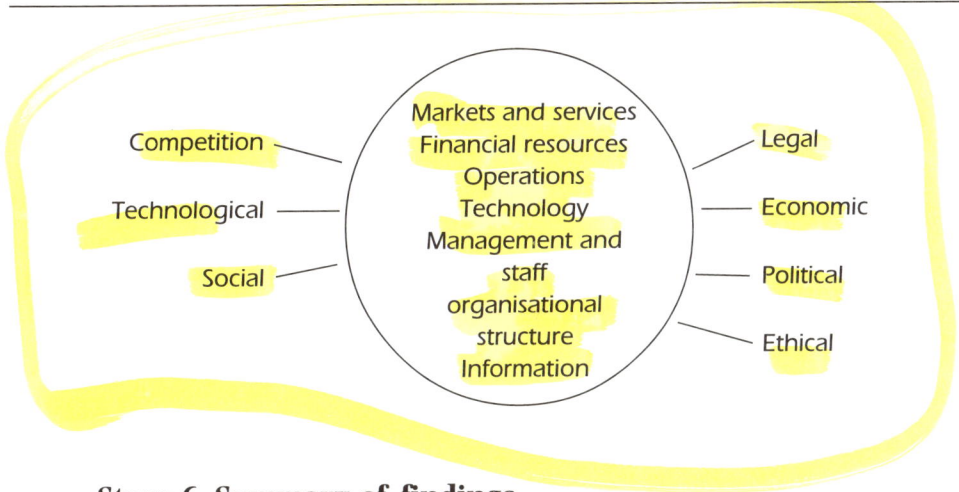

Stage 6 Summary of findings

The future role of the bank

2.13   It seems that the role of the bank is changing. Banking used to be about taking deposits and making loans. Customers based their purchase decisions on loyalty and established relationships. But banks today are part of an emerging financial services industry, which includes not only banks and building societies, but retailers like Marks and Spencer plc, Debenhams, etc, who are offering services such as credit cards and loans through their finance sections. Banks are also broadening their horizons and including stockbroking and insurance among their services.

2.14   The primary forces behind these changes have been:

- The Financial Services Act 1986;

- Economic change;

- Competition from other organisations.

2.15   The *Financial Services Act 1986* forced banks to decide whether to become tied agents or independent intermediaries in areas such as unit trusts. Most banks have become tied agents selling only their own products.

2.16   *Economic change* has seen pressure on interest rates drive away the corporate borrower who can access the multinational currency and stock markets more cheaply than using a bank. This applies to corporates raising funds and lending funds.

2.17   The commercial paper market, interest and currency swaps and Eurobond issues, to name but a few, mean that the corporation can lend or borrow more profitably by dealing directly, using the bank only in an advisory, fee-based capacity. Banks have to gain expertise and commercial standing in the Euro and world markets to earn fees rather than lend money. The bank has to decide whether the cost of entering these new markets will generate profitable fees.

2.18   *Competition* now comes from building societies, unit trusts, insurance companies, finance houses, international and merchant banks, stockbrokers and retailers. Awareness of competition is vital, but so is the decision on whether or not to compete. One thing to take into account in the competition is customer preference. Indications are that customers are no longer loyal to one bank. They are now looking more for convenience and the cost of their banking.

This has brought about increased competition and the need for banks to pay increased attention to better market segmentation, increased product lines, more delivery channels at lower costs, improved customer relations and improved cost control. As customers demand more accessible services, the delivery systems may have to change. Banks have a huge investment in their branch networks, but they may not be cost effective to operate. Banks have started to close unprofitable branches and restructure the profitable ones into personal/ corporate banking services. They are also examining new ways to deliver services such as home banking, ATMs (automatic teller machines), debit cards, EFTPOS (electronic funds transfer at point of sale), treasury management systems, and in the case of First Direct, a totally branchless, telephone-based delivery system providing a full range of banking services.

Modified objectives

2.19 Once the external and internal analysis for the bank has been summarised, the initial objectives can be altered into modified objectives (targets that are more realistic in the light of the external/internal analysis).

Student Activity 3

Do some research to find out the precise location in your organisation where corporate strategy and planning is carried out. Is it a separate Head Office function, or is it simply done by the Board of Directors, or is it separately done by major division heads? Write a half-page mini-essay on this, and critically comment on the way the corporate plans filter down to your office.

Stages 7 and 8 Development of corporate strategy and internal growth activities

2.20 To achieve these modified objectives, the strategies and plans have to be implemented and managed by the organisation. The objectives give targets for performance and provide a means of measuring progress. Both the objectives and plans are likely to be broken down into more manageable units. The concept of Anthony's framework envisages three levels of planning and strategy occurring in the organisation: strategic, managerial and operational.

2.21 The *strategic level of planning* is the one just discussed. It involves long-term planning by the organisation, considering both external and internal factors.

2.22 The *managerial level of planning* is concerned with obtaining and using resources effectively within the policies established by strategic decisions. It is concerned with all the operations of a company rather than one particular strategic decision and is often expressed in financial terms, e.g. the cost of training programmes. The middle manager occupies a key position at this level of planning and control. One system used to link the strategic targets to action plans for individual managers is Management By Objectives (or MBO). This turns strategic goals into action plans. It breaks down strategic goals into departmental and then individual goals. The goal an individual manager works towards must be agreed jointly with his superior and be in line with the overall goals of the department and organisation.

goal congruence.

2.23 Sometimes these action plans and their achievement may be linked to pay (performance-related pay). The system of MBO is examined in Unit 11. You need to be aware of its links with strategic planning and how it reduces corporate goals to individual ones.

2.24 The operational level of planning is concerned with the effective administration of specific tasks within a framework of procedures. It covers very short time periods measuring, for instance, the relationship between inputs of resources and corresponding outputs. It is this level of planning that most involves the lower management tier.

2.25 Once the strategic plans and objectives have been drawn up, then it is the responsibility of the middle and lower managers to implement them and monitor the progress of the organisation towards the goals.

Student Activity 4

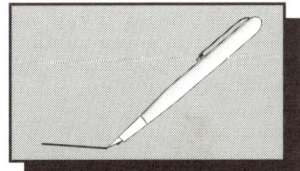

Summarise the main stages of the corporate planning process, in a diagram.

Stage 9 The evaluation of achievement

2.26 The final stage in the process of corporate planning is the review of progress against the plans and objectives. This review will indicate any shortfall in progress and result in action to increase resources or even alter the objectives.

2.27 How can an organisation decide if its strategic plans are working successfully? Braddick, in *Management for Bankers*, suggests that there are several key questions to ask:

- Is the strategy clear – in words and practice?
- Does the strategy exploit environmental opportunities?
- Is the strategy consistent with the company's competence and resources?
- Is the strategy internally consistent?
- Is the level of risk associated with the strategy acceptable?

2.28 Care must be taken to ensure objectives set for managers can be controlled by them, e.g. there is little a branch manager can do about costs since 70% of costs are accounted for by staff costs, which are within regional control. The manager can, however, have an effect on the income of the branch.

2.29 The success of the organisation will ultimately depend on the success of the corporate plan.

Summary

Having studied this unit carefully you should now:

- **be able to perform an external appraisal of on organisation;**

- **be able to construct a SWOT analysis of your own organisation;**

- **have examined the levels of corporate objective setting and planning;**

- **be able to discuss the relationship of evaluation to planning;**

- **be able critically to discuss your organisation's corporate planning and its relationship to planning in your location.**

Self-assessment questions

1. Which of the following can be termed corporate planning:
   (a) planning the next day's events;
   (b) forecasting labour supply for the next year;
   (c) deciding on one product rather than another;
   (d) planning objectives and activities for the organisation over the next five to 10 years?

2. Anthony's framework is a:
   (a) diagram of the corporate planning process;
   (b) description of the different levels of organisational planning;
   (c) description of the managerial functions;
   (d) device used in corporate planning.

3. An internal analysis involves:
   (a) assessing the current level of resources;
   (b) examining the bank's policies;
   (c) assessment of strengths, weaknesses, opportunities and gains;
   (d) assessment of strengths, weaknesses, opportunities and threats.

4. Why is the use of the word 'opportunity' unusual in corporate analysis?

5. Why is the use of the word 'threat' unusual in corporate analysis?

6. Why is the use of the word 'strength' unusual in corporate analysis?

7. Why is the use of the word 'weakness' unusual in corporate analysis?

8. Making predictions about future events is:
   (a) planning;
   (b) forecasting;
   (c) diagnosing;
   (d) analysing.

9. The main concern of planning is:
   (a) long-term future;
   (b) medium-term future;
   (c) any future events;
   (d) short-term future.

10. State any three of Braddick's key questions about banking strategy.

Unit 4

Financial Services in Context

1 Introduction

1.1 Much of the entire subject of management applies to any organisation, in any industry, large or small, in any culture. Banks and other providers of financial services are managed business organisations like many another. Much can be written about organisations, which have much in common and many differences, in terms of:

- Functions;

- Structure;

- Markets;

- Environments;

- Technologies.

1.2 It is tempting for bank management and staff to assert that their industry is different from all others; but then, it is equally tempting for those in the paint industry, or food supermarkets, or entertainment complexes, or education, to believe that their occupations are unique. In many ways, they have much in common; but there are distinguishing features which are not just the product or services themselves, but the internal and external differences based on having to offer those particular products or services.

1.3 This unit is decidedly not about the technicalities of banking, nor will it engage in explaining financial institutions at an elementary level. It is about the way in which banking and financial institutions both match and differ from others as managed businesses: financial services in context, in fact.

2   The changing nature of financial services

Merchant, retail and home banking

2.1   At this level the distinction between merchant and retail banking needs hardly be made. But for marketing purposes consideration could be given to adding a distinction: home banking and the revolution based in communication technology.

2.2   *Telephone banking* may have been inspired by the huge rise in insurance business achieved by innovative companies such as DirectLine. First Direct bank was founded on the basis of customer contact exclusively by telephone and the use of ATMs – and the large clearing banks saw fit to follow. Now most of their customers can use the telephone to transfer funds, pay bills, enquire of balances, order statements and chequebooks, institute and cancel standing orders, and the like. They can do this by talking to an operator, or using the telephone keypad.

2.3   *Home computers,* increasingly widespread in the UK and Europe, are now drawing the attention of banks wishing to provide service to current and new customers. The Alliance and Leicester and the Bank of Scotland caused something of a tremor in the early 1980s by providing a banking service which could be operated by a keypad attached to a television. Experiments on banking via the Internet will undoubtedly bear fruit when problems of security are solved.

Integration and diversification

2.4   Certain banking organisations decided in the 1980s to change their portfolio by buying into businesses other than banking. Lloyd's Bank tried the estate agency business, the Royal Bank of Scotland took over a travel agency. These ventures and others of the same sort were watched with care, but the experiment proved abortive. Peters and Waterman, in *In Search of Excellence,* suggested that the best organisations 'stick to the knitting' and work only in areas where they have expertise, and perhaps the banks learned that lesson.

2.5   The last years of the 20th century is seeing a realignment and change in the nature of banks, building societies, friendly societies and other financial institutions. In particular, building societies are either becoming banks or giving up their mutual status or both, led by majors such as the Abbey National and the Halifax. Shares have been given to members; and the profits shared with the shareholders.

2.6   The effect of the changes is largely to alter the competitive stance, in that profit is not just needed to amortise costs, but also to distribute. The responsibility of management is no longer to the members (depositors and mortgage holders) but also to the demands of the shareholders and the market. But the former societies have also made themselves freer to compete in wider, and sometimes more lucrative, markets.

Student Activity 1

By examining your bank's consolidated accounts, see if you can find owned subsidiary businesses. Using your analytical expertise, and canvassing the opinion of your managers, write a one-page mini-essay on the success of these subsidiaries, comparing and contrasting the direct financial subsidiaries with any which are outside the strict confines of the finance industry

CIB qualifications

2.7 The evolution of the Associateship of the Chartered Institute of Bankers is in line with changes in the business environment. To begin with, there are moves in the direction of offering NVQ national qualifications for people both within and outside the traditional banking industry; and the Certificate in Financial Services Practice and the Diploma in Mortgage Lending for building society staff, and the Certificate for Financial Advisers, and a Professional Investment Certificate, are now under the CIB flag.

2.8 While the ACIB has always been respected in financial circles, it struggled for recognition and particularly in terms of its level in comparison with the professional qualifications which were based on first degree or postgraduate studies.

2.9 Second, and with reluctance, both employers and staff in the financial services industry have had to acknowledge that careers in that industry are no longer necessarily linear and in the same organisation, and that qualifications should be easily 'portable'.

2.10 To associate the ACIB, then, with an honours degree in financial services from a highly reputable University clearly acknowledges the vicissitudes that the business faces at the turn of the 20th century.

changes not favourable

3   Deregulation and competition

The 1970s revolution

3.1 Towards the end of the 1960s three sets of changes caused the pattern of banking in the UK to take on a different aspect:

- Mergers;
- Banking technology;
- Computerised wage and salary systems;
- Inflation.

3.2 A plethora of *mergers* meant the formation of fewer, larger banks, and the foundation of such giants as Barclays, the National Westminster, the Midland, and smaller but equally composite groups like Lloyds and the Royal Bank of Scotland. Names like Martins, Glyn Mills, the District, the National, disappeared into the memories of traditional bankers.

3.3 There were rapid changes in *banking technology*, in particular in-branch on-line computing facilities. It was in the early 1970s that Williams & Glyn's Bank, as part of the Royal Bank of Scotland group, was the first domestic clearing bank to have all its branches connected via land-lines to a main-frame computer at its London Head Office. Simultaneously, it was possible to see the beginnings of cash transactions by automatic teller machines outside branches, albeit crude: for example, customers might be issued with six hole-punched cards which would deliver £20 each from the machine; but they would be 'sucked in' to the machine and returned to the customer with the next statement!

3.4   Simultaneously, there were massive advances *in computerised systems of wage and salary payments:* the ability to pay wages by bank transfer became very much more widely distributed, and it is clearly easier, simpler and cheaper than cash or cheque payment. Employers, with the enthusiastic co-operation of the UK clearers, strongly encouraged their staff to open bank accounts, and the 'great unbanked', as advertising agencies dubbed them, became a rapidly shrinking population.

3.5   In the mid 1970s there was massive *inflation,* over 25% in two successive years, for example. This raised the cost of the banks most significant outgoing – wages – and radically unbalanced interest rates. Many banks found them-selves in heavy cost-problems, and had to engage in stringent 'housekeeping' and cost-saving to maintain their business status.

Student Activity 2

Trace the name of your bank back to the mid 1960s: make a 'family tree'. See if you can find someone who has worked for you bank for, say, 25 years and make notes of their views on changes in your particular organisation over the time of their employment.

Competitive deregulation: the 1980s

3.6   In the 1980s there were changes in regulations which permitted banks to engage in mortgage lending and building societies to make personal loans for purposes other than house purchase, and changes in both regulations and attitudes concerning competition and advertising.

3.7   Many traditional bankers resisted this sort of change, indeed any change which increased the need to 'sell' and compete. If Head Office saw fit to en-courage them by training, it would be referred to as 'business development' at best, and certainly not 'sales' training.

3.8   They saw banking as an advisory profession, in the service of their customers *above* the interest of their employers. They felt that taking the customers of other banks was unethical: it was referred to as 'poaching' (an illegal act) and many engaged in rearguard pact with their local colleagues. Bank managers from dif-ferent banks would have weekly coffee-mornings and would discreetly discuss customers and particularly those inclined to dare to move their accounts.

3.9   A new generation of bankers came to replace the traditional managers to ensure that the banks would prosper in a leaner, sharper, more competitive UK environment as it developed through the years of Margaret Thatcher; and this was echoed throughout the world as many economies were inclined to, or had to follow suit.

Selling: the 1990s

3.10 Attitudes changed so much in the 1990s that many, if not most, banks now have a respected and valued selling function, either endemic to the manager's function or separately represented at every level. Selling is now an activity which managers may engage in up to regulatory limits, which, however, will only ever be removed consistent with rules about liquidity and cash-flow and proper operations, as we shall see.

4   Domestic banking on an international stage

Europe: the harmonising of financial services

4.1 The Second Banking Co-ordinating Directive, a set of proposals to come into operation at the foundation of the European Union in 1993, had the intention of harmonising banking activities throughout the EU and is complex and extensive. The implications for this subject have to do with the extension of competition, in that, for example:

- Banks would have a *single community licence,* and if it obtained approval in any one member state that would be accepted by any other state, and prudential control of branches in another state remains the responsibility of the home authority or government.

- The *range of financial activities* authorised in the home country would be recognised in any other member state even if any of those activities were not open to financial institutions in the 'host' state.

- Banks' *accounting practices* would be harmonised throughout the community.

4.2 As Europe becomes a social and economic reality, debate about the details and minutiae of this and many other trading directives proceeds apace. But towards the end of the millennium the intention of the European Union (formerly the European Economic Community, formerly the European Common Market) will inevitably be fulfilled, and cross-border business – and banking – will be a reality, despite the opposition of those who are wary of foreign influences. It would be very surprising if high-level informal approaches were not already being made between the boardrooms of wholesale and retail banking organisations across Europe.

4.3 Possibly further off is the establishment of a single European currency (ECU); but it does not take much of a flight of the imagination to envisage how much easier it would be for financial institutions, among many other businesses, to compete, and how much fiercer that competition would be, if foreign exchange was simply not an issue.

United States of America

4.4 The activities of American Express, MBNA, Diners Club and Citibank among others are the most obvious manifestations of American financing in the UK, and it is in the provision of credit that this activity is concentrated. This may be because in the USA most branch banks are limited to activity in one state, and national branch banking is the exception; while credit card companies have a wider scope, allowing national – and international – operations.

Other countries

4.5   There are major offices of prominent European banks in the UK's larger cities, with some quite large-scale business operations. But it is also interesting to note that where there are ethnic communities there are also banks from the Middle East, Asia and the Indian subcontinent which serve those communities both in the private and the business community.

5   Risk and regulation

5.1   There is a clear philosophical tension between risk, competition and the need for regulation to protect banks and financial institutions from failure, and consequently to protect their customers. The more risk, the more potential gain, but also by definition the more probability of failure; the more probability of failure, the more the need to protect by regulation.

Self-regulatory organisations

5.2   The Financial Services Act 1986 provided that providers of regulated investments must be authorised, among other ways, either direct by the Securities Investment Board (SIB) or by membership of a self-regulatory organisation (SRO), presently

- PIA   The Personal Investment Authority
- IMRO   Investment Managers Regulatory Organisation
- LAUTRO   Life Assurance and Unit Trust Regulatory Organisation
- FIMBRA   Financial Intermediaries Managers and Brokers Regulatory Association
- SFA   Securities and Futures Association

5.3   Membership is important to any who want to operate in the appropriate fields; but there is an argument that such voluntary and diverse organisations should be combined into one statutory body to put customers under an integrated protective umbrella.

5.4   One notable voluntary scheme, in line with the drive to be concerned for customers, is the Code of Banking Practice (1992, revised 1994). This sets out standards which customers can expect from providers, who undertake to tell staff and customers of its acceptance. It has merits in setting universal standards, but could be criticised in that such standards are more evident in the behaviour of organisations and staff than in paper declarations; and in any case, its provisions might have been overtaken in the competitive drive for customer care in the last decade of the century.

The role of a central bank

5.5   To an extent, the nature of a country's central bank makes a difference to its relationship with its government and with the banks for which it has some responsibility. For example, both the German central bank (Deutsche Bundesbank) and the Bank of England have two sets of 'customers' apart from those other few who enjoy the special privilege of historically-based accounts. They are the:

- Government's bank, and where the government 'borrows', finance is made available to facilitate its social programmes, its trade, its employment of staff, and so on.

- Bankers' bank, and strongly influence those banks which have to deposit or borrow via the mechanism of shifts in interest rates.

5.6   The difference is that while technically the Bank of England is owned by the treasury, it does not act or behave as a government institution: and neither government nor bank appear bound in any way to comply with the wishes of the other, but do so when there is common interest. This is, of course, usually the case, but disputes are notoriously possible, and in particular when the government differs from the bank in terms of the direction of interest rates to affect, for example, inflation or employment rates.

5.7   Where the central bank maintains no control over banking activities – and some former Soviet countries have flirted with this sort of arrangement – then there is unlikely to be any effective regulation, whether or not the government issues decrees to that effect.

Controlling liquidity and loan concentration

5.8   Both Government and central bank have a role in regulating the activities of the banking sector by the use of interest rates, but equally importantly by rules concerning reserves in terms of liquidity, to ensure that a bank can meet its liabilities. This arises from the fear of 'runs' on the bank: excessive demands at any one moment from depositors for their cash. It is done in various countries by:

- Demands for liquidity ratio maintenance   (Denmark, Central European countries);

- Control of cash flow   (UK, Canada);

- A combination of both   (USA).

5.9   The American authorities use liquid asset levels for small banks, and the CAMEL system for assessing larger banks:

- **C** apital adequacy;

- **A** sset quality;

- **M** anagement Ability;

- **E** arnings level;

- **L** iquidity level.

5.10   Maintaining levels of liquidity or reserves, even for reasons of safety, clearly limits an organisation's ability to extend or vary its operations, and therefore to compete. Additionally in most developed countries there are regulations about loan concentration, lending substantial proportions of a bank's assets to a single customer, especially in longer-term loans. This is because lending:

- To one business risks the bank's health, because it is dependent on the health of the customer;

- Substantially over a very long term is the equivalent of having equity in the customer's business and may affect the independence of decisions.

MPC
8 members
4 int
4 ext.
set inflation target
no attain.

Large exposure reporting'

Student Activity 3

Try to find out which are your bank's largest customers. If you can, confer with staff in the branch where the account is held, and enquire about whether there are any upper limits on lending to that customer.

Controlling operations

5.11 This unit would have to mention the problems encountered by Baring's Bank, in which one rogue dealer outrageously over-extended the bank in speculative activities, and the bank had to close its business as a result of the failure of that speculation.

5.12 Much of the blame might be allocated to a lack of supervision within the bank. However, the Bank of England had systems which might have prevented the overextension were it not for the fact that these systems traditionally were only applied *after* a problem was detected, and then not forcibly but in a traditional, gentlemanly manner.

5.13 New regulations were proposed in the summer of 1996 to provide for the requirement of organisations to employ people of expertise, to train people in such expertise, and for the organisations to be inspected in these matters on a regular basis. Time will literally tell whether these regulations will work, but the implications are costly for financial organisations, and again, the tension between regulation and the freedom to spend to compete is illustrated by this matter.

6 Consumer protection

6.1 Led by strong popular movement in the US, then in the UK, the voice of the consumer became strong from the 1960s onwards, quickly to be followed by a rich amount of consumer protection legislation covering the entirety of business.

6.2 Just to indicate this legal framework the following can be listed, *among others*:

- Consumer Arbitration Agreements Act 1988;
- Consumer Protection Acts 1961, 1987;
- Consumer Safety Act 1978;
- Data Protection Act 1974;
- Estate Agents Act 1979;
- Fair Trading Act 1973;
- Food Safety Act 1990;
- Hire Purchase Acts 1964, 1965;
- Misrepresentation Act 1967;
- Prices Act 1974;
- Sales of Goods Acts 1979;
- Supply of Goods and Services Act 1982;
- Trade Descriptions Acts 1968, 1972;
- Unsolicited Goods and Services Acts 1971, 1975.

6.3   In addition, there are EC directives and a vast amount of case law. The banking and finance business was in no way excluded from the provisions of many of these Acts. Indeed specific financial protection in the huge Consumer Credit Act 1974, affected and limited any (hypothetically) unscrupulous activity by lenders and offerers of credit, at least for loans up to £15,000.

regulated agreements

6.4   The specific nature and provisions of these laws and regulations are, again, not the concern of this course, but clearly such legislation provides yet more boundaries to the business and competitive environment of financial institutions. This is especially the case in an era where concern for the customer is now deeply established in the development of business, for profit.

Consumer care and service

6.5   In the late 1980s and early 1990s, as if centrally cued, all the UK clearing banks engaged in their separate customer care programmes. While each at first may have thought that they were unique in doing so, and that it would give them a competitive advantage, in fact since they were all engaged in such programmes it may have had only a defensive effect. The only real difference was that each bank had a different name for the programme. They all had in common:

- Creation or review of mission and vision statements;
- Public declarations of devotion to the idea of service;
- Re-orientation and training programmes for all staff;
- Senior executive staff actively and openly involved;
- Small local committees/quality circles for suggestions;
- Special programmes for those with customer contact;
- Review programmes for the design and operation of customer areas/queuing;
- Special telephone training, and new systems for response;
- Reward schemes for individual acts of good service;
- Redesign of the appraisal system to incorporate service performance.

6.6   It is notoriously difficult to alter the culture of an organisation, never mind an industry. Banks appeared to move from where it was felt that to hold the account of a 'valued customer' was nevertheless a paternal act (the customer was to be trained to behave properly). They moved to where 'customer is king' – and many care programmes led with such a slogan – and that to serve the customer was to become interested and concerned with what the customer wants rather than what the banks are inclined to offer.

Student Activity 4

Outline the main structure of any customer care programme your organisation has instituted in recent years. Write a half-page to a page essay on the results, both in terms of its effects on the customers, and of your bank's increase in business. You may find you need to consult your bank's PR or Marketing department to do research on this.

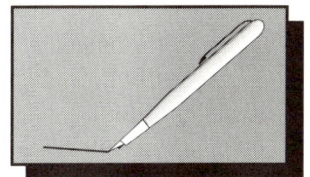

7 Business in the 2000s

7.1 People in the financial industry, more than most, will understand that forecasting the future is a risky business. However, it is fair to speculate about business trends on a very wide basis, and those trends indicate changes in the finance industry in:

- Wider global and European markets;
- Larger global and European business organisations;
- Developments in information and communication technology;
- Leaner and more purposeful structures and operations;
- Closer partnerships between employer and employee;
- Tighter integration between business operations and customer demands.

7.2 *Wider global and European markets* will develop as trade regulations are eased, possibly as trading partners engage in larger trading blocks such as the EU, transatlantic partnerships and the like. The finance business itself is already seeing wider markets than their own countries, and this trend should continue. As their customers become less parochial, banking and insurance will follow in support.

7.3 *Larger global and European business organisations* are likely to follow so that the markets may be served locally. If Marks and Spencer can open in Europe, the Middle and Far East, and in the US and Canada, and form business structures to accommodate the expansion, then so can many another. On the other hand, many UK areas of business and finance operations previously regarded as 'ours' will be owned by non-UK conglomerates. 'Our' water companies might be American or French-owned; 'our' stores by Egyptian companies; and if you reside in Stockport, your refuse is already being removed by an Italian company!

7.4 *Developments in information and communication technology* will be startling, and have startling effects. Voice recognition could soon replace the keyboard. Internet operations might make the concept of 'going to work' obsolete in many occupations: already with a lap-top computer, a portable telephone and a modem, most business operations can be carried out just about anywhere. Voice-based e-mail will make communication between people world wide instantaneous and ridiculously cheap. Financial transfer and record-holding will no longer need any physical transport of paper. The need for branches for simple financial transactions is already doubtful, and could be reduced to a minimum of consultative offices.

7.5 *Leaner and more purposeful structures and operations* will be demanded by ferociously competitive economies where shareholders, staff and consumers demand no waste and maximum return for the investment of their capital, their work-lives and their custom. Traditions will be less and less the basis of business relationships, and patient customer loyalty will be less likely to survive a better deal from another supplier where the customers themselves are under fierce competitive pressure.

7.6 *Closer partnerships between employer and employee* are likely. To retain the best of employees, organisations are likely to want to make their lives stimulating and comfortable. Trends are towards trusting, and empowering, well-trained and properly remunerated employees – those who will be left after the continuing automation of simpler operations – and many believe that the best and most competitive ideas for business advance originate with motivated staff at the 'coalface'.

7.7 *Tighter integration between business operations and customer demands* are inevitable. Any organisation, and especially financial firms, who believe that customers should take what they are given, will be beaten by organisations who are truly fascinated by the buying process and accommodate, even enhance it. It will be the market which will determine the entire shape of business in any foreseeable future.

customer driven

Summary

Having studied this unit carefully you should now:

- **place the financial services industry in its business environment;**

- **have become aware of the changing nature of the finance industry;**

- **recognise the role of regulation in the finance business;**

- **have an overview of the international aspects of financial markets;**

- **be able to distinguish between regulation and voluntary self-regulation;**

- **understand the role of consumer protection in financial business operations;**

- **be able to discuss the finance industry in a business future.**

Self-assessment questions

1. What was Peters and Waterman's advice about diversification?

2. What were the four major changes in the banking industry in the 1970s?.

3. Which European Union directive affected European banking in 1993?

4. What does the unit suggest is the major visible activity of US banks in the UK?

5. What do these initials stand for:

    (a) IMRO;

    (b) LAUTRO;

    (c) SIB?

6. Which notable customers do central banks serve?

7. What is the CAMEL test of a US bank's soundness?

8. Name at least four Acts which are concerned with consumer protection.

9. In which of these areas is there *not* likely to be major future changes:

    (a) larger global and European business organisations;

    (b) developments in information and communication technology;

    (c) leaner and more purposeful structures and operations;

    (d) greater numbers of employees in clerical positions?

10. Which one of these technologies are less likely to affect the business of the future:

    (a) voice recognition;

    (b) Nicam stereo TV sound systems;

    (c) voice-based e-mail;

    (d) electronic funds transfer?

Unit 5

People as Individuals, and Motivation

Objectives

After studying this unit, you should be able to:

- **know how psychologists classify individual differences;**

- **understand how transactional analysis shows the results of these differences;**

- **be able to reproduce and discuss major theories of motivation;**

- **understand expectancy theory and the nature of the model.**

---

1 Individual differences and their effect on relationships

1.1 People come to work with differing expectations about what they can gain from the organisation. One of the skills of management is to be able to realise and accept the various aspects of temperament and ability in individuals, and match these differences to job requirements, so the individual can achieve personal goals as well as gain the achievement of organisational ones.

1.2 Each person is a unique individual, but they also share features by which they can be compared with others. The uniqueness and comparability of each individual is referred to as 'personality'. It is difficult, although not impossible, to measure personality. Personality can be measured in terms of various characteristics; e.g., extroversion and introversion, sensing and intuition, thinking and feeling, judging and perceptive, neurotic and stable.

1.3 Eysenck suggests that there are two categories of personality-type: introvert-extrovert, and stable-unstable. The technical meaning of these are:

- *Introvert*: usually looks inwards for views of themselves and how they really are;

- *Extrovert*: usually looks outwards and wants to know what others think of them;

- *Stable*: emotionally unchanging and relatively constant;

- *Unstable*: very changeable and moody (*not* 'likely to go off the rails').

These can be placed on a diagram, with extrovert-introvert on one axis and stable-unstable on the other.

Student Activity 1

Surmise where you would be on the diagram. Start from the centre and guess how far out along each axis you would be.

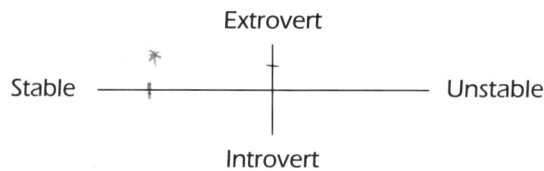

```
                        Extrovert
                            |
                  *         |
    Stable  ——————+—————————+—————————— Unstable
                            |
                            |
                        Introvert
```

1.4   The techniques that are used to measure personality differences are:

● Projective tests (see McClelland, and later in this unit on motivation);

● Questionnaires (personality and IQ);

● Tests of various abilities: spatial, verbal, numerical, memory, reasoning and perceptual speed.

1.5   The latter two means of assessment (questionnaires and tests) are used when selecting people for an organisation. They are therefore examined in more detail in Unit 9.

1.6   It is crucial that managers have an appreciation of the individuals working for them. To get the maximum effort from employees the manager must understand them. Different people might like different aspects of different jobs. Where managers have the opportunity to allocate tasks of various natures to staff, they are well advised to give some thought to how their personality will fit the role. Conversely, they can and should use aspects of personality as a diagnostic tool where staff are ineffective in their work roles.

1.7   There are five elements, according to Bennis, that managers should consider if they are to be effective in interpersonal relationships, the capacity to:

● Receive and send information reliably;

● Evoke expressions of feelings;

● Process information;

● Implement action;

● Learn in each of the areas.

Relationships at work

1.8   A major factor in the success of an organisation must be how well people work together, both as individuals within a group and as groups collaborating. *Personality* will be one factor that influences this relationship. Another is *structure*. Obviously the formal structure of the organisation places some individuals in a higher position than others. Many relationships are influenced by this status difference. Individuals tend to relate best to those of similar status. As well as relationships being influenced by status and personality, *role* also plays a part.

1.9   *Role theory* is concerned with the roles individuals act out in their lives and how the assumption of these different roles affects their attitudes to others.

1.10   Any individual plays a number of different roles, i.e. mother, daughter, wife, employee, supporter of sports club, amateur squash player, member of a political party, etc. Each organisation provides the individual with several different roles. Perceptions are influenced by these different roles, but in any situation one role is likely to have a stronger bearing on what individuals think and do.

1.11   An approach which has been used in examining the roles individuals play and the way they respond to others is *Transactional Analysis* introduced by Eric Berne (1968). Berne established that there are three ego states present in every individual:

- Parent;
- Adult; and
- Child.

1.12   People interact with one another, using any one of these states. When adopting the parent mode the individual can be critical and punishing or caring and protective. In the adult mode the individual stores and processes information, communicating in a mature way, whilst in the child mode the individual can be angry, frightened, insecure or curious, carefree and creative.

1.13   These states can be complementary in communication.

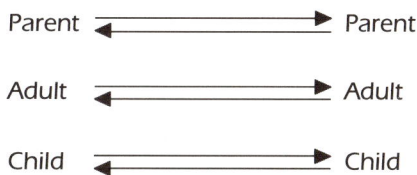

Parent ⟷ Parent

Adult ⟷ Adult

Child ⟷ Child

Or they can be crossed.

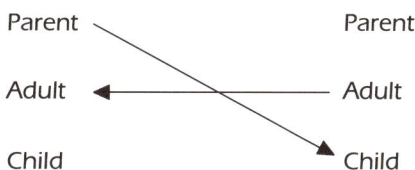

Parent   Parent

Adult ⟵   Adult

Child   Child

1.14   The more effective communication takes place in the complementary states.

Student Activity 2

Transactional analysis suggests that people in the various ego states use language appropriate to that state. For example, a Parent phrase might be 'How many times do I have to tell you ...'; an adult phrase 'He is 56 years old'; a Child phrase 'It's just not fair ...'. Think about, and think yourself into, these ego states, and suggest two more Parent, Adult and Child phrases.

1.15   Individual differences are a pervasive feature in organisations. They influence all aspects of managerial and organisational life and must be acknowledged as a topic of importance if a manager wishes to be successful. It will influence relationships with others, leadership style, the way the manager motivates others, administers the section, selects, trains, appraises and counsels staff.

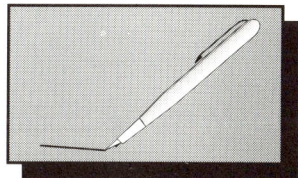

2 Definition of motivation

2.1   It is perhaps appropriate to begin this unit by defining what we mean by the term motivation. Schein, in *Organisational Psychology*, defines motivation as:

> Impulses that stem from within a person and lead him to act in ways that will satisfy these impulses.

2.2   The concept underlying motivation is that there is some driving force within individuals, which drives them to attempt to achieve a goal or objective in order to satisfy their need or needs.

2.3   Efficient organisations supposedly have a preponderance of 'good workers', who are highly motivated and derive a great deal of satisfaction from work. By contrast, other organisations appear to be overloaded with poorly motivated, dissatisfied employees. Motivational theories have attempted to explain and predict the development and satisfaction of human needs.

2.4   There are three major groups of theories or approaches to motivation:

- Traditional or Utilitarian view of man: the first and earliest approach;
- Human Relations View (also known as social or self-actualising man);
- The Complex Man View or Process Theories.

3 The Traditional view or Utilitarian Man

3.1   This traditional approach to motivation and encouraging a satisfactory level of employee involvement and effort is expressed in McGregor's Theory X:

3.2   People need to be controlled and threatened before they put in enough effort to work. It can be described as the carrot and stick approach to motivation.

4 The Human Relations view

4.1   There are a number of theories falling within this area. The earliest approach could perhaps be termed that of 'social man'. This view developed from the *Hawthorne Experiments* conducted by Elton Mayo. They supported the concept that man is a social animal, who gains a sense of identity, self-respect and fulfilment from his social relationships. To rationalise his work and take the social element out of it takes the meaning out of work. According to this theory the manager needs to build social relationships into the work situation and design organisations around work groups, so as to fulfil these social needs.

Self-Actualising Man

4.2   These theories developed from the concept that man is self-motivated and self-controlled. This view maintains that the usual managerial actions tend to reduce autonomy and so reduce motivation. This group of theories can be summarised in McGregor's Theory Y. People enjoy working and can exercise their own control over work

Student Activity 3

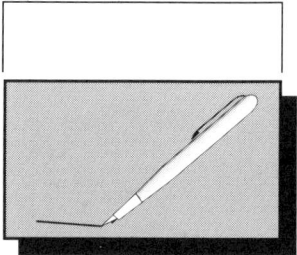

Fill in the questionnaire, based on one called 'How far will you go in life?' by Richard Christie.

How far you will go in life

4.3   In the statement below put a ring around the point on the scale which most closely represents your attitude.

		Disagree			Agree	
		A lot	A little	Neutral	A little	A lot
A	Generally speaking people won't work hard unless they're forced to do so.	1	2	3	4	5
B	The best way to handle people is to tell them what they want to hear.	1	2	3	4	5
C	Most men forget more easily the death of a close relative than the loss of their property.	1	2	3	4	5
D	When you ask someone to do something for you, it is best to give the real reasons for wanting it rather than giving reasons which might carry more weight with them.	1	2	3	4	5
E	Anyone who completely trusts anyone else is asking for trouble.	1	2	3	4	5
F	It is hard to get ahead without cutting corners here and there.	1	2	3	4	5
G	It is best to assume that everyone has a vicious streak and it will come out when given a chance.	1	2	3	4	5
H	One should take action only when sure it is morally right.	1	2	3	4	5
I	Most people are basically good and kind.	1	2	3	4	5
J	There is no excuse for lying to someone else.	1	2	3	4	5

Maslow's Hierarchy of Needs (1943)

4.4   This is one theory that could be said to belong to the self-actualising approach. Peoples' needs are arranged in a hierarchy; when one need is satisfied, individuals move onto the next level. Unsatisfied lower-order needs take precedence over higher-order needs and as the lower-order needs are satisfied, the higher-order needs begin to motivate behaviour. (See Fig. 5.1)

The implications of the hierarchy for management

4.5   The implications are that:

●   Management must find out where individuals are placed on the hierarchy.

●   The organisation will gain most by satisfying the lower order needs because then an individual will be motivated by praise rather than by money.

●   Organisations need to be able to satisfy different levels of needs for different individuals.

Figure 5.1 Maslow's Hierarchy of Needs

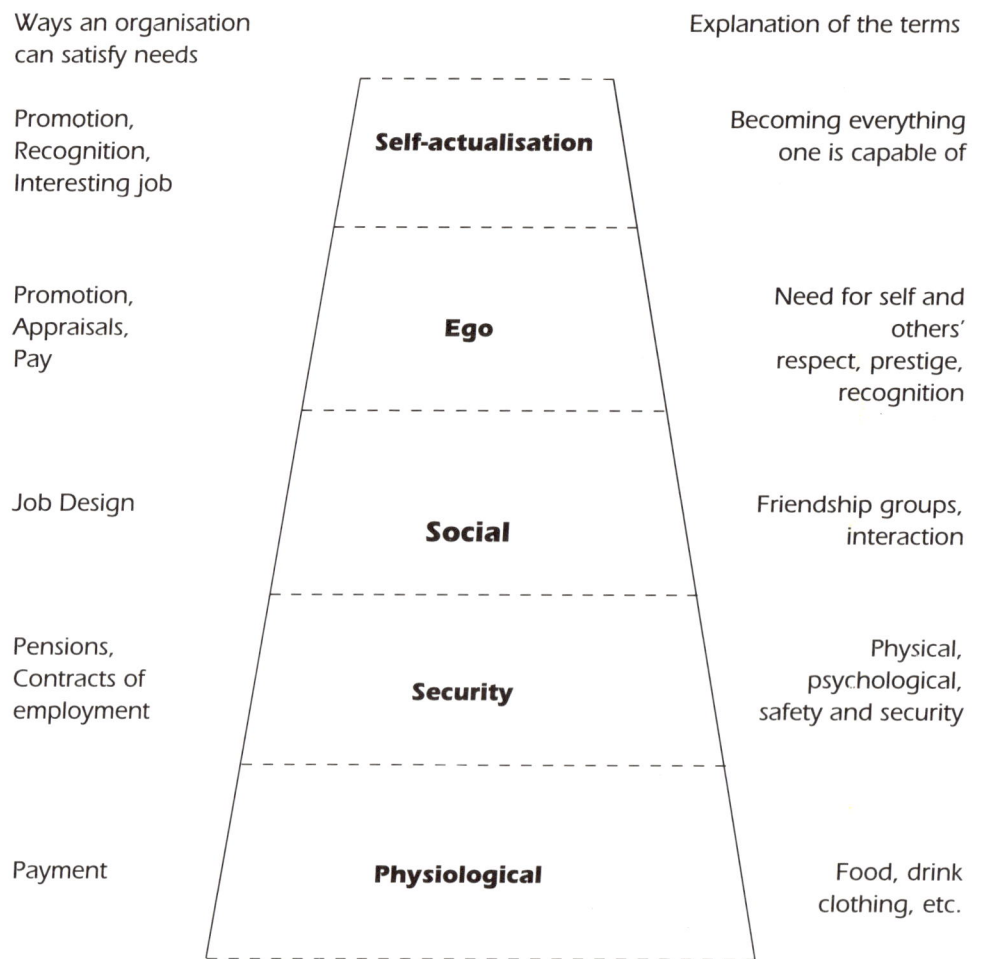

Ways an organisation can satisfy needs		Explanation of the terms
Promotion, Recognition, Interesting job	**Self-actualisation**	Becoming everything one is capable of
Promotion, Appraisals, Pay	**Ego**	Need for self and others' respect, prestige, recognition
Job Design	**Social**	Friendship groups, interaction
Pensions, Contracts of employment	**Security**	Physical, psychological, safety and security
Payment	**Physiological**	Food, drink clothing, etc.

4.6   Although Maslow's theory is intuitively appealing, when closely examined a number of problems seem to present themselves:

- *Can the theory be put into effect*, because there is no time-scale to indicate when satisfaction is supposed to occur at a particular level? The organisation will therefore need to be constantly checking and rechecking the satisfaction level of employees.

- Although Maslow implied the need pattern was the same in all individuals, it does seem to *vary from one person to another*, e.g. starving artists, who could be said to be on the ego level, without satisfying the physiological.

- It is *difficult to fit motivators into categories*, e.g. a company car satisfies *physiological* and *ego* needs.

- Research carried out into Maslow's theory has found *no empirical evidence to support his views*. Lawler and Suttle (1972) found no evidence to indicate that 'satisfied' needs become any less important than 'unsatisfied' ones, or that the satisfaction of lower-level needs raised the importance of higher-level ones.

Student Activity 4

Think about the bank's rewards for staff and fit them into the different categories of physiological, security, social, etc., on Maslow's hierarchy.

Herzberg's Two-Factor theory

4.7 This theory evolved in the late 1950s from a questionnaire answered by 200 engineers and accountants asking them what made them feel exceptionally good or bad at work. The items falling into the former category were:

- Achievement;
- Recognition;
- Work itself;
- Responsibility;
- Advancement.

4.8 In the latter category were:

- Company policy and administration;
- Supervision received;
- Salary;
- Interpersonal relations;
- Working conditions.

4.9 Herzberg drew the conclusion that characteristics in the work situation fell into two categories, those that:

- Led to satisfaction and were *intrinsic* to the job: 'motivators' (the first set of factors).
- Were *extrinsic* to the job: 'hygiene factors'. Although these could prevent dissatisfaction to some extent, they never provided true satisfaction (the second set of factors).

The implications for management

4.10 If managers wish to motivate employees they can only do so through job content. Pay increases or better working conditions cannot alone increase motivation, because it is a progressive need and the employee can never become completely satisfied. Autonomy and responsibility for organising and controlling one's own work is the real answer. No amount of environmental improvement can compensate for task impoverishment.

4.11 There are some problems with Herzberg's two-factor theory:

- The theory is *method bound*: if the same methodology is used the same results are always obtained, but if more searching questions are asked the results are not the same.
- The two groups of factors are *not mutually exclusive* as Herzberg suggested. Motivators can also act as sources of dissatisfaction.

4.12 However Herzberg's contribution is still considered to be important as he established the theoretical basis for job enrichment and new job designs.

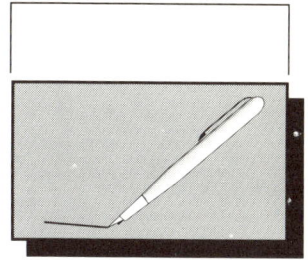

look at Handout in workshop 1.

49

Student Activity 5

Write three paragraphs of not more than 10 lines each answering the following questions, illustrating your answer with personal examples:

1 What are hygiene factors?

2 What are motivators?

3 How is it that a rise in wages can be described as either or both?

McClelland's theory

4.13 McClelland, who developed his theory in the 1970s, cited various needs and motives (over 40 in total), which are of importance to individuals and act as factors which influence behaviour and reactions. One of the needs which McClelland claims is of particular importance in today's competitive society is the need for *achievement*.

4.14 Individuals differ in the extent to which they experience this need. In order to assess this, McClelland uses TAT (thematic perception tests): a mixture of pictures to interpret, verbal questions and problems. The role of management is to determine the level of needs an individual possesses and assign organisational duties in line with this.

4.15 Some of the ways people might demonstrate a particular need:

- Need for *achievement*:
  - enjoys taking risks;
  - likes initiative;
  - enjoys new things and change, but is not so concerned about attention to detail.

- Need for *power*:
  - likes supervising others;
  - enjoys taking decisions;
  - uses his initiative;
  - has good ideas;
  - expresses himself well;
  - enjoys organising his own and others' work.

- Need to *belong*:
  - enjoys being a member of a team or club;
  - loyal to his department or team;
  - likes to share decisions;
  - likes to be popular and so is not good at criticising or disciplining others;
  - conforms to group norms and values;
  - good at communicating with others.

4.16 The problems with McClelland's approach are:

- A lack of empirical support for the theory;

- The unreliability of the TAT stories and pictures;

- The lack of attention given to the issue of how the needs interact with other organisational factors.

5   The Complex Man view or Process Theories

5.1   The more recently expressed views on motivation (from the late 1960s) accept that people may have hierarchies of needs, but maintain that these hierarchies can change as circumstances change. People are variable, having many needs and not necessarily finding fulfilment of all of them in any one solution. Individuals can respond to a variety of managerial strategies: their reactions are dependent on the situation and the needs which are dominant at the time.

5.2   This view of motivation, together with some of the problems associated with the earlier theories gives an indication that simple theories of motivation are not enough to account for behaviour in organisations. The theoretical models (often of dubious empirical validity) say little about the individual context, how individuals understand, attach meaning to and interpret the work situations they find themselves in.

Porter and Lawler's Expectancy theory

5.3   There are a number of theories very similar to that presented by Porter and Lawler, but theirs is perhaps one of the simplest to understand.

Figure 19.2 Porter and Lawler's Expectancy Model of Motivation

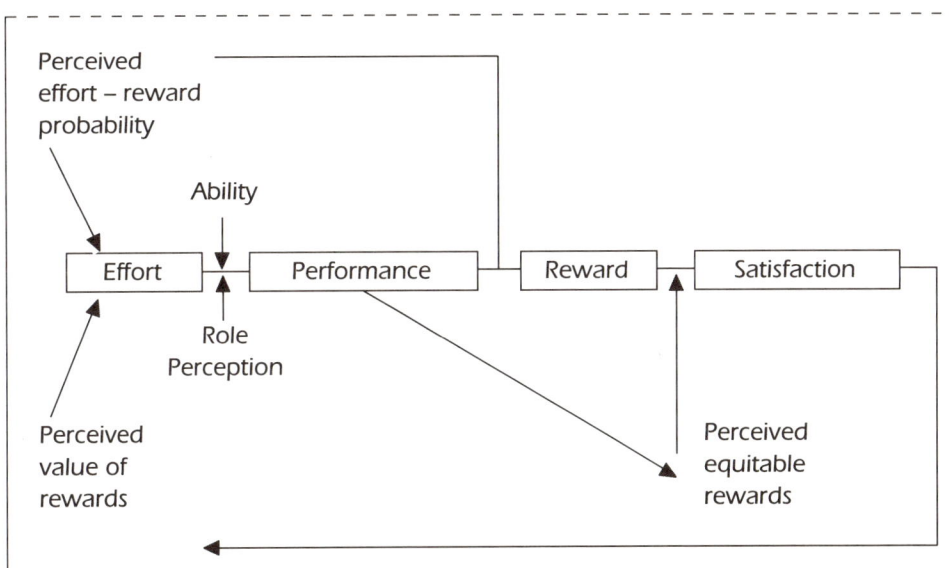

5.4   An individual has a need, say, for a pay increase. This leads the person to put in greater effort to secure promotion. However performance is also influenced by his ability and role perception (the training the individual received, work delegated, whether the individual has confidence in managerial ability, etc). If the individual receives the reward, i.e. promotion, satisfaction will be experienced and leads the person to put in greater effort again. If there is no reward in the form of promotion, the individual will feel dissatisfied and motivation will fall.

5.5 The advantages of this latest theory of motivation are that:

- It is a comprehensive approach incorporating many variables. Instead of promotion it could be examination success, a company car, etc.

- There is an emphasis on feedback and its importance.

- It takes account of the many intervening factors that determine motivation and attitudes to work.

5.6 The theory states that people are only likely to exert some effort when they value the rewards and see that they will get these rewards as a result of doing what is required. An individual's social background can greatly affect their valuation of different kinds of reward. Some groups may strive for improved social status, others will not. It cannot be assumed, and the theory quite rightly allows, that work is the central life interest. The importance of work may vary with socio-economic background, age, sex, etc. The theory also accepts that the people the manager is trying to motivate may not believe that their effort will result in the offered reward. Promotion is not always available. Similarly the effectiveness of effort is mediated by their own skills, the resources available to them, and their own perceptions of their role.

5.7 However, there are still a number of difficulties with the theory that have to be resolved:

- It has become very complex because it tries to incorporate so many variables.

- It tends to concentrate on prediction in terms of present events, e.g. how the needs relate to current work attitudes and behaviour, rather than how the needs arise in the first place. (Why does someone feel the need to be promoted in the first place?)

6 Conclusion

6.1 Students and managers often hope that there is a technology of motivation that can be applied to unmotivated employees. They are usually disappointed. The value of studying motivation lies in helping people think about their own views (perhaps prejudices) on the matter. The employees which managers are trying to motivate often see the world quite differently, and it may be the *employees'* perceptions that managers should consider more frequently.

6.2 Etzioni in the early 1960s claimed that employees could have any one of the three different attitudes at work:

- Alienated: preferring not to be a member of the organisation.

- Calculated: remaining a member in exchange for reward.

- Moral: feeling committed to, and sharing the goals of, the organisation.

Summary

Having studied this unit carefully you should now:

- understand the concept of individual differences;

- know at least one way of classifying them;

- have begun to contemplate interpersonal interaction via transactional analysis;

- have thought about and become able to discuss major theories of motivation.

Q

Self-assessment questions

1. In what two dimensions did Eysenck classify types of personality?

2. Define 'motivation'.

3. Which one of the following said that once a need was satisfied it was no longer a need:
   (a) Lawler and Porter;
   (b) Herzberg;
   (c) Taylor;
   (d) Maslow?

4. Which of the following could be said to describe Theory X:
   (a) man is energetic;
   (b) man is not given enough responsibility;
   (c) man is lazy;
   (d) man is rebellious?

5. Which of the following, according to Herzberg, is a motivator:
   (a) responsibility;
   (b) company rules;
   (c) working conditions;
   (d) salary?

6. In the Porter-Lawler model, ability has an effect on which of the following:
   (a) effort;
   (b) performance;
   (c) reward;
   (d) feedback?

7. Accurately draw Maslow's Hierarchy of needs, with an example at each level.

8. Accurately draw the diagram of Lawler and Porter's Expectancy model.

9. What are the major problems apparent in the Expectancy Model of motivation?

10. What were the three different attitudes to work on Etzioni's classification?

Unit 6

People in Groups and Teams

Objectives

After studying this unit, you should be able to:

- **define a group and discern between types of group;**

- **understand what makes a group effective;**

- **distinguish between groups and teams;**

- **know how individuals contribute in different ways to team working;**

- **have some ways of making group working more effective;**

- **have considered the problems of group conflict.**

---

1 Groups: a definition

1.1 On average, according to Handy (1976), managers spend 50% of their working day in one group or another. Senior managers can spend as much as 80% of their time in groups. They are an essential feature of working life, with most organisations broken up into departments or sections. Most organisational tasks require the co-ordination of these sub-units, so an understanding and appreciation of the nature and functioning of groups is essential if a manager is to 'manage' effectively.

1.2 There are many definitions available as to what constitutes a group. Mullins (1989) suggests that one essential feature is that its members regard themselves as belonging to a group.

1.3 Drake and Smith (1981) suggest that a group:

> ... consists of a number of people who have a common objective or task, an awareness of group identity or boundary, a minimum set of agreed values and norms which regulates their interaction.

1.4 Perhaps one of the most useful definitions is that provided by Schein (1980), who states:

> A psychological group is any number of people who:
>
> 1   Interact with one another
>
> 2   Are psychologically aware of one another
>
> 3   Perceive themselves to be a group.

2   Types of groups in organisations

2.1   There are two major types of groups present in organisations: the formal group and the informal group.

Formal group

2.2   This is a group created to fulfil specific goals and tasks related to the organisation's needs. They can be either permanent, e.g. the marketing department, or temporary, e.g. a steering committee.

Informal group

2.3   The informal group tends to develop from informal relationships (those which are unnecessary for the organisation), formed to satisfy needs beyond those of doing a job. Research studies (Festinger, Schachter and Back) indicate that informal relationships and groups are most likely to develop when people meet in the course of other activities outside of work. They usually tend to be horizontal cliques (with people of the same status), but vertical or mixed groups can also be formed.

2.4   Schein (1980) maintains that informal groups 'almost always arise if the opportunities exist'. They can work to the benefit and detriment of the organisation. The benefits of informal groups for the organisation and individual are that they:

- Provide social satisfaction for individuals.

- Aid communication within the organisation, providing an information flow where none usually exists.

- Provide pressure groups demanding action or changes within the organisation.

- Provide standards or norms of behaviour for their members; and

- The group members tend to have a common value system and certain shared views.

2.5   The problems of informal groups often arise from them serving a 'counter-organisational function', in that they tend to counteract any coercive tendencies of the organisation. They can become too powerful and act as a disruptive force within the organisation. In particular:

- They can provide resistance to change and alterations in work patterns.

- The norms and standards for the group can be inconsistent with those of management.

- They provide an active 'grapevine'.

- They can generate conflict when they clash with the organisation.

Primary and secondary groups

2.6   Another categorisation which is frequently mentioned is primary and secondary groups. Primary groups are usually small and the members are in regular contact, e.g. work departments. They are more cohesive and present a united front.

2.7   Secondary groups are larger in number, less personal and less cohesive. They are more difficult to communicate with.

Student Activity 1

Learn either Drake and Smith's or Schein's definition of a group. Write a paragraph of not more than 10 lines in which you reproduce that definition, explain its elements and use a group of which you are a member to illustrate its aptness.

3   Why do individuals form groups?

3.1   Groups fulfil a number of formal organisational functions and they can therefore be formed for reasons relating to the work process.

- Groups have productive functions. Certain tasks can only be performed through the combined effort of a number of individuals working together. They enable tasks to be completed more efficiently because of the benefits of multiple viewpoints and specialised knowledge.

- Groups make *work more palatable.* The group may encourage co-operation amongst its members, in order to modify formal working arrangements, sharing or rotating the unpopular jobs. Membership of groups can also fulfil other psychological functions.

- Groups provide an outlet for friendship and offer support and companionship. They can also help in solving work problems and reducing stress. (Maslow acknowledged the social needs of individuals in his hierarchy.)

- They provide a means of evaluating opinions and attitudes, and are a way of confirming one's identity, status, attitude, etc. They give the individual a sense of belonging as well as providing guidelines on acceptable behaviour and acting as a control on behaviour.

3.2   Social exchange theory (Kelley) maintains that the desire to join and remain with a group can be explained in terms of costs (anxiety, irritation, embarrassment) against rewards (increased self-esteem, praise and status).

3.3   Most research seems to conclude that groups fulfil both formal and informal functions; that is, they serve both the organisational and individual's psychological needs. The next issue that must arise is how an organisation can ensure its groups work as effectively as possible, and give maximum benefit to both the organisation and the individual.

Student Activity 2

Identify where a formal group at your place of work intersects with an informal group. Identify ways in which that phenomenon is of possible advantage to an individual and to the organisation, and of possible disadvantage to individual and organisation.

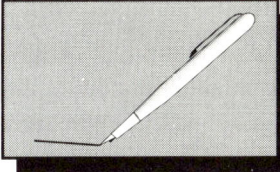

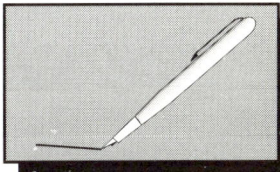

4 Effective work groups

Common factors

4.1 Research has revealed that there are certain common factors apparent in effective work groups. These factors can be divided into four major areas:

- Cohesiveness;
- Size;
- Supportiveness;
- Group roles.

Cohesiveness

4.2 The more effective group has similarities amongst its members in terms of background, status, objectives, norms and values. Similarity in levels of skill and ability also leads to greater cohesiveness. If a group fails to achieve its goals because of a lack of resources, either physical or material, then it develops a sense of failure and is unable to support and strengthen its membership.

Size

4.3 There also tends to be an optimum size in effective work groups. Between five and seven members is considered ideal. This gives enough individuals for there to be variety and multiple viewpoints, but people are not inhibited to speak or express their opinion.

Supportiveness

4.4 Groups whose members are supportive of others also tend to be more effective. Constructive criticism can be helpful to the progress of the group whereas destructive and excessively critical comments tend to destroy rapport and support among members. Resource support from outside the group can also be important.

Group roles

4.5 A group can be made more effective if, according to Belbin, individuals play different roles within the group. Belbin identifies eight different roles, i.e. a pattern of characteristics which define the way one team member interacts with another.

Group members and their roles

4.6 The following roles are present:

- The *Chairman,* controls the way a team moves towards the group objectives, making best use of available resources, recognising the team's strengths and weaknesses, ensuring best use is made of each team member's potential.

- The *Company Worker,* turns plans and ideas into practice, and carries them out efficiently and systematically.

- The *Completer – Finisher,* makes sure the team is protected as far as possible from mistakes, searches for the work which needs more attention and also keeps a sense of urgency about things.

- The *Monitor – Evaluator,* analyses problems, evaluates ideas and suggestions, so the team can then make an informed decision.

- The *Plant* (also called the Innovator), puts forward ideas and strategies, emphasising major issues.

- The *Resource Investigator,* explores and reports on ideas, developments and resources outside the group, creates external contracts and conducts negotiations.

- The *Shaper*, organises the way team effort is applied, directs attention to objectives and priorities and seeks to impose structure on discussion and the outcomes.

- The *Team Worker,* supports members in their strengths and helps improve weaknesses, fosters the team spirit.

4.7   To be an effective group, the team should have a balance of all these roles. Some members will adopt a primary role and others may have what Belbin refers to as a backup team role as well as their primary role.

4.8   There are other classifications of group roles. Benne and Sheates (1948) discuss task-oriented, group maintenance and self-oriented roles. In 1953 RF Bates categorised interaction in groups into various roles:

- The supportive roles: agreeing, showing solidarity, etc;

- The destructive roles: disagreeing, showing tension, etc;

- The task answer roles: with suggestions and opinions;

- The task question roles: asking for opinions and suggestions.

Student Activity 3

Choose a work group of which you are a member. Consider each of Belbin's roles, and write a sentence about how it is carried out, and by which member of the group. Write an additional short paragraph about which roles are not taken by any member and the effect of that on the effectiveness of the group.

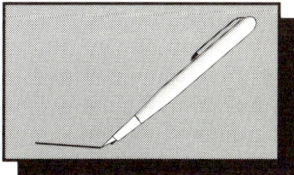

Task

4.9   The way the group copes or responds to the task also plays a part in influencing performance. If the decision required is urgent, then pressure is created and this can adversely affect performance.

4.10   It is also desirable for the group to have clear and common objectives so all action is directed toward the same end. Similarly, the type of leader, whether authoritarian or democratic, in charge of the group will affect their performance. (Leadership is explored in Unit 13 and the effect of leadership style on group members is examined there.)

4.11   Cohesiveness is also affected by the manner in which the groups progress through the various stages of development and maturity. Tuckman identifies four stages:

- Forming;

- Storming;

- Norming;

- Performing.

Forming

4.12 This is the bringing together of a number of individuals who formulate the initial objectives of the group. At this stage leaders, patterns of behaviour and roles begin to emerge. Members are attempting to create their identity within the group.

Storming

4.13 As people begin to know each other, so they start to present their views to the group, and disagreements and arguments begin to occur. It could mean conflict and the eventual collapse of the group, but if this stage is successfully passed then new objectives and operating procedures for the group can be established.

Norming

4.14 As the conflict is resolved so new guidelines and standards of behaviour will be established. The norms of the group govern members' behaviour, but not their thoughts. They are standards of behaviour to which members will conform and are unique to each group: its 'culture'. Norms are especially developed for those behaviours seen as important by the group. Norms are passed on from member to member and often initiating behaviours help to determine the later trends, i.e. the person who initially assumes leadership of the group will eventually be appointed chairman. Norms can sometimes be changed or introduced by an important incident which then sets a pattern. Norms could also be regarded as 'organisational legislation'. They do not have the force of law, but they still restrict behaviour. For instance, if a key member of a group works long hours and at weekends, that behaviour can spread and permeate through the group. Similarly, the amount of overtime can be established as a set amount each week. There are well-known experiments designed to illustrate the strength of norms of behaviour and the desire of individuals to conform to the norms.

4.15 Asch (1951) presented four confederates (people who were aware of the purpose behind the experiment) and one subject, all sitting in a group, with several lines differing in length. The subject was asked to join the four other people. They were shown the straight line 'X' and then three others for comparison and asked to judge which was nearest to 'X' in length. The confederates all said 'A' and although the subject initially cited 'B' he eventually agreed with the rest of the group and selected line 'A'.

4.16 Merei (1949) used as subjects children aged 4–11. After having observed the 'natural' leaders, the 'follower' children were put into groups until they developed norms of behaviour. The 'leader' children were then put into the 12 different groups at different times. In almost every case the group absorbed the leader, forcing their norms of behaviour upon him. The leaders, however, although accepting the norms of the group did find ways of influencing and changing them.

4.17 There can also be pressures to conform to norms in terms of output (Mayo in the Hawthorne Experiments, see Unit 5), and action may be taken by the group to ensure this occurs using:

- Withdrawal of communication;
- Direct communication about norms;
- Social pressures by isolating the nonconformist.

Performing

4.18 When the group has successfully progressed through the three earlier stages, it will have created the cohesiveness to operate effectively as a team. At this stage the group will finally be able to concentrate on the achievement of its objectives.

Environment

4.19 The work environment will determine which groups are formed in the first place. It is therefore obvious that throughout the life of the group the environment in which it exists will continue to play a significant part.

Signs of effective group working

Quantitative

4.20 These include:

- Labour turnover is lower;
- Accident rates are lower;
- Absenteeism is lower;
- Productivity is higher;
- Targets achieved;
- No wasted time.

Qualitative

4.21 These include:

- Interest;
- Strong agreement;
- Want development;
- Participation;
- New ideas;
- Good communication;
- Clear roles;
- Commitment to work.

Student Activity 4

Take a group of which you are not a member, outside or at work, which has undertaken a project of some sort. Look at the stages of group development suggested by Tuckman and write a short paragraph about attitudes and behaviour as it went through the stages.

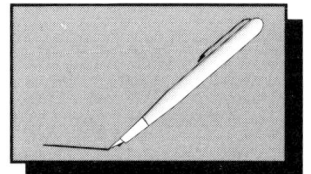

5 Encouraging the performance of a group

5.1 A leader of a group can help a group perform more effectively by:

- Establishing clear objectives for the group and individuals to follow.
- Motivating the members of the group, so they feel they are making a contribution to performance.
- Planning and setting timetables and targets to be achieved.
- Supporting and advising individual members: a leader may not be allocated the perfect team initially, but it is the leader's responsibility to build on their strengths and help them improve their weaknesses.
- Giving feedback and evaluation to the group so they know their progress and can be given coaching or training.
- Ensuring the resources are available for the group as they are needed: physical and financial.

5.2 The approach to leading and managing a group effectively is summed up in Adair's action-centred leadership, which involves concern for the task, the group and the individual (see Unit 13).

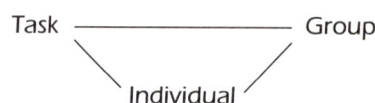

```
Task ———————— Group
      \              /
       \            /
        Individual
```

6 Group and individual decision making

6.1 Although groups are considered to offer many benefits for both the organisation and individual, there are certain situations when individuals working alone may be more efficient. Group decision making is, for instance:

- Costly;
- Time consuming;
- Can create conflict or be a compromise decision;
- Lacks confidentiality;

it can also be more risky.

6.2 By contrast, individual decision making is:

- Cheap;
- Quick;
- Confidential; and
- Risk aversive;

but it does not have the benefits of multiple viewpoints and specialist knowledge.

6.3 The final choice of either group or individual action will be determined by the:

- Time available; and
- Need for specialisation and confidentiality.

It will also depend on whether it is a routine or a non-routine decision, and the expense.

7 Groups: conflict and other organisational problems

7.1 In order that the organisation may achieve its goals, the work of each individual in a group must be directed toward certain objectives. Each member of a group, and indeed each group, develops its own role within the organisation. The role occupied by each person or group is a combination of personal and situational factors. In addition to these relationships, within and through a group, each individual will also have a set of relationships with others outside the group: customers, personnel department, trade unions, etc. Conflict frequently arises in the organisation because of the different roles occupied by individuals and groups.

7.2 Frequent examples of inter-group conflict caused by role conflict are given in research. One well-known experiment was that conducted by Sherif and Sherif (1961) in a boys' summer camp. A camp was organised so that two groups would form and become competitive, seeing each other in opposing roles. Other research has replicated the results. Each group begins to view the other as the enemy: distorting perceptions, seeing only their own *strengths*, not weaknesses, and seeing only the worst parts of the other group. Hostility increases whilst communication decreases and the conflict is thus allowed to increase.

7.3 Inter-group problems arise not only out of direct competition between clearly defined groups. They are also intrinsic in organisations and society, because of the basis on which society is organised. There are potential inter-group problems between men and women, older and young generations, higher and lower status, black and white. Any occupational or social group will develop 'in-group' feelings and define itself.

7.4 Inter-group conflict can be desirable in certain situations. Each group becomes more tightly knit and elicits greater loyalty from its members. The group tends to become more highly structured and organised, as well as more task-oriented.

7.5 The negative consequences of conflict (especially the lack of co-operation between groups) can sometimes outweigh the gains, and management may try to find ways of reducing tension. The conflict basically arises from a lack of agreement on the goals and role of each group, and so the first step must be to establish agreement and get the two sides working together.

7.6 The basic strategy recommended by theorists, therefore, is to locate the goals competing groups can agree on and establish valid communication.

Techniques to resolve conflict

7.7 Accepted techniques are to:

- *Establish a superordinate goal.* Find a goal all groups can aim for and that will require increased communication.

- *Inter-group training.* This involves bringing in a consultant to try to reduce conflict. The competing groups are brought into the training setting with common goals and asked to discuss and make a list of perceptions of the other group. These perceptions are then shared between the groups and, after private individual group discussion, there is a shared discussion on how to manage conflict.

- *Locate a common enemy.* Harmony can sometimes be established by bringing both parties together to fight off an enemy. For instance, conflicts between sales and production can be reduced, if both try to compete against another company.

- *Bringing the leaders of the groups into interaction.* Once the conflict between the leaders is resolved, they can influence the actions of their own parties.

- *The reallocation or restructuring of tasks and responsibilities.* Parties will no longer be competing for resources, etc.

7.8   Many theorists would argue that because of the problems encountered in reducing inter-group conflict, it is better if it can be prevented from occurring in the first place. This is difficult to achieve because the basic premise of many organisations is that division of labour makes for the most efficient organisations. The division of the work-force into functional or specialist groups is the ideal situation for inter-group conflict to occur. The possibility of it occurring can be reduced by:

- Relatively greater emphasis being given to total organisational effectiveness.

- A high degree of interaction encouraged between groups.

- Frequent rotation of staff between departments encouraged to stimulate a high degree of understanding.

- Win-lose situations avoided and groups not having to compete for scarce resources; rewards should be shared between departments.

7.9   An area of study which you need to be aware of is the topic of inter-departmental co-operation and the internal customer. It is essential that departments are encouraged to work together, especially where one is providing services for another (an internal supplier and customer). If departments are interrelated, budgets should be set recognising this relationship. Communication should be encouraged between the sections. The way in which the internal customer is treated is an indication of the way the external customer may be treated by the organisation.

7.10   A system should be introduced that ensures proper relationship management procedures are adhered to for internal customers.

7.11   Conflict can occur on both an interpersonal and inter-group level, and although there may be some positive benefits from a conflict situation, there are also many negative results. Some researchers would claim that rather than having to resolve a conflict situation, it is better to avoid it altogether.

Student Activity 5

Refer back to the text at 7.7–11, and consider these techniques very carefully. Like any such list, this one is incomplete. Add a way which, in your experience, can resolve conflict, and write a short paragraph which could be added as a last paragraph to the text.

Summary

Having studied this unit carefully you should now:

- **be able to reproduce a good definition of a group;**

- **discern between formal and informal groups;**

- **understand what makes a group effective;**

- **distinguish between groups and teams;**

- **be familiar with a model of how individuals contribute in different ways to a team;**

- **have some ways of making group working more effective;**

- **understand group conflict and methods of dealing with it.**

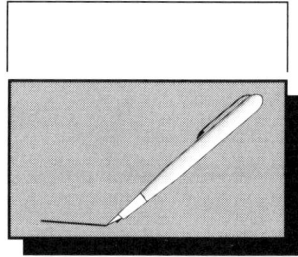

Self-assessment questions

1. Which of the following does not apply to Schein's definition of a group:

    (a) interact with each other;

    (b) meet frequently;

    (c) are psychologically aware of one another;

    (d) perceive themselves to be a group?

2. Asch's experiment concerned:

    (a) leadership of groups;

    (b) decision making by groups;

    (c) the establishment of group norms;

    (d) technology and groups?

3. Which of the following statements is true of a formal group:

    (a) it is not established by the organisation;

    (b) it always follows the organisation's objectives;

    (c) it fulfils a social purpose;

    (d) it is established by the organisation?

4. Which of the following does not describe the development of a group:

    (a) storming;

    (b) producing;

    (c) forming;

    (d) norming?

5. In what ways can groups put pressure on members to conform?

6. Why can informal groups be a problem in organisations?

7. What beliefs are expressed in Social Exchange Theory (Kelley)?

8. What are Tuckman's four stages in a group's development?

9. Group conflict is more likely to arise where:

    (a) two groups never communicate with each other;

    (b) they are in different geographic locations;

    (c) they compete for scarce resources;

    (d) each group has more than 15 members?

10. Which of the following is *not* likely to solve group conflict:

    (a) rotate staff between departments;

    (b) less communication;

    (c) clear role definition;

    (d) more communication?

Unit 7

Information, Technology and the Organisation

Objectives

After studying this unit, you should be able to:

- **know what Management Information Systems are;**
- **know how they operate in organisations;**
- **understand budgetary control;**
- **examine the role of Information Technology in business.**

1 What is an information system?

1.1 An information system is a means of processing data. An example would be changing the routine facts and figures of the organisation into information that can be used for decisions; in other words, getting the right information to the right people, at the right time. In business organisations the most common type of information system is a management information system. Kelly defines this as the:

> ... combination of human and computer-based resources that results in the collection, storage, retrieval, communication and use of data for the purpose of efficient management of operations and business planning.

1.2 The value of the information is measured in terms of the actions that management take as a result of using information. It follows that information specialists need to know what type of tasks and functions management perform, so that relevant information can be produced for them. Planning and decision making are the primary management tasks, and it is for these roles that information systems must be designed. Lucey states 'Planning is deciding in advance *what* is to be done and *how* it is to be done'.

1.3 Planning results in predetermined courses of action that reflect organisational objectives and plans implemented by decisions and action (see Unit 3). Information must, of course, be gathered in order to draw up plans of action. It is now possible for the entire information system of the bank to be integrated into a computer program so that specific information can be available for specific people or grades. This information is then available to simulate conditions for the future in the 'what if' format. For instance, the effect of an increase in interest rates can be calculated for a series of values, the optimum values for investment portfolios can be assessed and shares can be automatically put up for sale at a predetermined share price. Stock control by computer with 'just in time' and economic order quantities can ensure efficient ordering. There are many other examples of the use of information systems: manpower planning, personnel audits, customer records, budgetary control. Some of this chapter will be spent looking at one or two of these systems in turn.

2 The requirements of an effective information system

2.1 If any information system is to be acceptable to management and other employees, it must satisfy the needs of users in the following areas:

2.2 Requirements of an effective information system:

- *Timing.* It should be available as needed.
- *Appropriateness.* It should be appropriate to the needs of particular individuals and departments.
- *Accuracy and quality.* Information must be produced that is as accurate as required. Too much control is expensive and time spent on accuracy should be directly related to the importance of the information. The many errors of manual systems should be eliminated by the use of information systems.
- *Detail.* Important facts should be emphasised and stated in clear concise language to avoid ambiguity. There should be easy feedback if the information requires a response, so further details can be given if necessary.
- *Frequency.* This should be geared to the amount of time staff have to read, analyse and act on information being made available. There should also be signals that action is required.
- *Relevance.* If most of the information produced is not seen to be relevant, interest in the system will die. Occasional checks need to be made to ensure that the expected response is manned with the actual response that the information initiated. Areas where co-ordination exists and work between departments is integrated need special attention so everyone involved sees the relevance of the information.
- *Understandable.* The information should be comprehensible to those using it.
- *Flexible.* It should meet the changing needs of the organisation.
- *User-friendly.* The information should be easily available to staff.

Student Activity 1

Consulting a manager, think of an example of an information system in your office: possibly one where information is passed on a regular basis to Head Office. Write a short paragraph on how it satisfies the requirements of an effective system, as described in the section above.

3 The influences on the design of information

3.1 The different levels of management in the organisation are concerned with different decisions and so have different information requirements. According to Anthony there are three levels of planning in the organisation.

Figure 7.1 Some influences on the design of an information system from Lucey, *Management Information Systems* (1987)

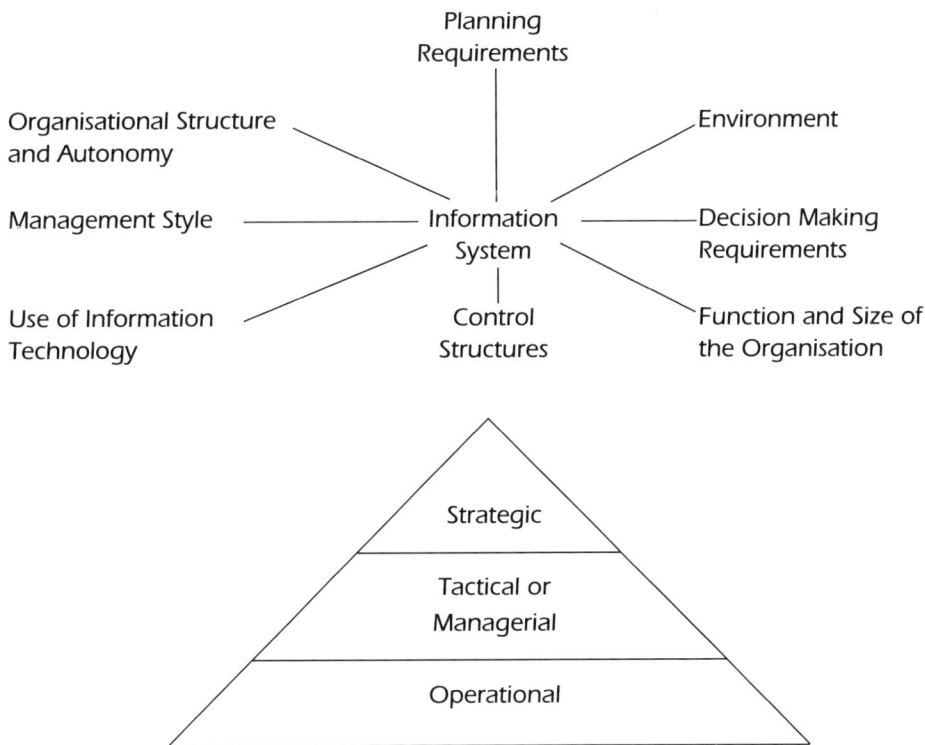

Planning
Requirements

Organisational Structure
and Autonomy

Environment

Management Style — Information System — Decision Making Requirements

Use of Information
Technology

Control
Structures

Function and Size of
the Organisation

Strategic

Tactical or
Managerial

Operational

3.2 Each of these levels has a different time span for planning: strategic being the long-term, tactical the medium and operational the short-term. They each have very different information requirements. Strategic planning is not programmable. It uses mainly external information. The operational level of planning utilises internal information that can be used in programmable decision making.

Figure 7.2 Information requirements of management levels

Strategic	Planning	Non-programmable decision making	External	Unstructured decision
Tactical	Control			
Operational	Information	Programmable decision making	Internal information	Structured decision

Management information systems at the operational level

3.3 These information systems are concerned with the implementation and control of the day-to-day activities of the organisation. These activities depend on the information system dealing with internal information. The effective and efficient processing of data is essential, since the controls are numerous and the monitoring constant. The volume of data is high and a response is needed rapidly so most responses are computer-based. Input at this level is data from operational transactions. Outputs are reports and enquiry handling,

69

e.g. the balance on AG Brown's account. Information systems at this level usually involve batch processing because data volumes are high.

Management information systems at the tactical management level

3.4 This level of management is used to implement strategic objectives and monitor operations. Control systems with information feedback are necessary for their monitoring role and management administer most of the known control systems using management by exception. In this situation budgetary control is where management is given a budget and told to report when the budget varies from the norm. So management by exception involves reporting variances from the set standards. Budgetary and other financial systems (which are covered in detail later in this unit) are a common example.

Management information systems at the strategic level

3.5 At the strategic level management decisions are external and concerned with the future. The information used is both qualitative and quantitative and is mainly external. At this level there are many of the 'what if' issues contained in the system, i.e. if interest rates rise by half a percent what is the likely effect on depositors, etc. Thus it enables management at all levels to assess risk.

4 Budgetary and financial systems

4.1 Budgets are financial statements prepared ahead of time, usually up to one year. They can, for instance, predict the cash requirements of the operations (operational budget) or the revenue or profit for a fixed period of time (revenue or profit budgets). Budgets are derived from organisational and then departmental objectives. The department will need to list all the activities involved in achieving objectives and the type of decisions to be taken. The relative importance of different activities needs to be recognised with the identification of key result areas. The key result areas are those activities which, if carried out well, will make a considerable contribution to achieving the objectives or, alternatively areas where substandard performance will lead to failure.

4.2 There then needs to be set a budget target (determining what is to be achieved by the important subsections of the department). These targets will be those areas that have been identified as key results and usually take the form of a standard to be achieved. These standards should be:

- Relevant;
- Measurable;
- Specific, e.g. not just prompt service but all queries answered in 24 hours;
- Attainable: otherwise frustration results.

4.3 The budget will be prepared by modifying past expenditure in the light of increases (or decreases) in expected costs. There should be flexibility to compensate for minor fluctuations.

4.4 The budget should be prepared so:

- Expected performance can be compared with actual performance;

- The variations between expected and actual performance can be assessed;
- The reasons for variations can be identified;
- Remedial measures can be instituted in good time;
- Information available is timely and accurate.
- Comparisons with other organisations are possible.

Student Activity 2

Again, consulting a manager if necessary, write a series of notes outlining the main elements and operations of the budgetary system which applies in your office. Write also a line of notes to show how it satisfies the specifications (a) to (f) above – or where it has shortcomings.

4.5   Horngren says three types of information are required:

- Score-keeping information;
- Attention directing information;
- Decision making information.

4.6   *Score-keeping Information* measures how well a business is doing and includes service levels achieved and profit information.

4.7   *Attention directing information* is the information that indicates to management a situation that needs attention and indicates where action is required. Service level figures and profit targets would be compared with budget and a variation highlighted. Management would then question:

- Why was there a variation?
- Did it relate to price or volume?
- Was it in a specific market or service?
- Was it failure to produce or deliver the required quality?

Thus an investigation could start into the causes of the shortfall.

4.8   *Decision making information* is usually presented on a routine basis in daily, weekly or monthly reports. It may come from routine reports or as the result of an ad hoc exercise. The routine information is based on new accounts and may indicate where there should be a switching of emphasis from the variances.

4.9   An example of budgets prepared for a branch could be in overall terms maximising profits, increasing deposits by 5% and mortgage lending by £600,000. For *maximum profitability* in a branch the main areas where effort could be concentrated are:

- Increasing turnover;
- Balancing deposits and lending volume (to avoid charges for using central funds and low profits on lending to head office);
- Reducing bad debts;
- Minimising costs: optimum cash level, staffing level, overtime.

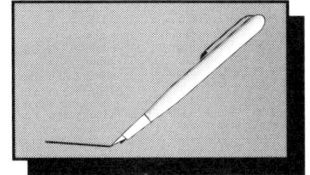

4.10   To *increase deposits* the key areas are:

●   Developing good business relations;

●   Quality of service: because the majority of new corporate business comes from recommendation by satisfied customers.

4.11   Areas to be examined by, say, the marketing department are the time and cash to be spent on advertising, sales promotion, sponsorship questionnaires and competitions, the quality of service-action (conducted in conjunction with personnel and training departments).

4.12   Each supervisor will then be given an individual target to control and keep.

5   Budgetary control

5.1   Tighter budgetary control is a measure of managing the cost of operations. This control can be achieved at managerial and operational levels. The stages in budgetary control are:

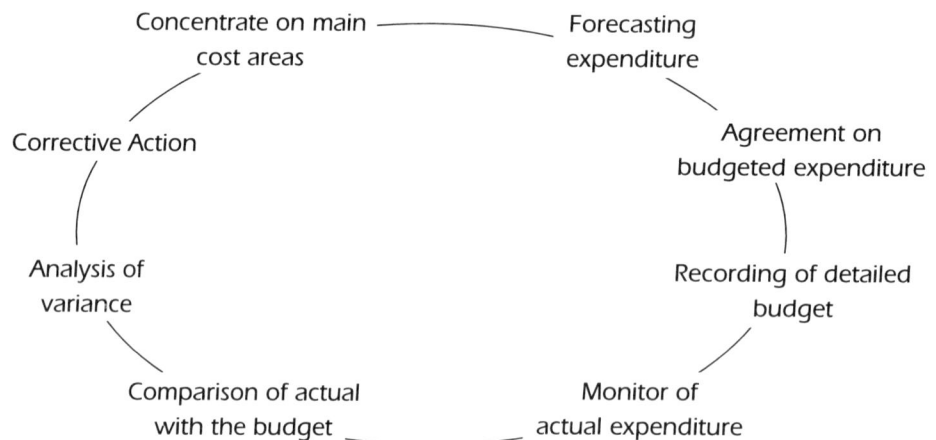

5.2   Budgets can cause problems with individual or team performance. Targets and costs can sometimes dominate behaviour so other equally important aspects of the job are ignored. Budgets can be time-consuming and rigid. This rigidity fits well in a stable working environment, but in a changing scene flexibility in both setting and maintaining budgets is needed.

5.3   If a budget is not properly managed, then there is a danger that managers will claim for an increase in demand and suppress a drop in demand having no incentive to reduce costs. The budget will therefore become inflated over a period of time. Conversely, efficient budgets provide managers with a chance to operate effectively the basic elements of management: planning and control.

6   What is information technology

6.1   According to the Department of Trade and Industry, information technology (IT) is the:

... acquisition, processing, storage and dissemination of vocal, pictorial, textual and numeric information by a microelectronics based combination of computing and telecommunications.

6.2   In other words it is the use of technology to gather, store and distribute information. The main factor behind the expansion of technology is the computer, which allows the electronic processing of information at a speed and in a quantity that would have been unthinkable 40 years ago. The banks have been heavy users of technology for some years. Since the late 1960s computers have been used in domestic operations.

7   Terms used in connection with technology

Databases

7.1   All clearing banks use mainframe computers to process cheques and credits from the customer. This involves all the current transactions on a customer's account and the balances that are owed to them or by them. Not all transactions can be kept in the memory of the machine and so printouts are given from time to time (a statement for the customer and microfiche for the bank). The banks have spent money on a computer system which will give a large database for the banks to use; that is, a pool of data to draw on. This can link customer names to the services which they actually use or potentially could use. Previously it worked only on account number. If the account details show the sex of the customer then the computer can tell the proportion of male and female accounts. Other information can be drawn from the data recorded, to find out the types of people the bank attracts, the type of services it may be appropriate to offer and the charges to be levied.

Mainframe computer

7.2   This is an expensive piece of equipment that is a number cruncher, designed to process many small items very quickly. Its value lies in the fact that it can eliminate paperwork and analyse the information quickly enough to allow management to make relevant decisions.

Minicomputer

7.3   This is also a powerful machine capable of running the accounting and other functions of a medium-sized business. It is used for running a network information system over a group of branches. This means that the information stored could be shared between branches as could the machines' analytical functions. Each branch would have its own input system and the minicomputers would have printers and screens.

Personal computers

7.4   These machines sit on an employee's desk to enable him or her to undertake specific tasks not usually connected with a mainframe or minicomputer, although they can be connected by the attachment of a modem. They can use many different programmes, word-processing, personnel files etc. They are simple to use and relatively inexpensive.

8 Examples of the use of technology

8.1 An example of the use of technology in banking is credit scoring. An applicant for a loan fills in a questionnaire and the answers are put into a computer. The program carries out a series of checks and tests and decides whether the loan should be granted. Previously all loan applications required a managerial decision. Now this is only needed for unusual requests, large loans or industrial applications. There are also programmes available to help in risk assessment. These will, with an input of forward forecasts, provide opportunities to do 'what if' projections.

Student Activity 3

Find a credit scoring form in your office or from a branch, or describe a credit scoring programme on your computer system. In what ways does it help the work of the lender, and in what ways does it limit that work?

Speed of information

8.2 In many instances computers can produce information quickly and efficiently for managers, but it is still the responsibility of managers to make the final decision. For example, Barclays found that its German operation was losing money and the information available indicated its future closure. However, it was established that the German operations produced a lot of profitable business for Barclays' Canadian subsidiary. A final human decision can therefore be essential. The speed of information is a major advantage.

8.3 Time can slant the relationship between a bank's assets and liabilities, between time horizons of short-term deposits and long-term loans. An alteration in interest rates, combined with the maturing of cheap deposits, can throw what was a profitable loan into loss. Technology can help improve this management of the balance sheet, because it can provide a quick response given a number of variables.

8.4 The bank also needs up-to-date information on what is happening in the marketplace. The better informed the bank is, the more valuable its advice to customers. The banks in the long term, with increasing competition, will be forced to use their capital more efficiently. The stock market judges banks by their return on equity, thus the bank's management must use the same measurements, balancing return against risk. This again uses a risk assessment programme and this information is available with technology. The profit, loss and revenue data can be provided swiftly and comprehensibly to top managers. The availability of such information has led to a scaling down of business in some areas, e.g. loans to first-class corporate customers need to be at too fine a margin over base rate to produce a reasonable profit.

Direct telephone lines

8.5 Ansaphones, mobile phones and faxes have revolutionised business. With a fax documents can be sent down telephone lines to anywhere in the world, producing a facsimile at the other end. Legal agreements can be checked internationally and signed within 24 hours.

Automatic Teller Machines (ATMs)

8.6   These are computer terminals which customers use. They depend on a card with a magnetic strip and a Personal Identification Number (PIN) which is used to authorise transactions. There are two varieties. One is 'on-line' and consults the customer's account details before issuing cash. The other is 'off-line' and depends on a predetermination of how much cash a customer can withdraw from a machine in a given period. The latter can stand on its own in any location. Other services available are balance details, statement print-outs and transfers between accounts.

Credit cards

8.7   These are always being developed to provide additional services for the customer. They can be used in ATMs.

Electronic Funds Transfer at Point of Sale (EFTPOS)

8.8   This system allows a customer to pay for goods by passing a debit card, e.g. Switch, through a magnetic reader. This checks the PIN, debits the customer and credits the shopkeeper immediately. This system eliminates the cheque and cheque card because the balance and legitimacy of the card are checked automatically. Whilst there were initial difficulties with both the retailer (cost-based) and the customer (awareness and fear of technology), the number of outlets offering EFTPOS as a payment method have grown rapidly.

Clearing House Automated Payment System (CHAPS)

8.9   This provides all branches of the banks with the ability to transfer money immediately from one account to another in the UK. It uses the computer terminal and codes to authenticate payment. However, CHAPS is not used for small payments, such as factory wages, which are dealt with via BACS.

Society for Worldwide Interbank Financial Telecommunication (SWIFT)

8.10   This is a system for the transfer of funds from one country to another. Messages are sent from one bank to another at high speed with complete security and at low cost using advanced telecommunications techniques.

Bankers Automated Clearing Service Limited (BACS)

8.11   This is a clearing house used by all bankers in the UK and owned by them. It deals with payments made by electronic means, but takes instructions from customers in many ways: via the customer computer, British Telecommunications, magnetic tape or computer discs. Main users are companies for wages, insurance companies for premiums, and building societies for mortgage repayments.

Telephone (remote) banking

8.12   Advances in technology have made it possible to transact bank business without entering a bank branch. Business can be conducted by telephone. An example is First Direct. Customers can call 24 hours a day and are directly connected to a banking representative using a computer terminal. At the press of a button the account details flash up and the banking transaction is carried out in the course of a conversation, e.g. balance enquiries, transfer of funds, payment of bills, etc. To ensure maximum security for transactions customers are provided with passwords. In all dealings with the bank customers are asked to verify transactions with passwords by giving two random characters from it and several pieces of personal information. Other banks are now developing a similar service.

Electronic mail systems (EMS)

8.13 This allows subscribers to communicate with each other on a screen rather than paper. It is quicker than normal postal systems but both parties have to be present if it is to operate effectively.

Screen based trading systems

8.14 These are used in the Stock Exchange to carry out transactions in the broking/jobbing markets.

Local area networks (LAN)

8.15 This allows communication between out stations on a local basis using high-speed lines. VAN (Value Added Network) are communication systems which allow a third party to communicate with the organisation operating the system, e.g. home banking.

Intelligent knowledge based systems (IKBS)

8.16 These will provide expert knowledge for people with the machine asking questions and then assessing the replies before providing information. This system could be used to identify the particular services a customer needs by asking questions about income, personal circumstances, existing financial services etc.

Fifth generation computers

8.17 This technology allows computers to carry out sets of instructions simultaneously rather than, as most do today, sequentially.

9 Effect of information technology

On customers

9.1 Customers have two opposing views. Some welcome the advantages and flexibility that technology brings, although ATMs are the only visible major use of technology from the customer's viewpoint at the present time. Some customers, however, see the information gathering and computerised accountancy as a threat. The Data Protection Act was designed to restrict the power of the computer to hold personal information.

On staff

9.2 Technology frees staff from tedious jobs and makes a company more efficient. If it is properly used it increases efficiency and therefore profitability enabling the bank to compete more effectively in the marketplace. The increase in efficiency and lower costs of using computers for administration, designing or controlling costs enables organisations to compete more effectively, to increase turnover and the number of services on offer.

On structures

9.3 The structure of banks will have to undergo change as the revolution in communication expands. The structure of head, regional and branch offices is changing and new methods of control and responsibility are being introduced. This will continue and the structure of banks in the future will be more homogeneous than before with the divisions being product-determined rather than geographically based. There will be an expansion in satellite banking with one major branch – the others will be just administrative and access organisations.

9.4 Technology will produce the need for organisational change. How should the banks approach employees about the need to change?

On an international basis

9.5 With communication links today, the money markets of the world work for 24 hours daily. The world is a global village for financial services and this enables companies to search worldwide for their finance. The shrinking of the financial world is the result of information technology. It has the effect of making it difficult for a country to change its financial policies without international effect and so slows down in some ways the process of change.

Student Activity 4

Discover and write down the major features, from the customer's point of view, of a telephone banking service.

10 The future

10.1 Banks and technology have so far faced two problems:

- They have invested vast sums of money in technology and sometimes *failed to find a large market* for the products that technology can produce, e.g. the initial reluctance to accept EFTPOS as a means of payment.

- Computer systems bought or built *could not do the jobs required of them*, e.g. Bank of America wrote off $80 million trying to get an accounting system for their trust business.

10.2 Although the introduction of technology has not always been successful in the past, it is likely that the future expansion of banking lies here. The youth of today is more familiar with technology and plans will have to be made for these customers in the future. Home banking will not just consist of being able to call up data, transfer money and other instructions. When technology has solved the problem of computer compatibility, there is the prospect of the cashless society. Cash would be delivered by a plastic card. The card is credited through a device attached to the home banking terminal when the money is needed. It can then be spent in shops by using a point-of-sale terminal. The cards can be used to send money from one person to another and losing the card is like losing cash. The card is simpler than the 'smart card'. It operates in a similar way to a 'phone card'. The technology exists and is being field-tested and banks will have to adapt their strategies to cope with this type of technological advance.

10.3 Technology has the capability to provide a comprehensive database for banks. This will mean that marketing of financial services can take a big step forward. The banks will now be able to inform customers of services they would

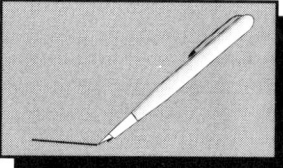

find useful from the data held about them. Marketing can be targeted to age, sex, social grouping, income, etc, and in the light of the existing banking services they are using.

10.4 The third area where development lies is in the area of risk assessment, with a programme that can help assess risk. It can be used for strategy and tactics. The bank could use the programmes to assess which customers are at risk by a rise in interest rates, the implications of a higher inflation rate, etc. The 'what if' scenario can also be applied to the bank's own strategy: whether to expand or contract business, loans or deposits in view of changing economic circumstances.

10.5 Technology is however only a means to an end. The goal for a bank is to sell financial services profitably. While banks are putting new technology systems in place, the organisation is dominated by those who choose the systems. It is necessary that in this development phase technology must be at the forefront of driving the banks to create new products and delivery systems to meet consumer demand. Today a massive amount of investment is needed to fund any operation that maximises the use of information technology and with progress the change will be on a larger scale affecting all aspects of the business.

Summary

Having studied this unit carefully you should now:

- **know what Management Information Systems are;**

- **know how they operate in organisations, including your own;**

- **understand the standards and requirements of budgetary control systems;**

- **have examined the role of Information Technology in business;**

- **have thought about IT at present and in the future in financial institutions;**

- **be able to discuss the role of information in efficient management.**

Self-assessment questions

1. What is an MIS? Fill out the initials and describe one.

2. Name five of the nine requirements of an effective information system

3. What are the three levels in Anthony's framework?

4. What should be the characteristics of standards in a budgetary system?

5. What three types of information are required, according to Horngren?

6. Which of these do not form part of a budgetary control system:
   (a) forecasting expenditure;
   (b) recording the detailed budget;
   (c) analysis of variance;
   (d) punishing budgetary excesses?

7. What is a database?.

8. What do the initials 'EFTPOS' stand for?

9. What do the initials 'CHAPS' stand for?

10. What does this unit imply is the greatest fear that customers have about IT?

Unit 8

Managing and Planning Human Resources

Objectives

After studying this unit, you should be able to:

- **distinguish between Human Resource and Personnel Management;**

- **trace the influence of these functions in the organisation;**

- **understand the objectives of HRM/Personnel departments;**

- **have an overview of HR/manpower planning;**

- **be able to calculate and use HR/manpower planning ratios.**

1 Definition of Human Resource Management and its relationship to other functions

1.1   One widely accepted description by the Institute of Personnel Management is:

> Personnel Management is that part of management concerned with people at work and with their relationships within an enterprise. Its aim is to bring together and develop into an effective organisation the men and women who make up an enterprise and, having regard for the well being of the individual and the working groups, to enable them to make their best contributions to its success.

1.2   This definition does not, however, indicate clearly that human resource management is a part of the general managerial process. An organisation has to use people, and most managers are, by the nature of their job, managers of resources: financial, technological and human. Although managers must deal with people, the organisation can also provide a number of specialists who can ease the load of the line managers and provide a specialist advisory service. They provide input into the planning, control and management of the whole organisation. Individual line managers are only able to see the specific needs of their own departments, not the organisation as a whole. Niven (1967) summarised this, writing for the Institute of Personnel Management:

> Personnel Management is the responsibility of all those who manage people as well as being a description of the work of those who are employed as specialists.

1.3   Northcott spelled out the relationship between the general structure of management and the specialised form of personnel management as he saw it in 1955:

- Personnel Management is an extension of general management ... prompting and stimulating every employee to make his fullest contribution to the purpose of the business.

- It is an advisory service and a staff activity with no obvious authority except that which arises from its terms of reference and the knowledge and skill of the advisor.

- It becomes organised as a function that is a body of duties brought together as the responsibilities of one person and carried out wherever they occur in the establishment.

1.4 To summarise, it is to be expected that every manager is involved in managing people, but the specialist function of personnel management has this as its primary objective and specialist function area.

1.5 There will, of course, be differences in the responsibilities of the Human Resource Director, who is concerned with the central functions of policy making, manpower, planning and reward systems, and the line manager's day-to-day activities in dealing with individuals and their problems. The latter could be termed the personnel duties of the ordinary line manager.

Student Activity 1

In chronological order from the time you first learned about the organisation to today, and into the future, list all the ways in which your Personnel or HRM Department has been and will be involved with your own career.

2 Why Human Resource Management has increased in importance

2.1 Over the last century personnel management as a specialist functional area could be said to have both increased in importance and expanded its areas of activity. A number of reasons have been put forward to account for this:

- Human resources are becoming increasingly expensive to employ. It is therefore essential that they are managed effectively.

- Social science research has emphasised the importance of increasing productivity and the benefits of having a satisfied work force.

- Legislation and the development of industrial relations has encouraged the emergence of specialists able to interpret and apply their skills to this area.

2.2 There is also evidence (Thomason) that over the last century these same factors have caused the activities of the personnel function to expand considerably. At the turn of the century welfare officers were appointed in some of the largest organisations to oversee the care of employees. This role developed into that of 'employment officers' responsible for the selection of staff initially, and then several years later, assuming charge of training. By the 1950s personnel officers were appointed on the basis of contribution to efficiency and 'better human relations in industry'. Training and education for personnel officers was continuing to expand and develop in line with job developments.

2.3   Many today see some differences in the terms Personnel Management and Human Resource Management. The former is concerned with the general management of people, whereas Human Resource Management focuses on the strategic management of human resources – that is, how they fit into the organisation, how they can best be managed and how selection, training and remuneration can best fit the model.

3   The key activities of personnel

3.1   The activities of the personnel function today can be divided into several key areas. These may vary from one organisation to another, depending on history, size, structure, philosophy, climate, etc. A number of these areas are explored in detail elsewhere in the workbook: manpower planning, selection training, reward systems, etc.

3.2   The major activity areas can be designated as:

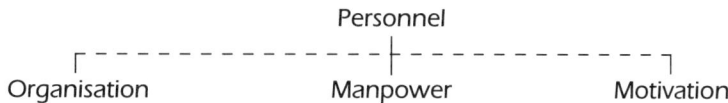

```
                          Personnel
      ┌ ─ ─ ─ ─ ─ ─ ─ ─ ─ ┼ ─ ─ ─ ─ ─ ─ ─ ─ ┐
 Organisation          Manpower          Motivation
```

The organisation

3.3   Key personnel activities within the organisation include:

- Deciding the department's objectives and priorities and designating activities;

- Determining the structure of the department and its relationship with other sections and departments;

- Determining the type and degree of service it will provide for others.

Manpower

3.4   Manpower planning involves a corporate overview of the current manning levels, the skills, qualifications and experience required for different levels in the organisation, and the current manning situation with anticipated trends, turnover, retirements, etc. From this information strategies can be devised to meet the bank's staffing requirements overall, incorporating recruitment, training and development, redundancies, etc.

3.5   This will, in turn, determine the recruitment and selection procedures and policies, e.g. whether the majority of new recruits are school-leavers, graduates or late entrants.

Motivation aspects

3.6   This is the area where the types and systems of recruitment training, education and career development are considered. Job design is also examined with reward and remuneration systems, job evaluation procedures, etc.

3.7   The industrial relations system, the degree and mode of communication, consultation, and participation, and the established grievance and disciplinary procedures can all have an effect on the organisational climate and motivation.

Student Activity 2

Obtain an organisation chart for your Personnel/HRM department. Now looking at the ways in which the department influences people's careers, can you identify from the chart different sets of functions in the department? How do they cluster? Write notes on this.

4   Objectives of the Personnel Department

4.1   The key objectives of a personnel department could be summarised as:

- Designing an organisational structure that encourages good communication, high morale, etc.;

- Obtaining and developing high quality employees;

- Attending to the organisational climate through the use of payment systems, industrial relations and other techniques;

- Meeting all the organisation's social and legal responsibilities.

4.2   Sir Leonard Peach of IBM identified the company's objectives or Critical Success Factors (CSFs) for Personnel as being:

- Maintaining the manager/employee relationship;

- Protecting full employment and promoting the wellbeing of the employee with excellent people management;

- Evolving employment practices and providing education programmes and full compensation;

- Encouraging unity whilst facilitating the management of differences.

4.3   Once objectives are decided then policies can also be agreed. For instance, does the selection process involve panel, or individual interviews; are tests to be utilised; and in the area of career development, is promotion to be zig zag, horizontal, vertical or largely through external recruitment? Employees' relations is another area where the policies of the organisation determine events: the procedure for electing staff representatives, whether productivity bargaining occurs, the policies for health and safety, welfare of employees, etc.

4.4   The policies of the personnel department not only determine how certain procedures are carried out but also have an effect on the relationships with other managers and departments.

4.5   It may be that the personnel department decides to take an active role in certain procedures, e.g. selection, training appraisal and promotion, or they may decide merely to offer advice to other departments on these areas, when asked.

4.6   There is no doubt, however, that once procedures have been determined by the personnel department they should be adopted and followed by other sections to encourage consistency and equitable treatment for all. The influence that the personnel department has over others not only depends on the particular area of activity in question (for instance, personnel will almost certainly be consulted on an area of employment law), but also the policy of the organisation, its structure and size.

4.7 We must emphasise that the management of people remains the direct responsibility of their supervisor, who should have the authority to deal with staff. The personnel department does not replace the direct relationship between boss and subordinate, but rather provides guidelines on policies and procedures together with specialist advice and services. Line management then utilises the central services provided by the personnel function, but accepts their role as front line personnel managers for their own staff.

5 Definition of Manpower Planning

5.1 Manpower planning has been defined as a strategy for the acquisition, utilisation, development and preservation of human resources. This is, however, a very broad definition which virtually covers the whole field of human resource management. It is perhaps more helpful to describe manpower planning as involving two key activities:

- *Assessing* the organisation's current manpower resources;

- *Anticipating* future demand for labour and predicting changes that will affect its supply.

In short, having the right people in the right place at the right time and in the right number.

5.2 There are two aspects to manpower planning. The first one is the macro aspect for organisations dealing with the broad strategy, e.g. the recruitment of 1,000 new employees per year. The other is individual career or development planning with training programmes and planned individual career progression. This unit is concerned with the former; the latter is explored in the next.

6 Why Manpower Planning is important

6.1 Manpower planning has become a key activity of increasing importance to organisations. There are several factors that have played a part in this development:

- Skill needs;

- Legislation;

- Cost.

6.2 As organisations have expanded their range of activities, so the *skills demanded of employees* have become more complex, thus requiring specialisation at an early stage in a career. This in turn means that changing individuals from one career stream to another no longer remains a possibility. So accurate assessments of future manpower needs within one discipline must be made.

6.3 Similarly, *employment legislation* aimed at protecting employees has increased substantially since the early 1970s, and it is now both expensive and time-consuming to reduce the work-force. Again, this creates pressure for the organisation to try and accurately predict future manpower needs.

6.4   With the *increasing cost of manpower*, organisations are more aware than ever that surplus manpower costs money. One factor that can lead to a more efficient organisation is to trim manning levels down to the size necessary for effective administration.

6.5   The process of manpower planning although seemingly straightforward in concept, is a complex process because of the objectives it seeks to achieve:

● Ensuring future manpower requirements are predicted accurately and fulfilled;

● Providing information for the development of training programmes;

● Anticipating redundancy and avoiding unnecessary dismissals;

● Predicting changes in society which may require organisational change;

● Assessing future accommodation requirements;

● Evaluating the feasibility of future developments in manpower terms.

7   The process of Manpower Planning

Student Activity 3

You are about to discover that Manpower/HR Planning is a matter of supply and demand. Write these headings on a sheet of paper divided by a line down the middle. Under each head, write a short list of, say, three or four items of what you suppose planners have to consider in drawing up a plan.

Figure 8.1 Stages of manpower planning

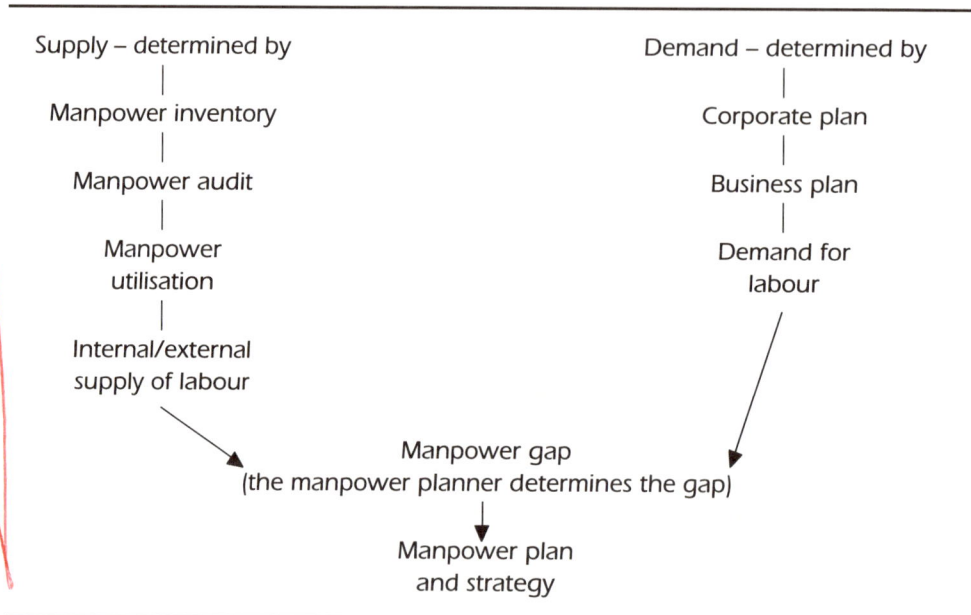

Supply – determined by

Manpower inventory

Manpower audit

Manpower utilisation

Internal/external supply of labour

Demand – determined by

Corporate plan

Business plan

Demand for labour

Manpower gap
(the manpower planner determines the gap)

Manpower plan and strategy

7.1   Although no one overall system of manpower planning exits, it is possible to describe in broad terms the different stages that exist within the process.

Manpower inventory

7.2 This stage involves 'stocktaking' the current labour resources within the organisation. The record systems for manpower are usually computer-based, and current manpower levels are categorised under various headings, such as department, occupation, age, pay, length of service, training, illness record, etc. Organisations can, therefore, gain information not only about the number of employees, but also the skill assessment of individual ability, including professional and academic qualifications, experience, etc. The organisation is then in a position to start making maximum use of its resources, with information for a macro system like manpower planning, and individual needs like placements available. This information could be used for sophisticated career planning systems.

Manpower audit

7.3 This stage provides a second factual base for manpower planning. It gives a detailed analysis of what is occurring within the work-force in the organisation. It provides information on absenteeism, labour turnover, man hours lost due to lateness, etc.

Labour turnover indices

7.4 There are various techniques which are used to measure wastage.

Crude labour turnover/wastage index

$$\frac{\text{Numbers leaving in one year}}{\text{Number of employees at the start of the year}} \times 100$$

7.5 This gives only a crude indication of labour turnover. Research has indicated that wastage is strongly linked to length of service, and employees with short service or younger employees are more likely to leave than any other group. Unless other statistics are gathered, using just this technique can be misleading.

Labour stability index

$$\frac{\text{Number of people with more than one year's service}}{\text{Number employed one year ago}} \times 100$$

7.6 This indicates the proportion of the work-force with longer service. It can be worked out for two or three years service, etc.

Half-life index

7.7 This is a measurement of the time it takes for a group to run down to half its size through wastage.

7.8 Attempting to run down an organisation by natural wastage does not tend to be successful. When an organisation stops recruiting, then the number of people with short service (and therefore the most likely leavers) decreases. The people left have lower chances of leaving and so the number of leavers is considerably reduced. The measurement and prediction of wastage must therefore take into account age and length of service.

7.9 This can be estimated using histograms which indicate the number of employees in a section or department of a particular age bracket.

Figure 8.2 Histogram classifying employees according to age

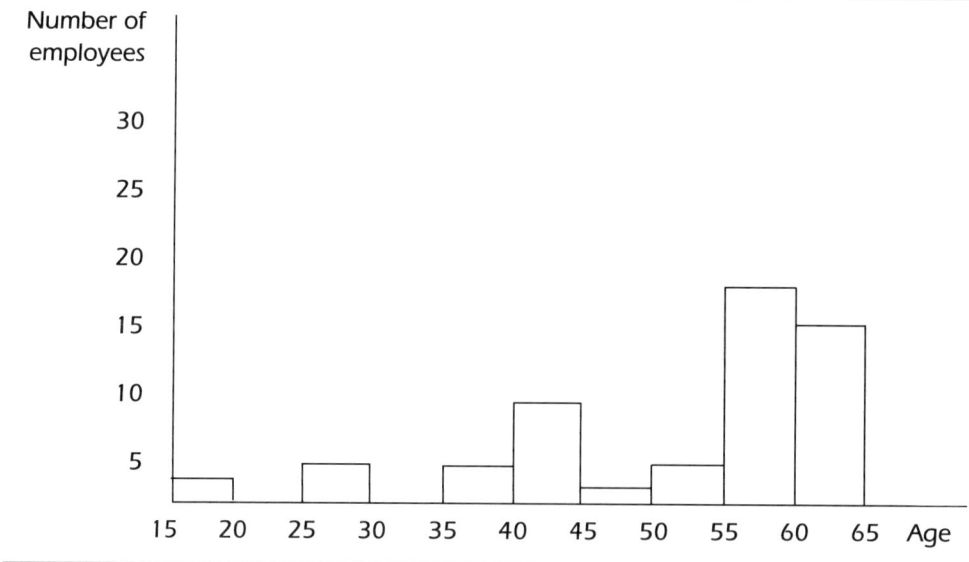

7.10 From the graph it seems that the department will face some problems with the age distribution of its employees. It is top heavy in terms of age, and over the next 10 years will lose just under 60% of its work force through retirement. There are important implications for recruitment and training if continuity is to be maintained.

Exit interviews

7.11 The other technique used in connection with turnover is exit interviews which try to establish the cause of employees leaving the organisation. It may result in simple changes being made that reduce labour turnover.

Absenteeism index

7.12 Another index not used directly in planning future manning levels but one indicating the health of the organisation is the absenteeism index.

$$\frac{\text{Number of days lost}}{\text{Total possible working days}} \times 100$$

7.13 Lateness can also be worked out so the percentage of working hours lost through late arrivals can be anticipated.

Student Activity 4

In consultation with your management, do some research to compile the figures you need to calculate a *Labour Stability Index* and an *Absenteeism Index* for your office. Calculate those ratios, and the write a paragraph on each, commenting on whether they are 'good' or 'bad' figures.

Manpower utilisation

7.14 The most efficient organisations make maximum use of their staff, and so an estimate of utilisation can be useful in manpower planning. This examines the effectiveness of jobs, their content through job analysis, the way they are performed (method study) and the time they take (time measurement). A

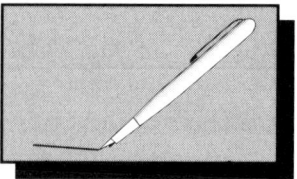

further economic analysis may be done of associated costs, for example:

- Recruitment;
- Induction;
- Training;
- Remuneration (basic pay, overtime, fringe benefits);
- Accommodation;
- Relocation;
- Severance pay.

Manpower gap

7.15 This is the difference between the current manpower situation and the anticipated future demand as derived from the corporate plan. Once the differences have been noted then remedial steps can be taken either to reduce, maintain or increase the labour force.

Manpower plan/strategy

7.16 The manpower plan provides a clear statement of the policy of the organisation (this is derived from the corporate plan). It should also give a set of measurable goals or targets which cover the management of human resources, and each part of the manpower planning process outlined with performance standards; for instance, the number of people to be recruited at the different levels: mature entrants, graduates, school leavers, etc, and the targets for training and development. The manpower planners must liaise with those responsible for the administration of training and development and the reward package generally, and with those providing the information, the executive corporate and strategic planners.

7.17 Several factors may need to be considered when drawing up a manpower plan. Many current manpower plans for financial service organisations involve large reductions in staff. The factors an organisation needs to consider when formulating such plans are:

- The overall strategic plan;
- What developments will affect the business;
- Sources of supply available (other than existing employees);
- Work-force requirements in terms of members, skills, location and age;
- General demographic, economic and employment trends;
- Criteria for selection for redundancy;
- Policy for redundancy – voluntary or compulsory;
- Necessity to maintain recruitment;
- Formulation of staff reduction programmes which will get support;
- Communication of redundancies to work-force, trade unions and the public;
- Provision of counselling;
- Costs – direct (redundancy payments) and indirect (advertising, etc.)
- Effect on the remaining staff and potential recruits;
- Needs for retraining or redeployment to fill gaps;
- Consequences for workload – has it dropped or been redistributed.

7.18 The strategy that the organisation draws up once all this information has been gathered does not merely contain potential recruitment needs but also attempts to estimate:

- Redundancies;
- The need for redeployment;
- Early retirement;
- Training;
- Transfers;
- Promotions;
- New job designs;
- Increased payments.

7.19 The manpower planning process is normally carried out centrally and on a regional basis.

Changing patterns of work

7.20 There is a trend towards more flexible patterns of work, e.g. part-time employees with school holidays and hours, job sharing and individuals starting on a second career after returning to the job market. There is also greater use of temporary contract staff.

Summary

Having studied this unit carefully you should now:

- **be able to discuss the distinction between Human Resource and Personnel Management;**

- **list and expand on the influence of these functions in the organisation;**

- **understand and display the objectives of HRM/Personnel departments;**

- **have an overview of HR/manpower planning, supply and demand;**

- **be able to calculate and use HR/manpower planning ratios to make a case.**

Self-assessment questions

1. Personnel departments are always responsible for:

   (a) staff morale;

   (b) personnel policies;

   (c) the administration of disciplinary procedures;

   (d) records of absenteeism.

2. The personnel department does not have as one of its roles:

   (a) manpower planning;

   (b) selection procedures;

   (c) social activities;

   (d) wages calculations.

3. The factor which will *least* influence the Personnel function is the:

   (a) size of the organisation;

   (b) structure of the organisation;

   (c) nature of the product or service provided by the organisation;

   (d) principles and values of the organisation.

4. What is the recommended age for retirement in your organisation?

5. Does it differ for men and women?

6. The manpower plan has an *active* part in:

   (a) management development schemes;

   (b) staff appraisal systems;

   (c) national unemployment problems;

   (d) supply and demand for staff in the future.

7. The supply of manpower is not *directly* connected with:

   (a) demographic trends in the labour market;

   (b) competition from other organisations;

   (c) retirement of staff;

   (d) current recruiting campaigns.

8. The manpower audit:

   (a) works out the costs of manpower;

   (b) works out theft levels;

   (c) provides a factual basis for manpower planning;

   (d) is concerned with an assessment of environmental factors.

9. How do you calculate a crude labour turnover index?

10. What is the name of the discussion when personnel staff discuss the reason for their departure with employees who leave the organisation?

Unit 9

Recruitment, Selection and Training

Objectives

After studying this unit, you should be able to:

- **understand the differences between recruitment and selection;**

- **know the steps through which organisations go to recruit staff;**

- **have examined selection techniques;**

- **understand the various ways in which people learn;**

- **have considered training programmes;**

- **have examined management development.**

---

1 Why the selection decision is important for the organisation

1.1 It is becoming increasingly important for organisations to recruit the correct calibre of staff. For banks this is particularly important because:

- Labour represents a high proportion of their costs.

- Banks wish to ensure that those they recruit are right for the job.

- A career in banking is still largely structured so employees progress in acquiring new skills through a hierarchy of positions. It is, therefore, important to select someone who can progress and achieve. The banks also acknowledge that some staff will not progress and achieve career development. This tiered recruitment pursued by many banks over recent years is one way of maintaining balance.

2 Recruitment and selection defined

2.1 There is some difference in meaning between the terms recruitment and selection. *Recruitment* refers to the analysis of a job and the features the organisation will look for in a potential employee, and attracting candidates to apply to the organisation and the offering of various terms and conditions of employment to a chosen potential employee. *Selection* refers to the assessment of candidates in order to choose the most suitable person, and describes a smaller part of the total process.

The process of recruitment

2.2   The process of recruitment and selection begins with the manpower plan, which represents concentration on those aspects of corporate strategy concerned with manpower. Through this process of planning, a manpower plan can be derived, which indicates areas in the organisation where there are likely to be shortages of people, and the number of people to be recruited to meet anticipated employment needs. This can be due to planned corporate change, redeployment, retirement, career progression, management development or people leaving the organisation for alternative employment. The manpower plan will also consider external factors which may play a part, such as population changes, technological advances, projected governmental policies and local variations.

2.3   A recruitment programme will be devised directly from these plans. An 'action plan' will be drawn up indicating the number and type of staff to be recruited, trained and developed. Although ideally there should be a continuous update, in many banking organisations there tends to be set time periods for recruitment: a major period, and a secondary 'topping up' (six months or so later).

2.4   Not only are the times for recruitment specified, but in the UK clearing banks the tiers of recruitment are also specified:

- School-leaver at 16 years of age with a minimum number of GCSEs.
- School-leavers at 18 years of age with 'A' levels.
- University graduates going to branch or departmental banking on a general graduate training scheme, or to departments to utilise specialist skills, e.g. economics or computers.
- Post experience recruits, from typists to senior executives, who have gained experience in other organisations. The bank itself may not be able to provide these staff through internal promotion because of rapid expansion or needing specialist expertise, e.g. recruiting new skills by employing accountants from the Inland Revenue.

2.5   The move towards centralised processing also has implications for staff recruitment. Obviously the vast majority of staff employed at the processing sites are operatives and carry out low grade work. They do not need detailed knowledge of the organisation's products or systems. Shift working increases the need for part-time staff. The employees in the branches need to have selling skills and administrative qualities.

2.6   At the moment a debate about two-tier recruitment is raging. Many argue that the banks create dissatisfaction by recruiting over-qualified staff for clerical jobs with little chance of promotion. It would be far better to recruit less qualified staff specifically for this work, although care still has to be taken to ensure that they receive some chance of promotion.

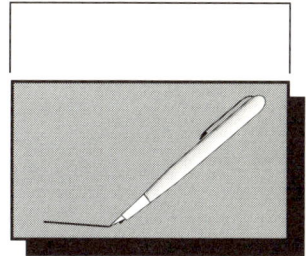

Student Activity 1

Write a step-by-step analysis of the stages of your personal recruitment to your organisation. Comment briefly on the qualities of each step: could you see the point of the steps? Were they well or badly carried out? If applicable, write also a brief paragraph about any steps which were left out or included which made the process untypical.

2.7   The policy of most of the major banks is to fill jobs from within the organisation. This means that most employees move jobs at fairly regular intervals within the same branch or sometimes to another location. The main area of recruitment is, therefore, among school-leavers, for clerical grades and graduates for fast management training.

2.8   For recruitment and selection to be effective at any level a series of well defined stages should be worked through.

Figure 9.1 Stages in the recruitment and selection process

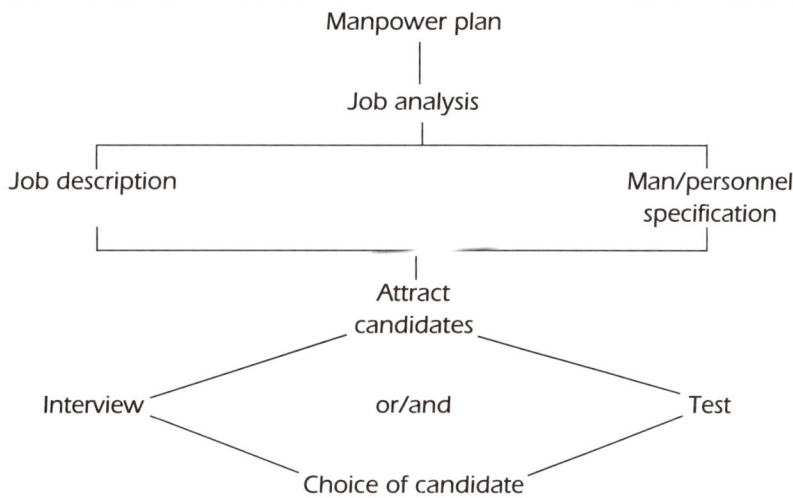

Manpower plan
2.9   From the manpower planning exercise, the organisation should have some idea of the numbers of people they wish to recruit and at which different levels for various jobs.

Job analysis
2.10 This involves the examination of what the potential employee will be required to do in any particular job. These facts concerning the job are then recorded on a job description (sometimes termed a job specification). The term job analysis can also be used to describe the process of drawing up a job description and man specification as well.

2.11 A structured approach to job analysis is desirable to ensure all aspects of a job are covered. This includes:

- *Objectives* – the aims and value of the job to the organisation;
- *Responsibilities* – to whom and for what;

- *Types of decisions* – are they authorisations, ratifications or verifications?
- *Attributes* – experience, skill, disposition;
- *Environment* – the nature of the environment.

Job description

2.12 This is an outline, in general terms, of the activities, tasks and responsibilities involved in a job. It is a written statement of job content. The job specification normally adds to this information giving details on the methods of performing the job and the skills and knowledge required (see the example below). It specifies the purpose of the job, its nature and responsibilities, where the position is located and to whom the individual is responsible

Figure 9.2 Example of a job description

JOB TITLE: Copy Typist/Word Processor
JOB GRADE: Grade 2
COMPANY/BRANCH/DEPT: Head Office
RESPONSIBLE TO: Typing Centre Supervisor
MAIN PURPOSE: To act as a member of a team providing copy typing service to a Head Office department.

1 Typing	
Type letters, memoranda, notes, reports, stencils, etc., from hand-written drafts in accordance with written instructions, or as instructed by the supervisor, following the standard practices laid down in the 'Typing and Word-Processing Guide'.	Accuracy, layout, quantity of material typed.
2 Photocopying	
Photocopying any documents attached or related to material being typed, as instructed. (Any general photocopying carried out by office juniors).	Quality of copies.
3 Housekeeping and General Working Conditions	
Maintain word-processor and clean typewriter and change ribbon as required. Keep desk and working are neat and tidy. Maintain stationery supply for daily use. (All stationery to be obtained through supervisor.)	Cleanness of typed work. Appearance of working area. Work not held up for lack of stationery.

AUTHORITY: To sign external letters on behalf of the originator but only when specifically instructed by the writer or Typing Centre.

2.13 All employees should have a job description because this forms the basis of the management of their performance. The description should be frequently reviewed because it can quickly become out of date.

Personnel specification

2.14 Once the job description has been drawn up, a personnel specification can be developed from the job analysis. This gives details about the type of person who is likely to perform well in the job. It is frequently laid out in a standard format, according to Rodger's seven-point plan.

- *Physical Make-up* (attributes of health, appearance, etc);
- *Attainments* (education, experience, training needed to begin post);
- *General Intelligence* (amount and power of reasoning ability necessary);
- *Special Aptitudes* (mechanical ability, artistic, verbal, spatial or numerate talents);
- *Interests* (when relevant to the job: outdoor interests, problem-solving hobbies);
- *Disposition* (dependability, acceptability, flexibility);
- *Circumstances* (family and home background, mobility, etc).

2.15 An example of a personnel specification following Rodger's seven-point plan, and referring to the earlier job is shown on the next page.

2.16 An alternative layout for the man specification and job description uses Munro-Fraser's five-point plan:

- Impact on people;
- Qualifications;
- Abilities;
- Motivation;
- Adjustment.

2.17 Both the Munro-Fraser and Rodger layout can be used as the basis for the later stages in the selection process, namely interviewing and advertisements.

Student Activity 2

It is likely that there is at least a job-specification, and possibly also a personnel specification, for your job. If you have them, make them available; if they exist and you do not have them, obtain them; if they do not exist, write some. Now compare them with the principles expressed in the unit above, and write a paragraph of not more than 20 lines about how well or badly they comply with those principles.

2.18 The organisation has, after completing the job analysis, description and main specifications, determined the job vacancy and likely qualities of the potential employee. Having determined what the organisation needs, time must be spent in attracting people to apply. For senior positions a technique termed 'head-hunting' may be used. An organisation will ask a specialist agency to recruit an individual for a post. The agency then approaches people already in positions and invites them to apply.

Attracting candidates

2.19 There are a number of ways of attracting people to apply for a post. The organisation can notify vacancies purely internally or use outside sources:

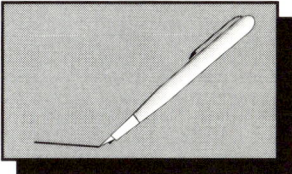

Figure 9.3 Specimen personnel specification using Rodger's Seven-Point Plan

JOB TITLE: Copy Typist

ATTRIBUTES	ESSENTIAL	DESIRABLE	CONTRA-INDICATIONS
1 PHYSICAL MAKE-IP	Over 18 years. Good health; normal vision and hearing (may be trained for audio typing); well-presented.	Over 21 years.	
2 ATTAINMENTS	General education to GCSE or CSE standard	'O' GCSE, or A or B grade pass in English. RSA 2 Typing; RSA 1 Office Practice or similar award. Previous work experience an advantage.	
3 GENERAL INTELLIGENCE	Average. Sufficient initiative and confidence to work without supervision.		
4 SPECIAL APTITUDES	Typing speed 40 wpm. Attention to detail	Typing speed 50 wpm.	
5 INTERESTS	(Immaterial – so long as normal working hours are not affected.)	Some outside interests at least (indicates a lively mind).	
6 DISPOSITION	Able to get on well as a member of a team; conscientious; reliable; punctual.	Willing to train for audio training/word processor.	Introvert; a 'loner'.
7 CIRCUMSTANCES	Available to work a normal working day. Easy access to and from work.	Able to work occasional overtime.	

press, specialist magazines, government or private agencies, school career talks or just the circulation of its recruitment literature, etc. It is essential that the literature gives as much relevant detail about the post as possible, so only those attracted to the job, who possess the minimum qualifications, will apply. The literature or advert should therefore list the essential qualities required, the primary benefits the job offers, its organisational position and context, the paper qualifications or acceptable alternatives, and the procedure for applications.

2.20 Banks normally spend more money and effort on recruitment literature than advertising. Careers officers, contact with schools, word of mouth and established reputations produce thousands of requests for literature. Advertising of posts is usually restricted to geographical or specialist areas where a need is unsatisfied. Whether, in view of future likely manpower needs and demographic trends, this situation will change, remains to be seen.

2.21 The applicant normally fills out an application form giving all relevant details. This information should enable the bank to filter out those candidates regarded as unsuitable. This is done by comparing details on a form against predetermined criteria on job specifications. Most application forms, particularly those for more senior posts, contain an 'open-ended' or 'tiebreaker' section, which requires the candidate to answer certain open questions. For example, 'Why do you wish to work for this organisation?' or 'Where do you see yourself in 10 years' time?' The pre-interview selection can also be made on the basis of these replies.

2.22 After an initial 'weeding out' the commonest form of filter is the interview.

3 The process of selection

3.1 Interviews offer a number of advantages to the organisation:
- They provide a lot of information, including personal details on the applicant, as well as providing direct information about the organisation to the interviewee.
- They can be used as a public relations devices.
- There is flexibility within the interview so gaps in information can be filled in.
- It is possible to assess personal ability to get on with the applicant.
- It may be the only suitable form of selection assessment; for example, applicants for very senior posts.

3.2 However, despite the advantages of selection interviews they can be *unreliable* (different decisions are made by different interviewers about the same person). This is especially true of unstructured and unplanned interviews.

3.3 Other disadvantages are:
- Interviewers have stereotypes of people and push interviewees into one category or another; and they also have a fixed idea of the type of applicant they want.
- Interviewers can make an accept/reject decision very early in the interview – in the first five to 10 minutes – and they then spend the rest of the interview looking for information to support this decision, rather than evidence to the contrary.
- Negative information has a greater impact on the interviewer's judgment than the positive.

- The assessor's judgment is affected by the previous interviewee, and he can be rated higher or lower because of this.

- The interviewer needs feedback on his performance in order to improve it, but because of the nature of the interview situation this is rarely given.

3.4 There are a number of techniques which can be used to try to improve the effectiveness of interviews.

Objectives

3.5 Make sure the objectives of the interview are clear and even set out in writing, if necessary, so it is evident what the interview should be trying to achieve.

Plan and structure

3.6 Plan the interview and structure it with an opening and close, and a clear idea of the questions that should be asked.

3.7 There are guidelines which can be followed and applied to many different types of interview: selection, customer, grievance, appraisal, disciplinary, exit, etc. The structure is basically the same for all these interviews, although the objectives and hence emphasis and tone may vary, e.g. a different tone and emphasis will be used in trying to establish what services the bank may be able to offer a new customer as opposed to disciplining an employee for persistent lateness. However, both are investigatory devices. The first establishes what services are needed and the second establishes why someone is late and how they can improve their performance.

3.8 A suggested framework of stages to be followed in the interview situation is given below:

- Objectives;

- Introduction;

- Investigation;

- Listen;

- Close.

Objectives

3.9 The objectives of a selection interview are to discover the candidates' suitability for a job, to leave candidates with a good impression of the company, and to ensure they feel they have been treated fairly. This means the strategy is one of asking and encouraging.

Introduction

3.10 This is an opening device, and involves greeting a customer or employee, trying to establish rapport, summarising the purpose of the interview and giving some information about your role as interviewer. This provides a bridge to lead on to the main part of the interview – the investigation.

Investigation

3.11 Interviews of any type are investigatory devices, involving questions and answers. For the selection interview, the applicant should be encouraged to talk to allow enough information to be gathered in order to make an effective selection decision. Sometimes this may involve gathering contrary evidence. For instance, an individual confesses to sometimes breaking procedural rules to give the customer a better service: is this behaviour an exception, and is the interviewee aware of the importance of rules? The interviewer must look for information to support or contradict what could be a negative point against the interviewee.

3.12 There are a number of different types of questions. Some are more effective than others in obtaining information. For example, an open-ended question might be, 'Why did you enjoy maths at school?' An example of a closed question is, 'Did you enjoy maths at school?' This evokes a 'yes' or 'no' reply.

3.13 *Open-ended* questions are: who, what, where, why, how, to what extent?

3.14 *Close-ended* questions are: do, are, can, could, have, is? Other questioning skills which can be used are:

- *Pacing*: ask one question at a time.

- *Tone*: try to keep it positive.

- *Tag 'why'*: ask 'why' in response to what an interviewee says to get more depth. 'You said you enjoy teaching others new skills. Why?'

- *Knowledge*: show you have done your homework, basing questions, where appropriate, on the interviewee's application form.

Listen
3.15 Analyse and integrate the applicant's information so it is a dialogue, and a conversation rather than a series of unrelated questions.

3.16 Focus on what the interviewee is saying, observe body signals. Take notes if appropriate. Don't interrupt. Check interviewee's understanding of the job and selection process. (In the disciplinary, appraisal, grievance and customer interviews, checking plays a very important part.)

Close
3.17 In closing the interview, the interviewer must check for agreement and understanding, summarise the key features of the process and establish follow-up procedures.

Key features
3.18 Throughout the interview process, there are three key features always playing a part that the interviewer must be aware of:

- *Body language*: interpreting and being aware of the interviewee's body language (nervousness, aggression, etc).

- *The environmental setting*: arrangement of tables and chairs, formal or informal, (maximising the environment for the purpose).

- *Interpersonal factors*: establishing rapport, how the individual would fit into the job; chemistry, charisma, etc.

Rating
3.19 Information having been gathered, the employee can be rated using the Munro-Fraser or Rodger scale. For instance on the Munro-Fraser criterion of motivation:

A: Exceptional drive and energy – goals are realistic and usually achieved although they are of a high level.

B: Makes very adequate use of the opportunities presented.

C: Adequate when working on routine tasks properly organised, with some limitations.

D: Very dependent on others for organising activities, with goals unrealistic or below what could be obtained.

E: Dependent on others for organising activities, requiring a disproportionate amount of attention not always available.

Student Activity 3

Obtain an application form for the level at which you entered your organisation; and call to mind your own recruitment interview.

(a) Evaluate the application form: were there any questions which seemed to serve no purpose? Were there any questions which were difficult to answer because they were badly worded? Were there any questions which were intended to be difficult, as filters or tiebreakers?

(b) Critically evaluate the interview: on reflection, did it really serve to indicate that you were right for the organisation? Was the form well-used to provide interesting and relevant questions? Did you 'get away with' anything?

Panel interviews

3.20 Because panel interviews involve a number of interviewers, they inevitably place the interviewee under stress. However, it does give the opportunity for a fuller assessment of the interviewee to be made, since other interviewers can assess the person once a question is asked and specialists can be involved in the panel. Discussion as to suitability can also occur; something not possible with the one-to-one interview situation.

Tests

3.21 As well as interviews, tests can also be used as a means of selection. They are popular particularly for school-leavers. There are tests for verbal and numerical ability, tests for spatial and computer skills (those skills not necessarily acquired at school but likely to be needed in a job), and intelligence and personality tests. The key feature is that the tests should be standard (administered in a consistent fashion), reliable (they test what they set out to do) and valid (in the sense that what they measure is a useful predictor of performance).

3.22 The appropriate use of tests depends on the users' objectives, their understanding of the test and the assessment of results in relation to the job. The only effective way to judge the test results is by comparison of the score with the scores of a representative or relevant group of people.

3.23 Tests and interviews can sometimes be combined over a period of several days at an assessment centre. However, because of the heavy costs involved, assessment centres are normally used for graduate management development programmes. Behaviour is observed over a period of 24 hours or more and the achievement of the group and individual assessed by several different specialist assessors. They use interviews, personal history, observation, case studies, leaderless group discussions, role playing and oral presentations. Social behaviour is also observed. The banks have specific needs as they are assessing individuals for a lifelong career (a heavy investment) and people recruited now will be managers in 15 to 20 years' time.

3.24   It is desirable that individuals are notified as soon as possible after the decision is made and the selectors are also prepared to discuss the reasons for the rejection.

4   Other interviews: appraisal, counselling, disciplinary grievance, exit and customer

4.1   Although the other types of interviews commonly used in banking are described in detail in Unit 11, you should be aware of the similarities found in all interview situations. If interviews are to be conducted successfully, the interviewer must ensure he is adequately prepared, having gathered any information necessary and be fully briefed on the situation. The interviewer must have an open mind, conduct the interview fairly, and encourage appropriate contributions from the interviewee. However, the objectives of the interviews will differ and these will, in turn, influence the balance of each of the different stages. For instance, the objectives of a disciplinary interview are to make the employee aware of the problem and advise the individual of the process and stages involved.

4.2   Guidelines for successful interviews:
* Preparation;
* Plan;
* Retain an open mind;
* Be fair;
* Encourage contributions from others.

5   Training: a definition

5.1   Training was defined by Pratt and Bennett (1979) as:

> The systematic development of knowledge, skills and attitudes required by an individual to perform a given task or job.

5.2   *Development*, on the other hand, implies the acquisition of knowledge or skills to be used in possible future jobs. It tends to be more person-centred.

5.3   This section will initially explore some of the principles and theories of learning, the concepts behind training and development practices. It then examines some of the training and development programmes used by banks.

Student Activity 4

Write a list of the last training activities in which you have been involved, up to a maximum of four. Write a preliminary analysis of the training: in a couple of sentences each was each activity well or badly:

- Designed in terms of content? How?
- Conducted by the trainers? How?
- Timed in terms of your work? Why?

6 Approach to learning

6.1 Learning is a concept applicable to all behaviour and is concerned with acquiring knowledge, attitudes, values and responses. It is essential to have some knowledge of how people learn in order to provide effective training. There are a number of different approaches which attempt to explain how people learn, but all involve the idea that there are different experiences which comprise the learning process. One approach – cognitive learning – says the process of knowledge is important and consists of two components. Much learning involves understanding or thinking about what is being learned, insight is needed in a situation if a person is to respond. Learning can also occur when knowledge is stored from past experience and then integrated, so the individual can adapt to new situations and achieve personal goals.

6.2 These concepts are perhaps best illustrated in diagrammatic form by Kolb.

Figure 9.4 Kolb's model of learning

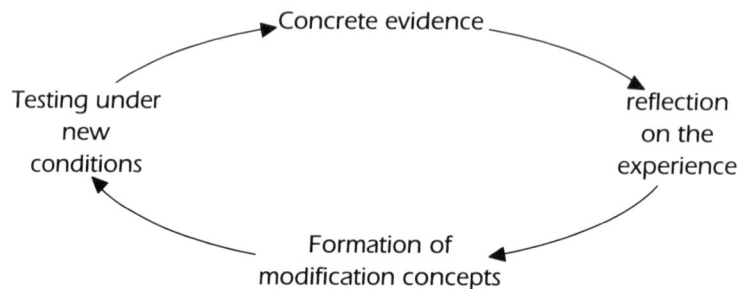

6.3 Kolb believed that some individuals were more competent or happier with particular learning concepts in the cycle.

6.4 Honey and Mumford have developed from Kolb's ideas four different categories of learning styles.

- Activists;
- Pragmatists;
- Reflectors;
- Theorists.

6.5 *Activists* enjoy the here and now and are dominated by current experiences. They like to be active in learning and enjoy new challenges. They are open-minded, but often act first without thinking.

6.6   *Pragmatists* are interested in experimenting with new techniques and ideas and learn best by linking learning with a real problem. They are keen to test things out but will reject out-of-hand pure theory.

6.7   *Reflectors* like to stand back, observe and collect data, then think about the information received before they act. They are thorough and methodical, but do not participate and are risk aversive.

6.8   *Theorists* like to analyse and synthesise, producing models and systems. They are disciplined, rational and objective, but do not like disorder and ambiguity. Everything is black and white.

6.9   Training for the individual often tries to incorporate several different types of learning experience with 'on-the-job' training as well as periods of training away from the job, thus allowing time to reflect on knowledge and experience.

Student Activity 5

First, look at Kolb's diagram. Given an absolute choice, at which one of the activities in the cycle are you most comfortable when you learn? Next, carefully read Honey and Mumford's classification of learning styles. Having done this:

● Try to rewrite each style in a short paragraph without looking at the text;

● Select the style you think best describes yourself;

● Write a further paragraph to say why you think you fit the selected style.

7   Why should training be carried out?

7.1   Today some form of training is carried out at all levels within bank because it:

● *Enhances performance.* It improves the individual's performance on a job through both induction and later training.

● *Saves time.* If people are not trained then they learn by performing the job and it takes much longer to reach the same standard.

● *Maintains skills.* Training also helps to maintain the skills of employees.

● *Increases motivation.* Training increases the motivation of employees by retaining their interest, hopefully resulting in reduced labour turnover.

● *Provides familiarity with all aspects of employment.* It is of mutual benefit to the organisation and individual for the employee to be well versed in all aspects of the job. Fewer mistakes are made and there can be cover for absent colleagues.

8   Different approaches to training

8.1   Despite the acknowledged benefits to be derived from training programmes, not all organisations exercise what could be termed effective training programmes. Four broad approaches to training have been discerned by Megginson:

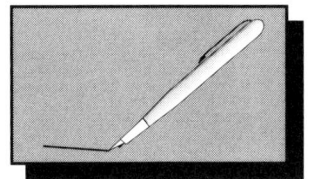

- *The Administrative Approach.* An organisation organises a variety of courses and sends all employees on them regardless of need, previous experience, etc.

- *The Individual Approach.* Employees select a course they would like to go on (usually run by an outside organisation), and ask their employers for permission to attend. The course is not really geared to the individual or organisational needs but rather has broader appeal.

- *The Organisational Development Approach.* All training is aimed at improving organisational performance generally and emphasises group activities such as decision making and problem solving.

- *Systematic Approach.* This is the final, and Megginson declares superior, approach as far as individual training is concerned. It can be described in diagrammatic form (see Fig. 9.5). This model acknowledges that there are certain situations which require training to be carried out, e.g. induction, promotion, new products or technology, changes in legislation. Less concrete indicators of a need for training may be absenteeism, high turnover, rising costs, low morale or conflict.

Figure 9.5 Systematic approach to training

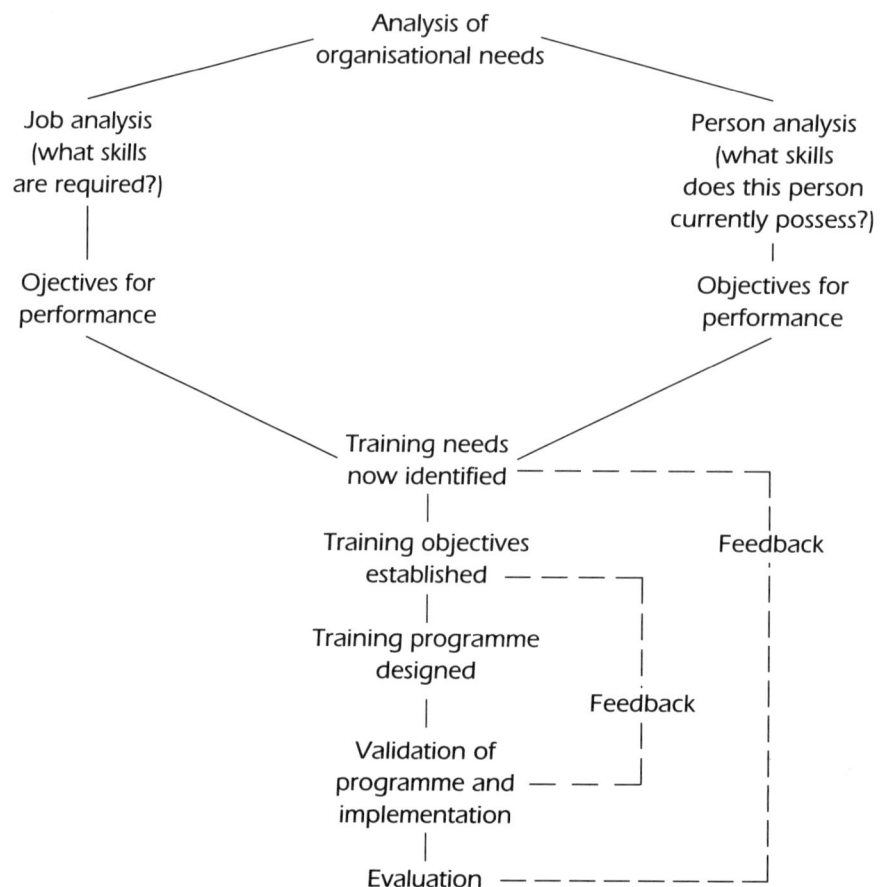

Systematic approach to training

Stage 1: Analysis of organisational needs

8.2   Is the organisation short of particular skills or jobs? Where and in what areas are further skills required?

Stage 2: Job analysis/person analysis

8.3   The job analysis involves an examination of the duties, responsibilities and skills required by the job. The person analysis may or may not take the form of the annual appraisal interview, assessing the ability and skills of the individual as well as shortcomings.

Stage 3: Objective setting

8.4   This involves setting objectives for job performance and what the individual is expected to achieve.

Stage 4: Identifying training needs

8.5   After objectives have been set, training needs can be identified. These can be influenced by changes in legislation, work systems and the type of services provided.

Stage 5: Establishing training objectives

8.6   Good training objectives are essential if effective training is to occur. What should be achieved by training must be stated exactly. Each training objective ideally consists of three parts and should specify:

● *Performance*: what the trainee has to be able to do;

● *Conditions*: under which performance has to take place;

● *Standards*: the level of performance expected.

8.7   When writing objectives the trainer should use precise words describing observable actions.

Stage 6: Training programme design

8.8   The exact content of the programme is determined by its design and the objectives are broken down, setting out in greater detail exactly what the trainee should do to satisfy the training objectives. The training media to be used is also established at this stage, as well as the type and place of tests and assessors.

Stage 7: Validation of the training programme and implementation

8.9   The format of the training programme – whether it is a formal course, on-the-job or open learning, etc – will have been decided at Stage 6. At Stage 7 an assessment of costs will be made, which may result in adjustments in training techniques as well as highlighting the need for additional facilities and increased resources. Whatever form the training takes it has to be validated internally before implementation.

8.10   *On-the-job* training techniques include:

● Job-centred learning;

● Sitting with Nellie (learning as you sit beside someone);

● Projects;

● Job instruction manuals;

● Management-by-objectives (discussed in Unit 11);

● Job rotation;

● Delegation;

● Programmed learning.

8.11 *Off-the-job training* techniques include:

- Lectures, talks, discussions;
- Case studies;
- Role playing;
- Simulation;
- Computer-based learning;
- Workshops;
- Textbooks.

Stage 8: Evaluation

8.12 The evaluation of training is the final but integrative part of any training programme. It can occur at several different levels and stages based on the individual's response to the training, others' assessment of performance, and the individual's contribution to the organisation.

8.13 Evaluation is concerned with the cost-benefit of training in monetary terms and the perceived value and usefulness from the point of view of the people involved and the work they do. It can occur for the employee on a number of levels.

- *Reaction level*: This occurs immediately after training is completed and involves asking the employees their opinions about it.
- *Immediate outcome level*. This is objective and involves testing the employee once training has been completed.
- *Intermediate outcome*. This is both objective and subjective and occurs some time, say three months, after training has occurred. It includes testing and asking the opinion of the trainee as to the value of the programme.
- *Ultimate level*. This is an assessment of the contribution of the training to the organisation.

8.14 Although these different approaches seem separate, most organisations provide a mixture of them all. The factor which connects all four approaches is the responsibilities of the individual, the organisation and the training specialist to identify and provide appropriate training opportunities.

9 Induction training

9.1 Induction training ensures that the new employee is adequately introduced to the job and the organisation. It is important that the inductee is aware of the plan for training so the programme can be followed.

9.2 The organisation also has certain legal duties to inform the new employee of regulations such as Health and Safety, contracts of employment. The Advisory Conciliation and Arbitration Service (ACAS) provide some guidelines as to items for inclusion on an induction programme. These are:

- Reception matters including introduction, PAYE and National Insurance number.

- Layout of the firm and department.

- Introduction to the department, its work and the inductee's job.

- Explanation of the conditions of service.

- Introduction to education, training and promotion.

- Safety and first aid.

- Company rules and procedures.

- Employee involvement and communication.

- Introduction to the company.

- Welfare and employee benefits.

9.3 These do not all necessarily need to be done within the first few days but different items could be timed to occur over a month after starting employment and some even before the employee officially starts, e.g. the history of the organisation and the company rules.

9.4 As well as providing the employees with essential information about the organisation and their jobs, induction training also helps to make employees feel part of the organisation. Many recruits leave within the first 18 months of employment – this is referred to as the 'induction crisis'. Sometimes this may be due to a wrong recruitment decision or the employee feeling the job was the wrong one or induction training being inadequate in preparing the employee, or alternatively, a feeling of not belonging to the organisation. An important aspect of induction is introducing employees to and integrating them into the culture of the organisation.

9.5 Problems can be created for an organisation if people leave within the first few months of their employment because of the:

- Cost of initial training;

- Image of the company with large numbers of former employees in the job market;

- Effect of high turnover rates on an organisation's work;

- Effect of high turnover rates on already established plans.

9.6 Employees must be made to feel part of the organisation as soon as possible. A number of steps can be taken to ensure this happens:

- Reception staff and other relevant employees are told of the newcomer's arrival.

- A desk is made ready.

- The new employee is shown where facilities, e.g. cloakroom, toilets, are.

- They are introduced to immediate work colleagues.

- The new employees are told of rules.

- They are given some work to do.

- There is an induction plan which is adhered to, whenever possible.

Student Activity 6

Obtain an outline of your organisation's Management Development Programme, consulting with your managers or your Training Department if necessary. Look at the programme of activities, and estimate the percentage of the total which consists of formal courses.

10 Management training and development

10.1 Management development is defined by John Humble as:

> ... a conscious and systematic process to facilitate the growth of managerial resources in the organisation for the achievement of organisational goals and strategies.

10.2 Many banks have management development units concerned with assisting the achievement of the business objectives of the bank. It therefore has an input into all the policies involving the resources of the business: manpower planning, organisational development, succession planning, including recruitment, appraisals and training.

10.3 Management development has become increasingly important because there is:
- An increasing amount of delegation for managers and they must be trained to cope with the extra demands this creates.
- An increasing specialisation of skills and this inevitably means increased training.
- Belief in the need for personal growth and development; and there has been
- An increase in higher education generally over the last 20 years and this has led to the expectancy that education will continue over a life time.

11 Content of a management development programme

11.1 As any management development programme will be focused on the role of the manager in organisations, we must first ask what does a manager do?

11.2 Mintzberg identified three major roles that a manager occupies (see Unit 12):
- *Interpersonal*: figurehead, leader, liaison;
- *Information*: monitor, disseminator, spokesman;
- *Decisional*: entrepreneur, disturbance handler, resource allocator, negotiator.

11.3 A manager will have various strengths and weaknesses across these roles and the skill of a management development programme lies in identifying the weaknesses and providing training. A number of techniques have specific application to management development programmes.

On-the-job

11.4 The include:

- *Coaching.* A senior manager will act as a coach, teaching individuals on a one-to-one basis about the job, how to identify problems, consider the options and evaluate them.

- *Action learning.* Small groups are formed (often from different departments) to work on current problems with the help of supervisors. It encourages a climate of self-help.

- *Job rotation.* Changing from one job to another in a planned pattern over a period of time. This encourages the acquisition of new skills.

Off-the-job

11.5 These include:

- Internal courses on knowledge, skills and general management.

- External courses run by a business school.

- CIB courses.

- Action centred leadership: developed from Adair's theories of leadership, which considers the achievement of the task, building the team, and the development of individuals.

- Assertiveness training: designed to teach managers how to establish objectives and attain them without being aggressive.

- Brainstorming: through creative thinking, ideas are called up and recorded in an effort to solve a specific problem. Initially, there is no criticism of the ideas, but later each one is closely examined.

- Case studies: a business problem is stated, which then has to be solved.

- Sensitivity training: a small group is formed and individuals are encouraged to analyse their own feelings, reactions and behaviours, thereby focusing participants' minds onto behavioural issues and interactions.

11.6 Today, the banks acknowledge that the effectiveness of their managers determine the effectiveness of the business, and the money invested in development and training will help to improve performance and therefore is money well spent.

11.7 No training or development can be successful without *motivation from the trainee.*

Summary

Having studied this unit carefully you should now:

- **understand the recruitment process;**

- **be able critically to analyse selection processes;**

- **know the steps through which your organisation goes to recruit staff;**

- **have examined job and personnel specifications and their role in selection;**

- **have considered interviewing as a selection tool;**

- **understand learning styles and be able to identify them;**

- **have considered the quality of training programmes;**

- **have examined the specific nature of management development.**

Self-assessment questions

Q

1. Which of the following is not considered in the recruitment process:

    (a) psychological testing;

    (b) physical attributes;

    (c) aptitude;

    (d) psychoanalysis?

2. The process of recruitment begins with:

    (a) job analysis;

    (b) interview;

    (c) advertising;

    (d) job description.

3. Which of the following does not appear in the five-point Munro-Fraser scale:

    (a) impact on others;

    (b) motivation;

    (c) personal history;

    (d) qualifications?

4. The most effective form of training is:

    (a) on-the-job;

    (b) off the job;

    (c) external;

    (d) through a variety of means according to needs.

5. Setting objectives and then comparing these to later performance is:

    (a) consolidation;

    (b) verification;

    (c) evaluation;

    (d) checking.

6. What are Rodger's seven points?

7. What are Munro-Fraser's five points?

8. What is the five-stage framework to be followed in interviews?

9. What are the criteria for good tests: what should they be?

10. What were the three methods of on-the-job training suggested as appropriate for management development?

Unit 10

Job Design, Job Evaluation and Reward Systems

Objectives

After studying this unit, you should be able to:

- **know ways in which jobs are designed and redesigned;**

- **understand the evaluation of different jobs;**

- **see how different salaries are applied to different jobs, and why;**

- **understand salary systems;**

- **be able to discuss performance related pay systems.**

---

1   Job design

1.1   The application of motivational theories has led to an increasing interest in job design and the effect of this on job satisfaction and work performance. New job design tries to accommodate personal and social needs at work through the reorganisation and restructuring of tasks. It therefore helps in enhancing personal satisfaction and makes the best use of people (an expensive resource today).

1.2   The emphasis in job design, according to Hackman and Oldham (1980) is in three key areas:

- Work should be experienced as meaningful, worthwhile or important.

- Workers must experience that they are responsible for the work outcome and accountable for the products of their efforts.

- Workers must determine how their efforts are working, the results achieved, and whether they are satisfactory.

1.3   These three features are most likely to be achieved if there is present:

- *Skill variety*: the degree to which a job requires the worker to perform activities that challenge a variety of skills and abilities.

- *Task identity*: the degree to which a job requires the completion of a whole piece of work with a seen outcome.

- *Task significance*: the degree to which the job has a perceivable impact on the lives of others.

- *Autonomy*: the extent to which the worker has freedom in scheduling work and determining how it will be carried out.

- *Feedback*: the degree to which the worker gets information about his efforts from the work or from his supervisors.
- *Development*: the opportunity to develop in the job.

1.4 There was an enquiry into job design in the UK during the 1970s entitled, *On the Quality of Working Life*. The research involved establishing evidence about desirable task characteristics aimed at increasing job satisfaction and motivation. It suggested:

- Combining tasks to create a coherent whole job, either using independent tasks or related ones, so their performance makes a significant contribution visible to the job holder;
- Providing feedback on performance both directly and through others;
- Providing a degree of discretion and control in the timing sequence and pace of work and effort;
- Including a degree of responsibility for outcomes.

1.5 Within the job there should be an opportunity for learning and problem solving within the individual's competence. It should be seen as leading toward a desirable future and be providing opportunities for development in ways that are relevant to the individual. The job should also enable workers to contribute to the decisions that affect their jobs, whilst providing adequate resources and support and ensuring goals and expectations are clear.

1.6 Within these criteria a number of different forms of new job design have evolved: job rotation, enlargement, group-working and job enrichment.

Job rotation

1.7 This is the most basic form of individual job design. Job rotation involves moving a person from one job or task to another. It helps to add variety and relieve boredom in the short term because it offers a wider range of tasks to perform. Normally the tasks are very similar and once a routine is established a worker can quickly become bored again. Job rotation may add to the range of skills a person possesses, but they are not usually skills of a different level.

1.8 Some theorists would claim that it is *not* really job design because it does not attempt to restructure jobs, but rather gives a worker the opportunity to do different tasks.

Job enlargement

1.9 This emerged during the 1940s and 1950s as a response to high task specialisation. It offers employees a greater variety of operations with longer cycle times, and it requires a wider range of skills. There is normally an enlargement of tasks horizontally as well as a greater latitude given to workers to determine methods and procedures.

1.10 It is not always a popular technique when employed in organisations. Workers may view it as increasing the number of routine boring tasks and as a means of increasing productivity and reducing the number of employees.

Job enrichment

1.11 The basis for this concept lies in Herzberg's two-factor theory. Motivators are intrinsic to the job and offer the opportunity for achievement, recognition, advancement, etc. The extent to which a person is satisfied by a job is determined by motivators.

1.12 Job enrichment offers vertical job enlargement. Workers are given greater autonomy over the planning, execution and control of their own work. It increases the complexity of work and provides a more meaningful and challenging job. It would mean, for example, not only assembling a product, but also pacing the work, receiving feedback on the product and checking its quality. It emphasises greater control for the employee.

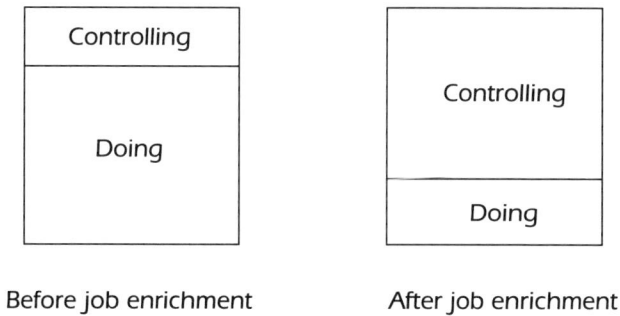

Controlling
Doing

Controlling
Doing

Before job enrichment   After job enrichment

Student Activity 1

Write a half-page account of a time in your career when you were the subject of job rotation (a change for the sake of variety), job enlargement (duties added to make the job more interesting) or job enrichment (more responsibility or more complexity). Were the variations well-timed, well-conducted, effective? Conclude your account with comment to that effect.

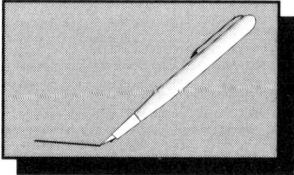

Group working

1.13 This emphasises the achievement of the group through its work. The group assumes greater responsibility for the effective performance of the work. Specific goals are set, but the members decide how the goals are to be achieved, and have greater freedom and choice and wider discretion over the planning and execution of control of their work as a group. The supervisor's role si to advise and support the group. This technique ensures the technological process is integrated with the social system and so becomes a socio-technical method.

1.14 Remember that these techniques are not mutually exclusive; they do overlap and interrelate.

1.15 Other associated factors can also affect job design, for example:

- Organisational structure;
- Technology;
- Management styles;
- Industrial relations;
- Personnel;
- Payment systems.

Conclusion

1.16 The organisation's choice will ultimately depend on its philosophy and structure. Is it job-centred or person-centred? Does it aim to achieve technical efficiency or individual satisfaction through work? How much organisational control and managerial direction can be surrendered to individual authority and responsibility? These and similar factors will determine an organisation's approach to job design.

2 Job evaluation: definition

2.1 Job evaluation is defined by Armstrong as:

The process of establishing the value of jobs in a job hierarchy.

2.2 It is possible to determine job values by negotiation or on the basis of broad assumptions about market rates and internal relations. A far more analytical approach can be adopted using a job evaluation scheme, with market rates and pay surveys. One of the major causes of industrial unrest is said to be the 'differential argument'. Individuals or groups believe they are not being fairly rewarded as individuals. A good job evaluation scheme should help to remove some of these major sources of conflict. However, conflicts still arise over the value assigned to a job by the organisation and the value the employee places upon the job. This is one area where grievance procedures can play a part. Reconciliation of differences in this area can be facilitated by training union representatives in job evaluation techniques. Remember, job evaluation is just concerned with placing a value upon a *job* itself, not evaluating the person doing the job. That is the role of appraisals.

3 Aims of job evaluation

3.1 The possible aims of a job evaluation scheme are to:
- Provide a *rank order* of jobs for the organisation. This can then be used to determine salary level and determine the status of any job position.
- Ensure judgments about job values are made on *objective grounds*.
- Provide a continuing basis for *assessing* the value of jobs.

4 Methods of job evaluation

4.1 There are two major categories of job evaluation techniques: the quantitative and non-quantitative. The *quantitative techniques* involve allocating points or values to the various elements of jobs, which are then combined to form a whole, whereas the *non-quantitative* method just involves the comparison of the whole or parts of jobs and places them in rank order.

4.2 There are two major non-quantitative schemes: job ranking and job classification, which is sometimes termed grade description.

Job ranking

4.3 This ranks whole jobs by comparing job descriptions. A paired comparison method is sometimes used, where two jobs are compared: two points are awarded to the higher ranking post, one where each is considered to be of equal rank, and none to the lower ranking job.

4.4 Livy (1985) illustrates this in diagrammatic form.

Figure 10.1 Livy's system of job ranking

	Securities clerk	Supervisor	Manager's clerk	Loans officer	Senior cashier	Cashier	Total points
Securities clerk	X	2	0	0	2	2	6
Supervisor	0	X	0	0	1	2	3
Manager's clerk	2	2	X	1	2	2	9
Loans officer	2	2	1	X	2	2	9
Senior cashier	0	1	0	0	X	2	3
Cashier	0	0	0	0	0	X	0

4.5 To ensure that this non-analytical system is as accurate as possible, the ranking should be undertaken by a number of individuals and one system agreed upon. Once ranking has been agreed, then jobs can be sorted into grades, in preparation for assigning salaries.

4.6 Ranking is an appropriate system of job evaluation where there are only a small number of different jobs, but it becomes more difficult where large numbers of different jobs are spread across departments.

Job classification or grade description

4.7 This job evaluation scheme begins with a series of hierarchical grades. Each one is then assigned a description or classification. The description has to cover the various duties that may be involved in the post, but include enough detail to make the classification of jobs clear. It must detail the type of work as well as the level of ability and provide key jobs for the identification of grades. Each job within the organisation can then be slotted into the appropriate grade. This is done using management knowledge or an assessment committee, who examine the individual job description and assign it to an appropriate grade.

4.8 The *quantitative* methods of job evaluation aim to make the process as objective as possible. However, even though these systems attempt to be more objective, they are still not completely so, because at some point human judgment is needed in the evaluation of jobs.

Points rating

4.9 This system breaks down each job into a series of factors. Each factor is allowed a maximum number of points. For example, for a clerical grade this may be:

	Maximum Points
Experience	20
Complexity	25
Discretion	15
Supervision	15
Responsibility for avoiding loss	15
Personal contact with customers	10
	100

4.10 Through the system of maximum points, each factor is being weighted to award importance. The total number of points awarded to a job will decide the grade of job:

     50 points = grade 1

     75 points = grade 2

     100 points = grade 3, etc.

Factor comparison

4.11 This is a similar technique to the first stage of points rating. It embodies the principles of points rating with ranking. Jobs are broken down into factors, but there is a limit to the number of factors that can be used. Initially, five factors are used in factor comparison:

- Physical requirements;
- Mental requirements;
- Skill requirements;
- Responsibilities;
- Working conditions.

4.12 There is an initial rating which comprises the rank order of jobs under the various factor headings.

4.13 All systems of job evaluation use job analysis and description. It is only when a job has been analysed and its duties described that it can be accurately evaluated and placed in a rank order.

4.14 Similarly the benchmark jobs, or an established system of grading like HAY/ MSL can be used. The benchmark jobs represent a particular grade within the job evaluation system. These jobs are recognised as standard and have an agreed value assigned to them and so provide help with the position of other posts. The HAY/MSL scheme is one commonly used in banks. This concentrates on know-how, accountability and problem solving as three key components in grading jobs.

4.15 Job evaluation does involve some subjectivity, as human judgment must be used in establishing an order of jobs or assigning values to them. This in turn means that the job evaluation system must allow employees the right of appeal against a particular evaluation. It will normally be heard by a separate appeal panel, who will check the job has been correctly evaluated using information previously provided and any new evidence.

Student Activity 2

Discover by research with your management and your Human Resource/Personnel Department what system of job-evaluation is used in your organisation, and what is done to keep it current. Study your system carefully, with any documentation you can acquire, so that you are able to write a lucid half-page description of it, including how the system is reviewed and updated.

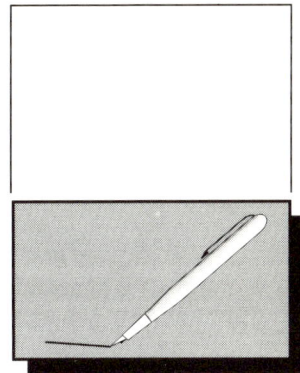

5 Salary administration: introduction

5.1 The job evaluation process places a particular job in a specific grade or at a particular point in a scale. The role of pay structures and salary administration is to assign a monetary value to the job. Determining the pay a job should receive is not an exact science. It does involve a number of intervening variables:

- Supply of and demand for a particular type of skill; for example, several years ago there was a shortage of computer specialists, so exceptionally high rates were paid for the posts.
- The difficulty of the job and the relative skills and responsibilities of the post.
- Existing pay scales.
- Unpleasant working conditions.
- Productivity/length of service/merit payments.
- The need to retain, motivate and attract staff to the posts.
- The value an organisation places on the job.

5.2 There are a number of different attitudes to salary administration. Some companies pay a full adult rate as soon as training has been completed, but there is little progression through grades, and increases are based on productivity bonuses and annually negotiated settlements. Other businesses, like the banks, expect staff to move through the grades, increasing salaries as they advance. There is an increasing trend in financial organisations to introduce performance-related pay.

6 Graded salary structures

6.1 There are a number of approaches to a graded salary structure.

Flat rate

6.2 One rate is paid for each grade and all trained employees of a particular grade will be on a common rate regardless of service. Sometimes additional long service awards are made.

Overlapping grades

6.3   This system allows staff to increase their salary over a period of years within one grade. Each grade has a minimum and maximum with a 'bar' acting as a cutoff point for the average performer. Only outstanding performers are able to pass through the bar. This system, through its design, accepts that those of a lower grade with considerable service may be of greater value to the organisation than newcomers of a higher grade.

Non-overlapping grades

6.4   This system differs from the overlapping one, because the maximum in the lower grade is equivalent to the minimum for the grade above.

6.5   In both the overlapping and non-overlapping systems, people move through from an entry 'learning zone' to a 'qualified zone' and 'premium zone', the latter being for exceptional performers.

Age-related scales

6.6   Before the more advanced job evaluation techniques it was common to pay a salary commensurate with age and experience. This is still commonly used as a system for trainees and those below adult rates, e.g. a salary for 16–18 year olds. The employees may be paid a 'birthday increase'.

Salary progression curves

6.7   These can also be referred to as maturity or career curves. They aim to link increases in salary over a period of time to increased maturity or experience. They are normally used for professional people. The system assumes that they develop within their discipline as a result of their experience. Sometimes more than one rate of progression is provided, when there are different rates related to initial entry qualifications and the individual's rate of progression.

6.8   The essence of the salary progression curves demands that salary administration is flexible, so employees may advance according to ability.

Student Activity 3

Discover by research with your management and your Human Resource/Personnel Department what are the top and bottom rates of salary in your own grade, and the top and bottom rates of salary in the grades above and below your level. Draw a diagram of how all three relate, and make observations about any overlap.

7   The requirements for an efficient salary system

7.1   Most salary systems provide the opportunity for progression, either according to age or experience. This opportunity to progress provides motivation for improved performance in the future, as well as encouraging 'high flyers' to remain with the firm. In order to ensure that a progressive system is as efficient as possible and can be easily controlled, it needs to:

●   Be divided into defined areas or zones;

●   Have incremental systems to indicate the rates at which individuals can progress;

- Have guidelines for determining merit increments.

7.2 Incremental systems can vary from rigid, fixed procedures to flexible systems where management has complete discretion over the award. Within the bank the incremental system is fairly tightly controlled with a scale of increments according to performance.

7.3 With less opportunity for promotion and fewer layers of management, many banks are moving toward performance related pay (PRP). In this way good performance can continue to be rewarded and recognised without promotion.

8 Salary scales v performance-related pay

Salary scales

8.1 The *advantages* of using a salary scale are:
- It is clear and available, i.e. published, to employees;
- It is predictable, so budgets can be anticipated for employer and employee;
- It offers incremental rises;
- Performance bonuses can still be incorporated.

8.2 The *disadvantages* of using a salary scale are:
- It is paid irrespective of results, so incentive can be lacking;
- It is rigid;
- It encourages promotion because this is the only way of really increasing income substantially;
- There can be anomalies between grades.

Performance-related pay

8.3 The *advantages* of performance-related pay are:
- Rewards should be related to effort;
- There is not the same necessity to promote to increase rewards;
- The system can be integrated with corporate goals and an MBO system;
- It is easy to incorporate if it uses quantitative measures;
- It can be used to reward correct behaviour;
- It encourages the achievement of targets and increased productivity can fund the increased pay.

8.4 The *disadvantages* of performance-related pay are:
- It is not always easy to set targets for individuals to achieve – some are qualitative rather than quantitative measures – and this can be time-consuming and costly;
- The setting, monitoring and evaluation of performance against targets is time-consuming;
- It is not easy for the employee to budget because this income is uncertain;
- Salaries cannot be published, as there is no uniform standard or scale;
- It can be difficult to judge performance objectively, especially where the employee's performance may be measured in qualitative terms.

123

Student Activity 4

Create in a few lines your definition of performance related pay, and check it carefully to see if it clearly defines any such system which is implemented in your organisation.

Salary planning

8.5　This system ensures individuals are correctly placed within their salary range in relation to performance, and that they move through and between grades at a rate appropriate to their progress and potential. In the short term, salary planning can be done using projection to show the various rates at which people can progress through a salary range. It can be used to indicate what a current or future increase should be and also to compare an individual's progress with the standard, and with that of his or her contemporaries.

8.6　Although these planning systems can be used to check individual progress, such detailed analysis is not always feasible. If the system incorporates certain features then it is more likely to be regarded as fair by those involved. The features that will encourage these attitudes are:

● Salaries calculated as systematically as possible;

● Clear explanation to those involved;

● Equitable application to all staff.

8.7　As with job evaluation, the system should operate so it is understood by those involved, allow for individual or group appeals and be open to review if it is not working properly.

Salary budgets

8.8　A salary budget is a statement in quantitative and usually financial terms of the planned allocation and use of resources to meet the needs of the company. Budgets are based on planned levels of activity or output that determine resources and the number of staff in each category. The budget should take account of monies available to the company. This in turn affects the ability to pay general and individual merit increases, the numbers employed, or both. Historical control over salary costs can be achieved by comparing budgeted costs with the actual cost, analysing variance and deciding on corrective action such as a reduction in manning levels or limiting merit and other increases.

8.9　Within most salary structures there is a range of additional benefits available for different categories of staff:

● Bonus schemes: profit-sharing, etc;

● Non-contributory pension schemes;

● Low interest loans/housing assistance for transfers, etc;

● Sick pay;

● Paid holidays;

● Company cars;

● Medical benefits.

Summary

Having studied this unit carefully you should now:

- **know about job design;**

- **characterise job-rotation, job-enlargement and job-enrichment;**

- **understand systems of the evaluation of different jobs;**

- **distinguish between job ranking, job classification, points and factor comparison;**

- **be able to analyse salary structures;**

- **understand what constitutes an efficient salary system;**

- **be able to discuss the pro's and con's of performance related pay.**

Q

Self-assessment questions

1. The basis for job enrichment is derived from:

   (a) Maslow;

   (b) McClelland;

   (c) Herzberg;

   (d) Porter and Lawler.

2. The problem with job rotation is that:

   (a) people do not get to know their job properly;

   (b) people fear redundancies;

   (c) people become more likely to leave;

   (d) it allocates more responsibility.

3. Basic salaries in the UK banks are *not* based on:

   (a) length of service;

   (b) grading system;

   (c) HAY/MSL system;

   (d) job evaluation.

4. Which characterises the UK reward system in banks:

   (a) payment by results;

   (b) piecework;

   (c) payment on commission;

   (d) starting pay according to qualifications?

5. A grading system which takes account of experience rather than just grade is:

   (a) an overlapping system;

   (b) a non-overlapping system;

   (c) merit increases;

   (d) an age-rate scheme.

6. What are the three main aims of a job-evaluation system?

7. What are the four main ways of rating jobs?

8. Where is it likely, if at all, to see age-related scales of pay?.

9. For what pragmatic reasons are banks introducing performance related pay?

10. Give three advantages of a system of performance related pay.

Unit 11

Appraisal, Discipline, Grievance and Employment Law

Objectives

After studying this unit, you should be able to:

- **understand appraisal systems and their application;**

- **be familiar with the elements of grievance procedures;**

- **be familiar with the elements of disciplinary procedures;**

- **know about employment law and discrimination;**

- **know about legal matters of employee health and safety.**

---

1   The purpose of appraisals

1.1   Personnel appraisal is a system used by organisations to assess an employee's current performance and sometimes future potential. It can be used as a source of information for a variety of purposes:

- Manpower planning;

- Promotion;

- Succession plans;

- Training;

- Career development;

- Payment of annual bonus.

1.2   Appraisals can also be used for the study of competencies needed to perform a particular job to the required level. When used in this context, appraisal forms should include description of good and poor performance levels so a person's level of competence can be judged.

1.3   Appraisals can be said to provide information for both the organisation and the individual. For the organisation *they*:

- Provide information about employees for manpower decisions.

- Reveal the adequacy of other personnel procedures, e.g. selection and training. If there is a poor match between people selected for a job and the job itself, this will be revealed in the poor performance of the employee.

- Indicate improvements in performance due to training or development programmes.

- Can be used as the basis for determining salary reviews.

- Help to identify potential and lead to recommendations for the next job and training.

1.4   For the individual the appraisal provides:

- Information and feedback about performance, and future potential with training recommendations; and this feedback

- Should increase the motivation of the individual through a combination of praise and suggestions for improvements. The theoretical support for this lies in Maslow's Hierarchy of Needs (ego needs), Herzberg's motivators and Porter and Lawler's theory of motivation (see Unit 5).

1.5   It is desirable that an organisation should be clear about the purpose and nature of the appraisal system. Appraisals can be completed to allocate rewards and benefits (reward review), for the improvement of current job performance (the performance review), for the prediction of the level and type of work the individual will undertake in the future (the po*tential review*). Randall, *et al* (1972), suggest each appraisal should serve only one purpose, otherwise their value is seriously undermined. For instance, an individual may have shown vast improvement in performance yet still only be just above average. The rating given to that person under the reward and performance reviews will be quite different from the potential review (the individual's potential is still limited, despite the improvement in performance).

1.6   Ideally, whatever appraisal system is adopted it should:

- Give feedback on the employee's work (the importance of this is indicated in Porter and Lawler's theory of motivation; see Unit 5);

- Make salary and promotion decisions as fair as possible;

- Give employees an opportunity to participate in decisions affecting them;

- Allow for career planning, training decisions and counselling.

1.7   Appraisals are difficult to carry out because the system tries to measure performance and categorise and comment on an individual's job behaviour.

Student Activity 1

Obtain a blank appraisal form for your level in your organisation (and for other levels if possible) together with any available notes of guidance for appraisers and appraisees. Study the documentation carefully, and write notes on what purpose you believe it is intended to fulfil.

2   The format of appraisals

2.1   To achieve the objectives identified above the principles and format of the appraisal system must be agreed:

- The criteria on which performance is to be assessed must be agreed, e.g. accuracy of work, neatness. There are often problems in deciding representative criteria.

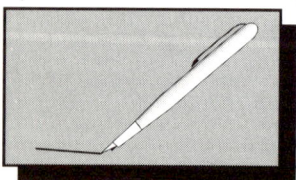

- The standard to compare performance against – perfect, average or historically, against each individual's own performance in the past – must be determined.

- A layout must be selected for the form. There are a number of different types of format.

Overall assessment or written statements

2.2   This format requires the supervisor to 'assess the performance of X, paying attention to areas for improvement'. Alternatively it may provide some guidance to help the appraiser focus on specific areas, e.g. relationships with colleagues. The problems with this type of format are that they are tedious to complete, their quality depends largely on the literary ability of the supervisor, and they are difficult to use when comparing staff. Some of the headings can be vague and difficult to interpret, e.g. 'application' is a term frequently seen on the form, but it could be interpreted as 'hard-working', 'adaptable', or 'suitable for the post'.

Ratings, gradings, scales

2.3   Under this system the supervisor rates the extent to which a subordinate possesses or has demonstrated a variety of traits, say foreign exchange knowledge.

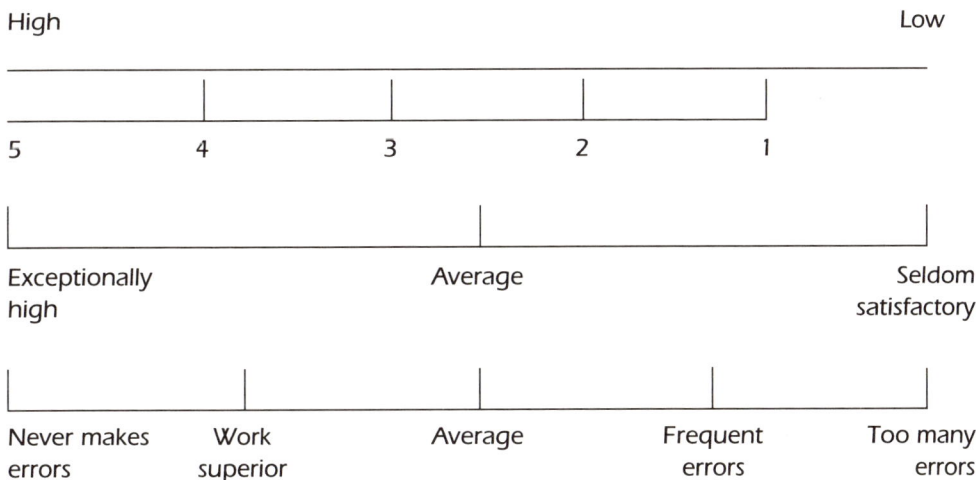

High   Low

5	4	3	2	1

| Exceptionally high | | Average | | Seldom satisfactory |

| Never makes errors | Work superior | Average | Frequent errors | Too many errors |

Poor 1–6, Average 7–18, Good 19–25

2.4   Grading uses verbal descriptions rather than numerical scales.

The problems of rating

2.5   The main problems are that:

- The criteria for scales are not always connected with the job of the person being rated.

- The scales do not include suggestions on how to improve performance.

- It can be difficult to identify training needs from the scales.

- Supervisors tend to rate most employees as average rather than rate above or below average. This is called the central tendency effect.

- It is difficult equitably to arrange rewards in line with ratings. However ratings forms are quick to complete and easy to interpret.

Ranking

2.6 Ranking involves placing employees in order, according to their performance. It is most commonly used as a system to allocate rewards or merit payments. Ranking can use one of three techniques.

- *Paired comparison.* Every employee in a department is compared with every other employee, drawn up from best to worst.

- *Alternative ranking.* This involves picking out the best and worst employees. Once these are eliminated the process can be repeated with the remaining staff.

- *Forced distribution.* Employees can be placed in a category, the:

Top 10%	Excellent
Next 20%	Above average
Next 40%	Average
Next 20%	Below average
Bottom 10%	Poor

Problems of ranking

2.7 The principal ones are that:

- It is a difficult system to use with large numbers of employees.

- The system does not indicate the degree of difference between employees.

- There are difficulties in trying to compare the performance of staff from different departments.

BARS (Behaviourally Anchored Rating Scales)

2.8 This appraisal system tries to identify in more detail key behaviours within a job and then places a person on a scale. For example, 'customer relations':

7 Willing to help a customer at all times. If he/she does not know the answer, he/she will go to great lengths to provide good service.

6 Courteous and helpful at all times.

5 Courteous.

4 Knows duties of job and fulfils them; can sometimes be helpful.

3 Sometimes appears rude to the customer when under pressure.

2 Rude and offhand with customer when under pressure.

1 Rude and offhand with customers for much of the time.

2.9 A different series of rating scales have to be drawn up for each job and it is therefore a time-consuming and costly system to introduce.

Target based reviews

2.10 Because financial institutions are concentrating on missions and objectives to a greater extent than ever before, employee appraisals seem to be coming into line, and it is regarded as valuable to include, or even to base an entire appraisal system on, targets and the extent of their achievement: they are using the idea of setting performance standards and measuring success to assess contribution.

2.11 Essentially, together with other requirements already discussed for a good overall system, there should be at least these stages on the form and in the ensuing interview:

- Detailed review of each of the immediate past period's targets.

- Review of the extent to which that target was reached, missed or achieved.

- Adjustment of such similar targets for the ensuing period.

- The addition, if appropriate, of agreed new targets.

- Agreement of the training or resources needed to meet the fresh set of targets.

2.12 The responsibility for the substance of each stage lies with the appraiser or the appraisee in different proportions, but note the last: as we shall see under MBO, people cannot meet targets unless they are equipped to do so.

3   Common problems in completing appraisal forms

3.1 Recognised common problems are:

- The *strictness or leniency of supervisors* completing the appraisal forms may vary.

- The assessment of individuals is often based on *personality rather than results*. Personality traits do not usually determine the standard of performance and they are, by definition, enduring and not within the individual's scope to alter. The appraisal should be based on results not behaviour.

- The *halo effect*, which is the tendency to assume that because an individual possesses some positive characteristics they are entirely without fault.

- The most recent events and problems with performance tend to dominate the assessments, rather than those incidents occurring nine months ago.

- Personal bias by the supervisor.

- Contrast effect, which is the tendency to rate an average person unfavourably because of exceptional performers in the group.

- Administrative problems because of the time appraisals take and the paperwork involved. There is also the necessity to see that comments or promises made in the appraisal are followed, through training courses, job experience, etc.

- The concern of organisations for a system which can be applied with a degree of consistency across the entire organisation creates problems because of the many different assessors and jobs involved.

Multiple reviews

3.2 Some organisations use a system of multiple appraisers so that the employees are assessed by their supervisors, but also assess their own performance. Other colleagues and managers with whom employees interact may also be asked to appraise their performance, as well as the subordinates they manage.

4   Management by objectives

4.1   This is an alternative system used for measuring the performance and the contribution of managers in an organisation. It is in operation today in several banking organisations. Its founder was Peter Drucker who defined it in 1954 as:

> A system that integrates the company's goals of profit and growth with the manager's needs to contribute and develop himself personally.

The system can perhaps best be understood by examining the stages in diagrammatic form.

Figure 1.1   Management by objectives

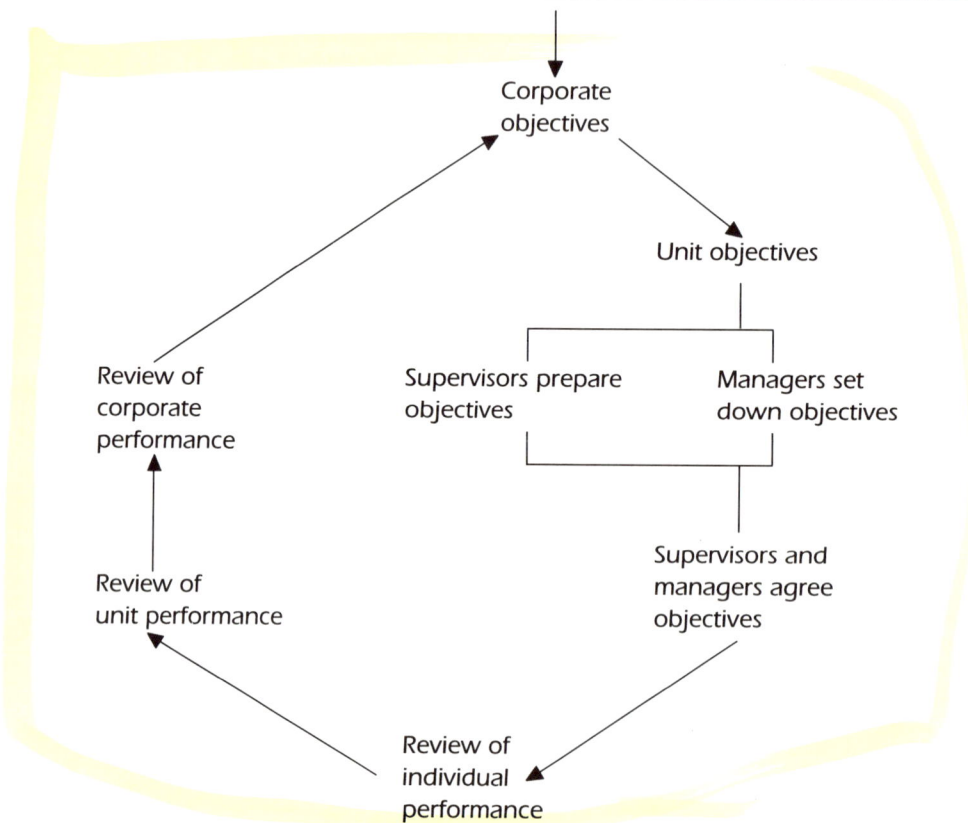

4.2   The system is designed to ensure that employees are working towards goals in line with those of the organisation, thereby increasing the motivation of the individual as well as making a more valuable contribution to the organisation. The information training managers receive is relevant, being related to performance, and the achievement of managers can be measured against set goals.

4.3   The benefits of the system according to Drucker and Humble (a promoter of MBO in the UK) are:

- Individuals aim for goals that contribute to organisational effectiveness.

- Managers are involved in setting targets for themselves and this increases morale.

132

- MBO can lead to the identification of problems in achieving high performance.

- The scheme aids management development and training, whilst increasing organisational efficiency.

4.4 However, despite many articles produced to indicate the advantages of MBO and citing practical examples of successful application, many commentators have criticised its use in the UK. The major problems seem to stem from the fact that the type of managerial philosophy common in the UK is at variance with the ideology of MBO. It is seen as a means of control in the UK, rather than encouraging the active involvement of managers. There are also difficulties in establishing meaningful goals for managers to achieve over a relatively short time period (say six months to one year) and follow-up activities like training may not happen. MBO can also create competition between departments and for some sections and individuals it can be difficult to set goals.

5 Appraisals and MBO interview

5.1 The main stages in the appraisal interview are:

- Preparation;

- Introduction;

- Investigation;

- Listen;

- Close.

Preparation

5.2 The appraiser should consider the objectives of the interview as part of the preparation. An appraisal form should be completed, reviewing the previous forms that have been completed. The appraisee should be given the opportunity to review their own performance. The appraiser should examine previous targets, and strengths and weaknesses. An open mind should be kept about improvements. The appraiser should have an outline plan for the interview and arrange for a room, with no interruptions.

Introduction

5.3 The appraiser should open the interview by trying to relax the appraisee and establish a rapport. The purpose of the interview and the rough plan should be outlined. The appraiser should give a summary of the employee's strengths and be positive about these aspects of performance.

Investigation

5.4 The appraiser should ask the employee to analyse their performance, discuss it and then they should evaluate the performance together. The appraiser should be aware of the wording of the questions and use open terms (who, what, where, when) to ensure a responsive answer is given. Closed questions elicit a one word answer or at best a short reply, while leading questions contain the seeds of the answer in the question. The appraiser should also avoid overloading the appraisee with critical comments as this can have a negative effect on motivation.

Listen

5.5   The appraiser should listen to what the employer suggests for improvement, encourage self-analysis and agree an action plan.

Close and evaluate

5.6   The appraiser should offer help with training and guidance and summarise the new goals and standards set, agreeing feedback times. The appraiser should also assess their own performance in the interview.

Student Activity 2

Look carefully at your organisation's appraisal form. Is any of it target-based, i.e. does it require the setting of targets for the future period as opposed to simply reviewing the past period? *If so*, using your experience or imagination, slightly redesign it so that it is more detailed and specific, or write a short note on why it is already detailed and specific enough. *If not*, design a new section for it which requires forward planning of a target-setting nature.

6   The grievance and disciplinary process

6.1   A grievance procedure is the specified procedure which is to be followed in an organisation when an aggrieved employee wishes to take a grievance to the higher levels of the organisation. The disciplinary procedure is that which must be followed when an organisation feels an employee has not maintained its disciplinary standards.

6.2   The procedures which organisations follow for dealing with grievance and disciplinary action are to some extent determined by law, although each organisation specifies its own particular procedure.

Student Activity 3

In consultation with your managers or your Personnel/HRM department, obtain a copy of your organisation's Grievance and Disciplinary procedures (tell them why you want them!). Use them to compare some of the ensuing sections with your own system, making notes as you go.

6.3   Operating grievance and disciplinary procedures is an area of employment law where managers may be frequently involved. It often causes anxiety amongst managers when they have to use grievance and disciplinary procedures, because of the fear of mistakes occurring. It is necessary for organisations to possess both a grievance and disciplinary procedure under the Contracts of Employment Act 1972 and the Employment Protection (Consolidation) Act 1978.

6.4   The procedures adopted by a company should conform to the guidelines contained in the Code of Practice issued by the Advisory Conciliation and Arbitration Service (ACAS). The Code also contains information and advice about the operation of such procedures. A grievance or disputes procedure should describe the stages for dealing with disputes in the organisation when the issue is first raised, say at a clerical level, until it is referred (if it is not settled at an early stage) to outside conciliation.

6.5 The procedure exists for both union and non-union employees. It may be that for trade union members there is a national agreement between employer and union.

7 Grievance procedures

7.1 The grievance procedure should be written down, specifying to whom the employee takes the grievance and the right to be accompanied. No industrial action should be taken until the procedure is exhausted, and time limits should be set for completion of one stage in the grievance procedure before moving onto the next (five working days is normal).

Stage 1

7.2 All queries and grievances should be raised initially by the employee with the employee's immediate supervisor. An employee may choose to approach a shop steward or representative first, so the issue can be raised jointly or by the shop steward on the employee's behalf. The supervisor will try to resolve the issue and give an answer within *five working days*. If it cannot be satisfactorily resolved, the matter will be referred to Stage 2 of the procedure.

Stage 2

7.3 If the employee is not satisfied by the supervisor's answer, the issue will be referred to the departmental sectional manager. At the meeting there may also be in attendance a trade union representative and personnel manager. The departmental manager, following discussions with the personnel manager, should give an answer within five working days of the matter being raised.

Stage 3

7.4 If the union representative is not satisfied with the answer given by the departmental manager, the matter will be referred to a senior manager, who with the personnel manager, will discuss the matter with the union representative and senior union representative. Again five working days are allowed for an answer. In some organisations the procedure ends here. In others it is referred to a mediator or joint consultative body.

7.5 It is normal for the personnel department to be informed when a grievance procedure starts. Everyone can then be treated in the same way. It is also the right of the employee always to have a representative present.

8 Disciplinary procedures

8.1 It is normal for an employer to have a disciplinary procedure for employees, therefore ensuring standards can be maintained.

8.2   A key aim of the disciplinary procedure is to try to achieve a change in behaviour on the part of the employee concerned, so further action is unnecessary (assuming there is an indication that the problem is one of employee behaviour). Employees may be unaware of what is expected of them, and so it is desirable that there is a general understanding of what constitutes a misdemeanour and what the consequences might be. Also, individuals should be given warnings of what will happen if they fall below the required standard. The procedure also ensures all individuals are treated consistently. The proceedings may indeed reveal mistakes by management in failing to communicate disciplinary rules, and it may be that after discussion it is felt to be unfair even to classify it as disciplinary action.

8.3   It is important that the procedure be followed in disciplinary action, otherwise an eventual dismissal may be considered unfair, if inappropriate action has been taken.

8.4   In the banks there are certain guidelines established:

- The procedure must be in writing.

- It must specify to whom it applies.

- It must provide for speedy action.

- It must allow employees the right to be accompanied.

- No action can be taken until it is investigated and employees must be given the right to state their case before action is taken.

- No employee can be dismissed for a first breach of discipline, except in cases of gross misconduct.

- Employees must be given an explanation of the penalty imposed and a right of appeal.

8.5   The reasons for dismissal are contained in the Employment Protection (Consolidation) Act 1978:

- Incapable of performing the job or appropriate qualifications absent;

- Misconduct;

- Redundancy;

- Contravention of duties or restrictions imposed by law by continuing employment;

- Other substantial reason to justify dismissal.

8.6   A dismissal is unfair if insufficient reason is given or the dismissal is not reasonable in the particular circumstances, i.e. the employee has not received a copy of the disciplinary rules. The employee is entitled to a written statement giving reasons for dismissal.

Stage 1

8.7   A verbal informal warning is given to the employee in the first instance, or where it is a minor offence. The warning should be given by the employee's immediate supervisor.

Stage 2

8.8   A formal verbal warning by a supervisor or manager.

Stage 3

8.9   A written or formal warning is given to the employee in the first instance with a more serious offence, or after repetition of minor offences. This is given by a senior manager. This states the nature of the offence and specifies future disciplinary action which will be taken if the offence is committed again within the specified time period. A copy of the written warning is placed on the file of the employee's personnel record but destroyed in 12 months if the performance is satisfactory. The employee is required to read and sign the formal warning and has the right of appeal if it is believed the warning is unjustified.

Stage 4

8.10   A final written warning is given by a senior manager and, in some instances, the personnel department.

Summary dismissal

8.11   An employee may be summarily dismissed in the event of gross misconduct (as defined in the company rules). Only senior managers can recommend summary dismissal and action should not be taken until the personnel manager has discussed the case and the appeal procedure has been carried out.

Appeals

8.12   In all circumstances, an employee may appeal against suspension or dismissal. The personnel manager should be present and the employee may be represented. The appeal is conducted by a member of management. Appeals should be held as soon as possible.

8.13   If an appeal against dismissal is rejected, the employee has the right to appeal to a chief executive. The personnel manager and employee representative may be present.

8.14   An employee can appeal against a dismissal considered unfair before an industrial tribunal. The employer is required to demonstrate that the dismissal has been fair and reasonable. Sometimes sanctions other than warnings and dismissals may be given, for example the removal of discretionary pay or demotion.

9   Grievance and disciplinary interviews

Preparation

9.1   In the case of disciplinary interviews the manager has time to prepare. In the case of grievance interviews, the manager may not have the time to prepare for the initial interview. The manager should ideally carry out a full investigation into the circumstances of the case. This should be done speedily, and the observations and memories of witnesses should be included. The manager should get as much information as possible so the facts are understood. In the disciplinary procedure the employee should be interviewed to establish their version of events and the representative be told a disciplinary interview is to occur.

9.2   After the preparation the stages are the same as those introduced for the selection interview:

- Introduction;
- Investigation;
- Listen;
- Close.

9.3   In the introduction the manager should explain the stages in the disciplinary and grievance procedure; what the issue is; who is present and why; and what will happen during the interview. If the employee is not accompanied, remind the individual of that right.

Grievance procedure

Investigation
9.4   Hopefully the manager may have some idea of the nature of the grievance and should aim to find out as much as possible. Braddick identifies three areas for investigation:

- Background;
- Circumstances;
- Latent and manifest causes.

9.5   The manager must be aware that there are symptoms and causes. Often it is only by digging deeply that the true cause can be found and thereby solve the problem. It is for this reason that the manager should be prepared to keep an open mind, asking open and probing questions.

Listen
9.6   The manager should listen to the employee and not try to offer solutions at this stage. Most grievance procedures include a time period for the manager to consider the situation before offering a solution. After the initial meeting the manager should consider the facts raised by the employee, the possible action paths and implications of each.

Reply and close
9.7   After the various action paths have been considered the manager should call a further meeting to give a response and try to close the issue (although this may not be possible if the manager does not have the proper authority). In the closing solution the manager should aim for a win/win situation so both employee and employer are satisfied. If the issue is not closed, the further stages in the grievance procedure should be outlined.

Disciplinary procedure

Investigation
9.8   After the introduction to the interview, the manager should give the reason for the warning and ask the employee to comment. The manager should specify standards, restate what the employee is required to achieve and question the employee about any help needed to meet these standards.

Listen
9.9   Listen to what the employee requires and agree to help.

Close

9.10   Specify what the employee should do in order to have the warning removed, recap on the appeal procedure and ask if there are any questions.

9.11   In both grievance and disciplinary procedure a written record should be kept.

Why have a grievance and disciplinary procedure?

9.12   Basically:

- It is a statutory obligation under Employment Protection (Consolidation) Act 1978.

- The needs of the organisation and individual may not always coincide and so reconciliation or severance procedures must be seen to be fair by all concerned.

Student Activity 4

Find the definition of 'misconduct' and 'gross misconduct' in your organisation's disciplinary procedure. Make notes of the definition and the procedure involved. Now create a scenario or short story of an example of such conduct (either misconduct or gross misconduct) as it might have manifested itself in your office, and continue the story through the way your management, possibly including yourself, applied the procedure.

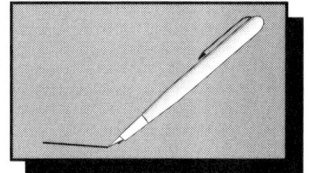

10   Legal aspects of employment

10.1   Most employment legislation has been drafted over the last 20 years and it is during this time that there has been a considerable increase in the degree of protection awarded to employees by statute. Although you need to be aware of the scope of legislation and its general provisions, you must also understand the implications for the organisation manager and individuals. The student activities are designed to supplement knowledge from this point of view.

Terms and conditions of employment

10.2   Under the Employment Protection Consolidation Act 1978 (EPCA), employees have the right to obtain within 13 weeks of the start of employment a written statement from their employer setting out their terms of employment. It must identify:

- Job title.

- The employer and employee.

- The time employment began.

- When continuous employment began and if any previous employment counted towards this, e.g. maternity leave. This has an effect on redundancy payments, sick pay and dismissal.

- Scale and timing of remuneration.

- Holiday entitlement.

- Hours of work.

- Sick pay and provisions.

- Pensions.

- Periods of notice.

- Rules relating to the job and whether there is a contracting out certificate for the job.

10.3   The employees who are excluded from these arrangements are those employed on a temporary basis or for less than 16 hours a week.

10.4   All employees also have a right to receive an itemised pay statement and should be informed of grievance and disciplinary procedures; especially what constitutes a dismissal. The organisation must also inform employees where the health and safety requirements are displayed.

10.5   Although these terms are specified, there are other conditions of employment enshrined in common law (case law) which the employer and employee are expected to observe, e.g. duties of care, co-operation and loyalty. The conditions laid out in the terms of employment must, however, conform to individual rights of employment, e.g. every employee has the right to at least one week's notice.

10.6   Some other rights of the employee under the EPCA 1978 are:

- When an employee is suspended by an employer on medical grounds the employee is entitled to remuneration for 26 weeks.

- An employee who is a union official has time off work with pay for trade union duties.

- There is also time off work for public duties, e.g. to be a JP. The employer is not obliged to pay for absences.

- Employees are also entitled to time off with pay to look for work if they have been continuously employed for two years and have received notice of redundancy.

Student Activity 5

You discover after a subordinate has been working with you for a year that he has a medical condition which was not detected at his pre-employment medical and which means you should not have employed him in the first instance. He did not tell you at the time. As he explained when challenged, 'If I had told you the truth you would not have given me the job. I lost seven jobs because I did tell the truth.' He is not only a satisfactory employee, he is first-rate. He is very popular with his colleagues. Customers particularly seek him out and speak well of him. His conduct is exemplary and his results are outstanding.

List the questions which need to be asked in investigating this case, and set out up to three alternative actions which might be taken.

Discrimination and the law

Maternity rights

10.7   An employee cannot be dismissed because she is pregnant, if she has a minimum of two years' service. She is also entitled to statutory maternity pay with the right to return to work of a similar nature, provided she works up to at least 11 weeks before confinement and returns within 29 weeks. She is also entitled to time off work for antenatal care.

Rehabilitation of Offenders Act 1974

10.8   It is an offence to discriminate against someone with a spent prison sentence.

Disabled Persons Acts 1944 and 1958

10.9   This places a duty on employers of more than 20 employees to employ a small percentage of registered disabled people.

Sexual and racial discrimination

10.10   There are two major pieces of legislation designed to protect against discrimination at work: Sex Discrimination Act 1986 and the Race Relations Act 1976. The Acts are very similar in terminology and can be discussed together.

10.11   The Acts made it unlawful to discriminate against a person on sexual or racial grounds, and cite a number of specific situations. Discrimination can be direct or indirect. Direct discrimination is treating a person less favourably than another on grounds of sex or race. Indirect discrimination is applying to one person the same requirement or condition applied to others but:

● It is such that the proportion of women (or persons of a racial group) who can comply with it is smaller than the proportion of men;

● Which cannot be shown to be justified irrespective of the sex, colour, race, nationality, ethnic or national origins of the person to whom it is applied;

● Which is to the person's detriment if they cannot comply with it.

10.12   To require applicants to be over six feet tall would discriminate against women, unless it could be justified by the nature of the work as advertised.

10.13   It is also unlawful to discriminate in respect of access to opportunities for promotion, transfer, or other benefits.

10.14   Under the Equal Pay Act 1970 a woman is entitled to equal pay if she is employed on like work with a man in the same employment area, or the work requires the same or greater skills than a more highly paid man in a different job. The Act is enforceable before an industrial tribunal after application by the aggrieved party. From 1986, the Sex Discrimination Act extended these provisions to previously exempt private households and small companies. With the Employment Act of 1989 it equalised pension and redundancy rights.

10.15   There are in addition codes of practice issued by the Commission for Racial Equality (CRE) and the Equal Opportunities Commission (EOC). The codes offer guidance to employers but are not enforceable by law, although they are taken into account by an industrial tribunal when considering a case.

10.16   The financial service organisations have recognised for some years the under-representation of women in managerial positions and in response have tried to provide equal opportunities for all employees. Most, if not all, financial service organisations are Opportunity 2000 employers (the business-led initiative launched to improve the position of women at work). Many employers are now providing a work-based crèche, job share opportunities and flexible working arrangements for some of their staff. Recruitment, assessment and appraisal are often competency-based which tries to eliminate any bias against female employees.

10.17 The objectives of an equal opportunity policy could be expressed as being to:

- Increase the number of women entering the bank with expectations of being treated as equal with male counterparts;
- Ensure women are promoted on career paths and become more assertive;
- Increase the numbers of women in managerial positions;
- Eradicate assumptions that men are career-minded and women are not;
- Increase the number of applications from ethnic minority groups and to encourage the view that the bank is an equal opportunity employer.

10.18 To fulfil these aims, it seems that an equal opportunities policy should embrace the following areas:

- Creating posts which have responsibility for equal opportunities.
- Monitoring of equal opportunities.
- Review of training material and access to training.
- Review of recruitment and selection procedure.
- Review promotion, appraisal, career development.
- Reassess career path and structure.
- Examine job descriptions and evaluation.
- Examine payment structure.
- Examine disciplinary and grievance procedures.
- Review pension arrangements.

Related issues for the future of banking

10.19 Consider the following.

- There will be a growth in part-time employees, and these will be mainly women. However, it is thought that there must be more effort to make part-time work more satisfying, with better terms and conditions.
- The introduction of technology provides advantages in providing jobs for women in small service branches and operations centres, but this may mean a lack of career opportunities.
- The advance of two-tier and three-tier recruitment will affect women because many experience later career development and may not have the opportunity to progress within this system.
- Population trends indicate that fewer 16 and 18 year olds will be available for work and this may encourage retraining mature female staff. Demographic trends with a drop in 16–28 year olds could be favourable for the mature employees.

Student Activity 6

By research with your Personnel/HRM department, discover or estimate what proportions of staff are male and female at different levels of your bank, and diagram this by means of a histogram or any other graphical means. What conclusions do you draw from the diagram?

Welfare and conditions of work

10.20 There are two major pieces of legislation that affect the banking organisation: Office, Shops and Railway Premises Act 1963 (OSRP) and the Health and Safety at Work Act 1974 (HASAW).

Office, Shops and Railway Premises Act 1963

10.21 This Act extended the requirements of the Factories Act 1961 to people employed in offices. The main provisions were:

- Suitable and sufficient toilets and washing facilities provided and maintained with proper lighting and ventilation.

- Stairs and gangways of sound construction with handrails and no obstructions.

- Drinking water provided.

- Places for hanging clothes.

- Seats for employees.

- Facilities for eating food.

- No person under 18 years of age using dangerous machinery.

- No one may lift a heavy load which could cause injury.

- First aid boxes should be provided.

- No overcrowding of rooms, with 40 square feet or 400 cubic feet for each person.

- Reasonable temperatures: no less than 16°C after the first hour, and thermometers to check the temperature.

- Fire precautions and accidents should be reported.

10.22 The Act also allowed for a compulsory inspection of the premises by inspectors.

Health and Safety at Work Act 1974

10.23 The Act has the following objectives, to:

- Secure health, welfare and safety for people at work.

- Protect others from risks arising at work.

- Control the use and storage of dangerous substances.

- Control the emission of noxious or offensive substances into the air. The Act specifies a range of duties for both employer and employee, enforceable at criminal law.

10.24 The *employers' duties* are:

> To ensure as far as is reasonably practicable the health, safety and welfare of all ... not only employees but those affected by your products or plant.

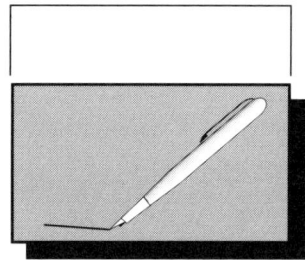

10.25 Employers must:

- Provide information, training and supervision;
- Issue a policy statement;
- Consult the trade unions;
- Establish safety committees.

10.26 The employees' duties are also important, because safety at work cannot be achieved without the interest and support of employees. In particular, employees have a duty to take reasonable care for their own and others' safety. There are two offences: 'horseplay' and 'deliberate disregard of safety requirements'.

10.27 Trade unions have a right to appoint safety representatives to look at hazards and complaints and make representations.

10.28 There are two enforcement agencies. The Health and Safety Executive, whose inspectors have the right to enter premises, examine them and question employees. However, the role of inspectors is to pursue the cause of safety, not just apprehend wrong doers. The Health and Safety Commission is responsible for issuing codes of practice, new regulations and general research.

10.29 Penalties can be invoked against a company or individual. Some directors and managers as well as safety managers can be prosecuted under the HASAW Act. For managers to be prosecuted, it has to be shown that a breach has occurred through their consent, connivance or neglect. The maximum punishment for an offence is two years imprisonment. This can be invoked for refusal to comply with a notice, breach of general duties, or a grave or repeated breach of a relevant act.

Summary

Having studied this unit carefully you should now:

- **understand appraisal systems and their application;**
- **be familiar with your own system, its qualities and shortcomings;**
- **be familiar with the elements of your own grievance procedure;**
- **be familiar with the elements of your own disciplinary procedure;**
- **have thought through the application of these procedures;**
- **have considered important issues in employment law and discrimination**
- **know about legal matters of employee health and safety.**

Self-assessment questions

1. Which of the following is not a ranking technique:
   (a) paired comparison;
   (b) elimination;
   (c) alternative ranking;
   (d) forced distribution?

2. Appraisal should be done:
   (a) annually;
   (b) every six months;
   (c) whenever it is felt to be necessary;
   (d) every nine months.

3. Appraisal interviews are normally between:
   (a) staff member and immediate superior;
   (b) staff member and immediate superior and manager;
   (c) staff member, trade union representative and manager;
   (d) staff member, manager and colleague.

4. Why are appraisals valuable for an organisation?

5. Why are appraisals valuable for an employee?

6. What do the initials ACAS stand for?

7. Name three reasons for dismissal enshrined in the Employment Protection (Consolidation) Act 1978

8. Which four Acts of Parliament affect the rights of women in employment?

9. Which of the following could be said to be a provider of security in the welfare services:
   (a) contracts of employment;
   (b) canteen facilities;
   (c) a kind manager;
   (d) short working hours?

10. Under the HSAW Act, what are the employer's responsibilities?

Unit 12

Organisational Theory and the Role of the Manager

Objectives

After studying this unit, you should be able to:

- **understand the role of the manager;**

- **have learnt about the various schools of management thought;**

- **have considered the major functions of the modern manager;**

- **be clear about the relationship between manager and subordinate.**

1 The manager: an introduction

1.1 Although many definitions of the role of the manager are available, all appear to have a common thread. A manager is one who is responsible for getting things done through other people instead of doing the job himself. With stated objectives to achieve, he or she directs human activities with the help of other resources. The manager does not only have to get things done, he or she also has to ensure they are done as effectively and efficiently as possible, because this is the key to a successful organisation. Drucker in his book *Management* (1974) summed this up:

> Every achievement of management is the achievement of a manager. Every failure is a failure of a manager. The vision, dedication and integrity of managers determine whether there is management or mismanagement.

1.2 Today there is considerable interest in considering management in a specialist area in its own right. The Management Charter Initiative is one example. Leading managers and their representative organisations summarise in the charter the skills, techniques and personal qualities needed by an effective manager.

1.3 Writings on organisation and management have existed for many years. However, the development of management thinking as we view it dates from the end of the 19th century, when large industrial firms were established and the problems of managing large-scale resources were realised. Before we examine current thoughts on the role of management it is helpful to examine the historical views, the development of management thinking and what might be termed management theory. McGregor in *The Human Side of Enterprise* (1960), emphasises the importance of this study:

> Every managerial act rests on assumptions, generalisations and hypotheses – that is to say on theory. Our assumptions are frequently implicit ... theory and practice are inseparable.

1.4 Mullins also believes the study of management theory to be crucial. He gives the following reasons:

- What leading writers say is an important part of the study of management;
- It is necessary to examine the inter-relationship that exists between theory and practice;
- An understanding of the development of theory helps in understanding how management has progressed;
- Many of the ideas and concepts introduced by the theorists are of importance and value to the manager.

1.5 For ease of study it is usual to divide the writers on organisations and management into three major groups. The groups are distinguished by basic differences in their approach and thus we can identify the main trends and frameworks of analysis. However, within this framework, we can identify a number of subdivisions. These show the complex nature of the theories and writings on management.

1.6 The first and oldest of these three groups or 'schools' is the *Classical Approach*. This could be said to comprise three slightly different approaches:

- Scientific management;
- Administrative management;
- Bureaucracy.

1.7 All three approaches examine the technical and economic aspects of organisations, but tend to neglect the psychological and sociological.

1.8 The second school or group is the *Human Relations* school and it emphasises the study of behaviour, examining specifically individual and group productivity, individual development and job satisfaction.

1.9 The Classical and Human Relations schools have now been overtaken by a more comprehensive approach to the study of management. The *Systems School* views organisations as a system – an inter-related set of activities that converts inputs to outputs – and so studies the key elements in an organisation, how they interact with one another, and the influence of the environment of the organisation. It therefore examines people, structure, technology and environment. The most recent development of systems theory has been termed *Contingency*, because it emphasises the need to look at specific circumstances or contingencies when designing organisation or management systems.

1.10 The three schools have developed very approximately in a chronological manner.

1.11 Each school has gradually expanded the theoretical base of knowledge and added to managerial concepts and ideas about the organisation. Although we can distinguish these three schools or approaches, remember that the boundaries of each are not always clearly visible.

```
Systems: 1950s–present
(Contingency)

Human Relations: 1920s–1950s

Classical: 1880s–1920s
```

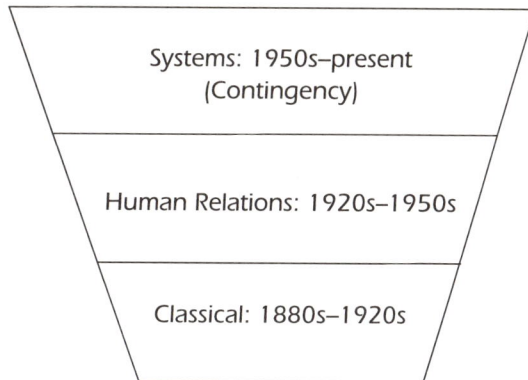

2   The Classical School

2.1   The work produced by all of the Classical writers had several common features. They emphasised the:

- Purpose and structure of organisations;
- Technical requirements of each job;
- Principles of management.

2.2   They also assumed all behaviour was rational and logical. However, despite these similarities there are significant differences in approach identified as Scientific Management, Administrative and Bureaucracy.

Scientific Management

2.3   Probably the best known proponent of Scientific Management is Frederick Wimslow Taylor (1856–1917). An engineer by training, he joined the Midvale Steel Works as a labourer and rose rapidly through the ranks to become Foreman and later Chief Engineer. He eventually became a consultant and devoted his time to the propagation of his ideas.

2.4   He first published his ideas in a paper, *A Piece Rate System*, published in 1895. This was expanded in two later books: *Shop Management* (1903) and *Principles of Scientific Management* (1911).

2.5   Taylor stated that the principal objective of management should be to obtain *maximum prosperity for the employer*, coupled with *maximum prosperity for each employee*. For the employer this did not just mean large profits in the short term, but the development of all aspects of the enterprise to a state of permanent prosperity. For the employee 'maximum prosperity' did not just mean immediate higher wages, but his physical and technical development so he could perform efficiently in the highest grade of work for which his natural abilities fitted him.

2.6   Taylor laid down four underlying principles of management:

- *The development of a True Science of Work.* The establishment of a 'large daily task', classified after scientific investigation as the amount to be done by a suitable, selected and trained person under optimum conditions. For this he would receive a high rate of pay – much higher than in other 'unscientific' factories. He would also suffer a loss of income if he failed to achieve this performance.

- *The scientific selection and progressive development of the workman.* To receive this high rate of pay, scientific selection would occur to ensure the employee possessed the physical and intellectual qualities necessary to achieve output. Taylor stated that it was the responsibility of management to develop workers, offering them opportunities for advancement which would enable them to do the highest, most interesting and profitable class of work, within the confines of the organisation's operations.

- *The bringing together of the science of work and the scientifically selected and trained men.*

- *The constant and intimate co-operation of management and men (in a spirit of hearty co-operation).* There is almost equal division of work and responsibility between management and workers. The management takes over all the work for which they are better fitted than the workmen, i.e. the specification and verification of methods, time, price, quality and standards of the job, and the continuous supervision and control of the employee doing it.

2.7   By science Taylor meant systematic observation and measurement (hence today he is known as the father of work study). He often quoted the 'science of shovelling': the determination of an optimum load, that a first class man can handle with each shovelful, and the correct design of shovels to handle loads of different materials.

2.8   The insistence of maximum specialisation is also fundamental to Taylor's thinking. He believes that the four management functions (production, finance, personnel and marketing) should be separated out and performed by different specialists, each responsible for controlling different aspects of work. Taylor calls this system 'functional management', and likens it to the increased efficiency that can be obtained in a school where classes go to specialist teachers for different subjects, compared with a school where one teacher teaches all subjects. Taylor also formulated the 'exception' principle: all management reports should be condensed, giving details only of *exceptions* to established standards or averages, so gaining an immediate picture of progress. This is now termed Management by Exception.

2.9   Taylor's methods and principles have been followed by many others: Gantt, Frank and Lilian Gilbreth. However, even in his lifetime, Taylor's ideas were widely criticised and even today are often misunderstood. Few managements, although willing to practice work study, will introduce one of his basic tenets, that there should be no limit to the earnings of a high producing worker. Taylor requires that:

> ... both sides take their eyes off the division of the surplus as the all-important matter and together turn their attention towards increasing the size of the surplus.

Student Activity 1

Look carefully at your place of work. Name and make notes of three manifestations of the philosophy of Taylor which you see still operating, nearly a century after Taylor's ideas were first mooted.

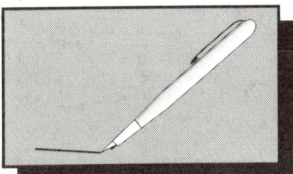

Administrative Management

2.10   The second subdivision within the Classical school is that of administrative management. It is probably best reflected in the writings of Henri Fayol (1841–1925), a practising industrialist who started writing in 1916 (two years before his retirement). It was first translated from French into English in 1949 under the title *General and Industrial Management*. Fayol, although acknowledging the importance of specialist commercial activities, concentrated in his writings on managerial aspects of organisations which he felt had not been explored to date.

2.11   He writes about management's role in organisations, involving a series of activities, which he are common to all managers, whatever their role in industry:

- Forecasting;
- Planning;
- Organising;
- Commanding;
- Co-ordinating;
- Controlling.

2.12   Fayol goes on to define 14 principles of management which he believes should be applied in organisations if maximum efficiency is to be achieved.

- *Division of work.* The work is to be divided amongst all within the organisation, so the burden docs not fall too heavily on any one person, i.e. work and responsibility should be shared.
- *Authority.* The right to give orders should be commensurate with responsibility.
- *Discipline.*
- *Unity of command.* Employees should have to report to only one head.
- *Unity of direction.* Everyone should be working towards the same end in the organisation.
- *Subordination* of individual interest to general ones.
- *Remuneration.* Pay should be fair to both employees and the firm.
- *Centralisation.* Control should be retained centrally for maximum efficiency.
- *Scalar chain.* There should be a clear line of authority from the top to bottom of the organisation.
- *Order.* The organisation should be ordered with a place for all employees and activities.
- *Equity.* Employees should be treated fairly and equitably.
- *Stability of position.* Employees should experience stability of position and long-term appointments, and no unnecessary change should be introduced.
- *Initiative.* All levels within the organisation should be encouraged to show initiative.
- *Esprit de corps.* A spirit of harmony and co-operation should exist within the organisation.

2.13 Many of Fayol's principles of management are still respected today as being good practice, e.g. unity of command. However some aspects of his work have received additions from later behavioural theories, e.g. the role of management now normally has the concept of motivation added to the list.

2.14 Fayol represented a revolutionary approach to business. He believed management should be taught how to manage and founded the centre for Administrative Studies. His writings had a profound influence on business, the army and navy in France.

2.15 Fayol's thoughts and writings could be said to be closely related to Weber's work on bureaucracy although it is believed that the latter's writings were not known to Fayol at the time.

Bureaucracy

2.16 The writings of Max Weber (1864–1920) expounded the concept of bureaucracy. His major work was research and study on the concepts of power and authority, and the writings on bureaucracy developed from this. Weber was interested in why people in organisations obey orders. He distinguished between *power* (the ability to force people to obey regardless of resistance) and *authority* (the right to expect obedience). He distinguished between various types of authority shown in organisations (see Unit 19):

- *Charismatic authority*, derived from the influence of one man on the organisation (personality);
- *Traditional authority*, based on precedent; and
- *Rational-legal authority*, based on the use of rules and procedures and applicable to any office.

2.17 Rational-legal-authority, which Weber regarded as the proper type, led him to develop the concept of bureaucracy as the ideal organisation. This type of structure uses rational-legal authority as the basis for its offices. The term 'bureaucracy' has rather negative connotations today, with images of red tape and unbending rules, but in management theory the term is used merely to describe the structural features of a particular type of organisation.

2.18 Weber in fact suggested that it was a superior type of organisation:

... the decisive reason for the advance of bureaucratic organisation has always been its purely technical superiority over any other form of organisation.

2.19 Weber, in his writings attempted to identify the main features of bureaucracy:

- A *hierarchy of authority* exists within the organisation and is assigned to various positions, *not* people.
- The work of the organisation is allocated to these various positions in a *division of work*.
- There is a high degree of *task specialisation*.
- A formally established *structure of rules and regulations* ensures uniformity of decisions.
- Officials are expected to *administer impartially* these rules.

- Employment and promotion is on the basis of *technical qualifications and merit, and is for a lifetime*.

- Reward for effort is *regular payment on a fixed scale*.

2.20 Weber maintained that the growth of bureaucracy had come about because of the increasing size and complexity of organisations. This dictated the need for specialisation which in turn led to a need for procedural rules. However, this can mean that managers become merely administrators rather than having the opportunity to show initiative or discretion. Other criticisms of bureaucracy are related to this; being governed by rules, a lack of responsiveness, lack of flexibility and inability to change.

2.21 As with the other Classical writers, Weber takes no account of individual or group feeling in the organisation. Argyris (who today is one of the major critics of the bureaucratic organisation) claims that bureaucracies restrict the psychological growth of the individual and cause feelings of frustration and conflict.

Student Activity 2

Taking Weber's list of the characteristics of bureaucracy, consider your own organisation. While it may not be entirely bureaucratic in this sense, there will probably be *specific* examples of each feature which can be observed. Make notes of such examples specific to your own organisation.

3 The Human Relations School

3.1 The Classical approach lacked any consideration of human behaviour and how this could be influenced by and influence organisations. The Human Relations approach redresses the balance. It emphasises the creation of an environment which encourages individuals to work towards organisational objectives. The study of organisations develops into the study of human behaviour: how and why people behave and act as they do.

3.2 The Human Relations approach examines specifically individual and group productivity, individual development and job satisfaction. For convenience, we group the areas of study into:

- Individual needs and motivations;

- Behaviour of work groups;

- Behaviour of supervisors/leaders;

- Inter-group behaviour.

3.3 The start of the Human Relations approach is generally assumed to be the famous Hawthorne Experiments at the Western Electric Co in Ohio, USA (1924–1932). The experiment was originally designed to examine the effects of the environment on productivity. Elton Mayo, who was responsible for their supervision, began by examining the effects of the intensity of lighting upon productivity. The results however showed that productivity in the experimental groups increased even when lighting conditions deteriorated.

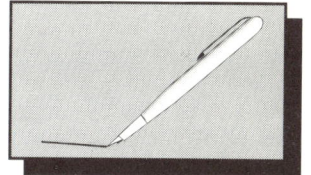

Productivity also increased in the control group although lighting levels remained unchanged. Something, other than environmental conditions had clearly affected productivity. Other experiments then followed.

3.4 Six female employees (all friends) were transferred from their normal area of work to a separate room and a series of changes were made to their working conditions: hours of work, rest pauses and refreshments were all varied. A sympathetic observer was also present. Productivity continued to increase after all but one of the changes. The researchers concluded that the extra attention given to the employees and the interest in them shown by management was the main reason for higher productivity.

3.5 The experiments also involved introducing similar conditions with a group of men and a series of interviews with employees about the work and their attitudes and feelings.

3.6 The Hawthorne experiments would seem to be a significant milestone in that they emphasised the importance of people in an organisation, work groups, leadership and motivation, communications and job design.

3.7 The major criticism that has been levelled at the Human Relations writers is that they may have been concerned with 'people without organisations.'

3.8 The systems approach (below) tries to some extent to remedy this, being concerned with the 'formal organisation' of the Classical school as well as the 'people' of the Human Relations school.

4   Systems School

4.1 The Classical and Human Relations schools have now been succeeded by a more comprehensive approach to the study of management. This systems approach views organisations as a system (an inter-related set of activities, converting inputs to outputs).

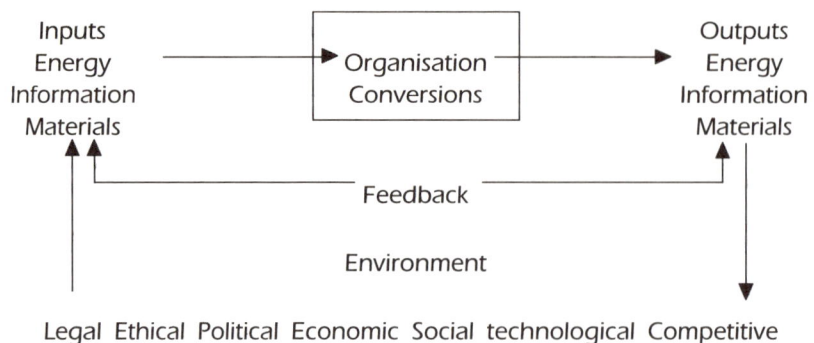

```
Inputs                        Outputs
Energy        ┌──────────────┐   Energy
Information ──▶│ Organisation │──▶ Information
Materials     │ Conversions  │   Materials
              └──────────────┘
                  Feedback
                 Environment
```

Legal Ethical Political Economic Social technological Competitive

4.2 This approach studies the key elements in an organisation, how they interact with one another and the influence of the environment. It therefore examines people, structure, technology and the environment, and their effect on each other. The most recent development of Systems theory has been termed 'Contingency' because it emphasises the need to look at specific circumstances or contingencies when devising organisational and managerial systems.

Definition

4.3   Lucey in *Management Information Systems* (1987) states:

A system is a set of interdependent parts that together form a whole or perform some function – the parts must be interdependent or/and interactive.

4.4   Organisations, by definition, are open systems because they interact with their environment. Each system is composed of *subsystems*, e.g. the organisation has financial, production and marketing subsystems. Where each of the subsystems meet, the boundaries are called *interfaces*. The internal boundaries are determined by organisational policies, e.g. personnel may select individuals for posts or it may be the job of individual departments. There are also decision making, information and communication systems.

4.5   The first paper produced on the organisational concept of Systems theory appeared in 1951, written by two members of the Tavistock Institute of Human Relations EL Trist and KW Bamforth entitled *Some Social and Psychological Consequences of the Long Wall Method of Goal Getting*. The work of the Systems School developed from that of the Human Relations School, who had investigated the relationship between job satisfaction and productivity. Although no clear cut relationships between job satisfaction and productivity were demonstrated, other as yet unidentified factors were obviously playing a part. It seemed that there was one factor, technology, which could play a part in causing a lack of job satisfaction.

4.6   The Systems school developed this idea, but stressed that attitude and morale amongst employees was caused by a variety of factors, not just one.

Student Activity 3

Draw up a systems diagram of your office or section, with one specific example of an input, a conversion, an output, feedback, and some environmental influences.

4.7   It is perhaps easiest to present the Systems views in an historical format. There was originally a 'hand-got' method of mining which was based on small group organisation at the coal face, consisting of interdependent working pairs of colliers (a hewer and his mate), assisted by a boy trammer. The group would be allocated its own small face to work and it was common practice for them to make their own contract with management. There were common pay bonuses shared equally between colliers.

4.8   This was replaced by increasingly mechanised methods of coal production known as 'conventional long wall'. The length of the coal face worked was increased and there was an increasing degree of specialisation. The work cycle of cutting, filing, pulling and stonework was now allocated to different groups operating on different shifts. However this system of working created distinct problems and led to a need to preserve the socio-psychological advantages of composite work groups. The need to improve economic performance was accepted through longer faces and a three-shift cycle.

4.9   The same technology continued to be used, but the incoming shift took up

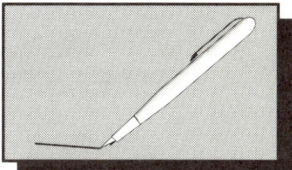

the cycle at the point vacated by the previous shift. This task continuity made the cycle groups become self-maintaining. The group shared pay equally and became self-selecting. The influence of technology and work structure on productivity was thus established.

4.10   The study of management and organisations then expanded further into what is known as the *Contingency School*. Their work has so far indicated that there is no one best way of designing organisations to meet their objectives. Organisations must adapt themselves to circumstances.

Advantages of the Systems School

4.11   These are that it:

- Helps identify problem areas quickly.

- Provides a means of systematising factors and influences in the organisation.

- Aids the understanding of the contribution of each part of the system to the whole.

- Indicates the importance of communication and information systems.

- Indicates the interaction of the environment with the organisation.

Disadvantages of the Systems School

4.12   These are that:

- It is difficult to understand and apply directly to organisations.

- To understand how a large complex organisation works needs a highly sophisticated approach.

- It is difficult to see how the subsystems interact and define the boundaries of each.

- In examining systems the people element tends to be overlooked.

Contingency School

4.13   As a result of research into the electronics industry in the UK, Burns and Stalker were able to distinguish two systems of organisation: mechanistic and organic.

4.14   According to Burns and Stalker the mechanistic system is characterised by a high degree of specialisation, a rigid hierarchy of authority and responsibility with clearly defined boundaries of rights and privileges. Communication is vertical (between superior and subordinate), rather than lateral. Loyalty and obedience are essential prerequisites for employment. This system was perceived by Burns and Stalker to be most appropriate to those firms operating in stable conditions, as everyone knows what is expected, what their responsibilities are and the need for loyalty to the organisation.

4.15   The organic structure is more appropriate, according to Burns and Stalker, to conditions of change because an individual's responsibility and job definition are never clearly defined. The individual's job and role are seen as being directly related to the goals of the firm, to which the individual contributes his special knowledge or abilities. Responsibilities are given to those best qualified in the sense of knowledge and skill rather than position. Control, authority and communication are in a network. Structure and responsibility are directed towards organisational goals, not individuals. A consequence of the flexibility of the organic structure is the sense of insecurity expressed by members, who can never be sure where their job and responsibilities end.

4.16 An organisation has a need to gain the right structure for its particular circumstances, yet a mechanistic organisation by its very history is likely to experience a resistance to change, and so be unable to make the transition to an organic structure if the need should arise.

4.17 Joan Woodward was involved in research between 1953 and 1958 into the relationship between organisational structure and technology in Essex manufacturing firms. She isolated three major types of production systems that seemed to show some relationship to structure:

- Unit and small batch;
- Large batch and mass production;
- Process production (continuous production as for chemicals).

4.18 The organisations using process production tended to use decentralisation and delegation more than the large batch systems and the span of control of middle management (the number of subordinates reporting to one superior) tended to decrease with technical complexity (there were fewer people to report to one superior in process production). The more complex the technological process, then the greater the chain of command. The span of control of the chief executive also increased with technical complexity.

4.19 The organisations which fell into the median range of their particular production system tended to be more successful than those at the top or bottom. Woodward's findings again emphasised the contingent factors influencing organisations.

4.20 Lawrence and Lorsch undertook studies of several firms in the plastics, container and consumer food industry. They were not only interested in structure but also how specific departments were organised to meet different aspects of the environment in which the firms operated.

4.21 They found in their study of six plastic industry firms that the most successful ones were those with the highest degree of collaboration among departments and those whose managers responded well to the particular functional needs of their departments.

4.22 In their later research Lawrence and Lorsch concluded that the extent of collaboration and responsiveness will vary according to the demands of a particular environment. The mechanisms which the organisation use to make it successful vary. In mechanistic structures they are more likely to use policies, rules and procedures, whereas in the organic structure teamwork and mutual co-operation are used.

4.23 The Aston Studies (based at Aston University) examined organisations as complex systems, arguing that there are four basic types:

- *Work-flow Bureaucracy*: high standardisation of procedures and specialisation.

- *Personnel Bureaucracy*: some centralised procedures but production systems localised.

- *Implicitly Structured Organisations*: low standardisation.

- *Full Bureaucracy*: highly structured with high specialisation. Banks could be said to fall into this category. There has been a slimming down of banks in the late 1980s with fewer layers of management and less central control.

Problems and advantages of the Contingency Approach

4.24   A number of problems could be said to exist with the Contingency Approach. Child (1984) cites them as being:

- Causality: it cannot be certain that organisational performance does not have an effect on structure rather than vice versa.

- The measurement of performance used in the contingency studies has not always been precise.

- Some organisations may be able to ignore environmental contingencies and still function effectively, e.g. those in a monopolistic position.

- Although firms may be affected by a number of contingencies, it has not yet been established which are of importance to whom.

4.25   In *defence* of Contingency Theory, Robey (1982) maintains that it has provided a wealth of empirical research and it draws the attention of managers to factors that should be considered in organisational design. He concedes that one difficulty with the Contingency approach is that it emphasises differences between organisations to the exclusion of similarities.

4.26   It should be concluded, as Mullins (1989) states:

    that although there are limitations to the Contingency approach ... it does direct the attention of the manager to the situational factors to be considered in the design of organisation structure.

4.27   The Contingency Approach draws attention to the situational variables which account for differences in the structure of organisations. It is more concerned with variances than similarities, and rejects the idea that there is one best structure. The success of the organisation is more dependent on the ability to assess situations and respond accordingly.

5   The manager today

5.1   As there are many hierarchical levels in the organisation, so there are various managerial levels. A senior manager will spend much of the time thinking of the long-term future direction of the business, and although a branch manager may also think longer-term, the greater concern is achieving weekly and monthly goals. Lower managerial levels are more concerned with daily goals. There are also various specialisations in the bank today; for example, computer analysts, economists, and personnel directors who run departments or sections providing detailed advice for the running of the organisation.

5.2   Most managers have two main areas of activity: people management and process or business management.

6   Major functions of a manager

6.1   Although many definitions of the role of the manager are available (the earliest attempt was by Henri Fayol), they all have a common thread: a manager is the one who is responsible for getting things done through other people instead of doing the job alone. With stated objectives to achieve, the manager directs human activities with the help of other resources.

6.2   Many writers seem to agree that there are six main functions of management.

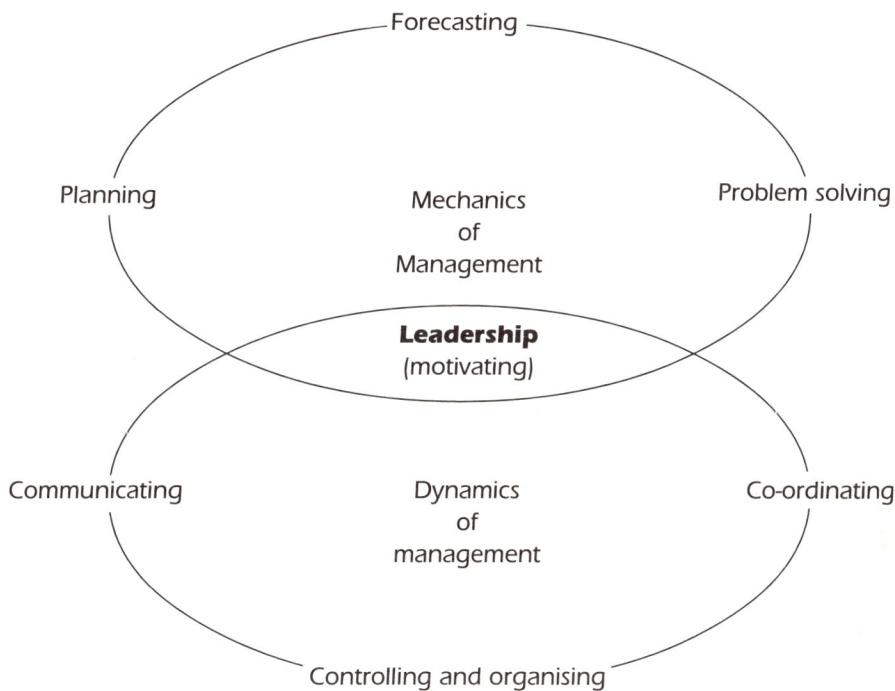

```
                        ┌─── Forecasting ───┐

   Planning                  Mechanics              Problem solving
                                of
                            Management

                            Leadership
                            (motivating)

   Communicating             Dynamics               Co-ordinating
                                of
                            management

                        └─ Controlling and organising ─┘
```

Student Activity 4

Think of the activities of your manager, and select out the six main functions detailed in the diagram above. Over the last few weeks, your manager should have engaged in all of them: make notes of observable examples of when your manager did each one, with comment on whether they did them well or badly, i.e. whether the outcome fulfilled the organisation's objectives, in your opinion.

Forecasting

6.3   Most managers have, as part of their job, to look ahead and anticipate events. The extent to which they are required to do this varies according to their level of responsibility in the hierarchy. At the lower levels they are more concerned with implementation of strategy rather than devising strategy themselves.

6.4   Forecasting implies both pro-active and reactive approaches. A pro-active approach is required when a manager examines international and national

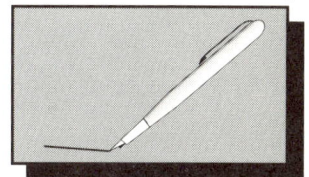

economic systems, customers, competitors and business development areas. This could be described as looking for opportunities.

6.5 A reactive approach is looking for threats. The UK financial services industry has some reactive forecasting with quick responses to threats like telephone banking and insurance systems. At lower management levels forecasting takes the form of deciding on possible future action to meet a target.

Planning

6.6 Planning implies the establishment of organisation, breaking down duties, devising a programme and objectives for a department and allocating the work. It calls for forecasts and demands that managers look ahead and anticipate future events.

6.7 Plans are important even when change is introduced to help establish key tasks, key result areas, targets and monitoring.

6.8 Planning involves a series of stages.

- *Determine the aims of the job.* A key area of activity is to communicate the aims to all those involved, so they know what is required of them.

- *Estimate and secure the resources* required. Managers need to ensure the cost of the resources required in the plan will not outweigh the benefits. For one-off projects the task of securing resources can be difficult, and not all the resources will be needed for the life of the project.

- *Identify key result areas and key tasks within them.* Key result areas are crucial to the success of change and within these certain key tasks need to be completed. In order to take and pass an examination people have to enrol or to plan a course of study, pay for entry to the examination and devote time to studying the subjects.

- *Define success criteria.* This involves specifying how you will know you have succeeded. These can be defined for different stages in the process. Taking an examination as an example, the first stage is being accepted on a course, then purchasing a notebook, etc.

- *Set standards of performance.* These give expected measures of performance whilst activities are ongoing rather than at the end of the activity. These standards should be specific, measurable, achievable, relevant and trackable. (SMART is a useful mnemonic for remembering them.)

- *Define short term goals and first steps.* This needs to be completed so the individuals know where to start and what to aim for.

- *Set individual targets.* This is needed so each individual knows not only the overall objectives but also what is required for each person.

- *Set up monitoring systems.* This is an important stage because it ensures that plans are proceeding smoothly.

Problem solving

6.9 This involves the manager seeing difficulties, preferably before they arise, and planning action to cope with the problem. There is a series of well-defined stages in the problem solving process.

- Selecting and defining the problem;
- Gathering data about the situation;
- Examining the situation to identify failings and irrelevancies;
- Develop a new improved situation;
- Install the plan in practice;
- Maintain the plan, modifying it where deviations have occurred.

This process is examined in detail in Unit 16.

Co-ordinating

6.10 This means the co-ordination of materials, equipment, financial and human resources to ensure the production of goods or services. This is crucial where a project or expansion project is involved, as all activities should proceed at a common pace.

Controlling and monitoring

6.11 This is concerned with evaluating performance and taking steps to bring it into line with plans. It presupposes that plans are already in existence, otherwise there is nothing to control, aim for or measure performance against. From the plans targets are derived and performance can then be measured against these targets. Appropriate action can then be taken to eliminate the variance or adjust the plan so it reflects what can be achieved.

6.12 There are four main ways of controlling:

- By checking up on key events;
- Using 'milestones' (reporting on all levels of activity at certain points);
- Management by observation – the manager observes informally to make sure it matches progress;
- Management by exception – reports are submitted if there is a variance between the plan and the performance.

6.13 Budgets are one of a number of techniques used to control output and expenditure (see Unit 7).

Communication

6.14 This is, according to Williamson in *Business Organisation* (1981), a 'process whereby messages are transmitted from one person to another'. Communication is fully discussed in Unit 14.

Summary

6.15 Discussions on the role of the manager can be found in the earliest organisational writing. The principles of planning, organising, co-ordinating and controlling are derivations of the classical school of theory, namely Fayol and Taylor. The ideas of problem solving and communicating are conceptual additions from the Human Relations and Systems Schools of thought. In recent years there has been some interest in creating a management charter which will detail the skills and techniques necessary for a successful manager: the Management Charter Initiative.

7   Managerial roles

7.1   As well as the functions and processes management are involved in, it is possible to identify the various roles they occupy. Mintzberg (1973) classified these into 10 different roles, divided into three major groups:

- Interpersonal roles;
- Informational roles;
- Decisional roles.

Interpersonal roles

7.2   These arise from the managers' relations with others. The manager is a figurehead, representing the organisation and its policies, i.e. signing documents, etc. The manager is a leader, responsible for staffing and the motivation of subordinates. There is also a role to play in liaison with managers and others outside the manager's unit.

Informational roles

7.3   The manager has an important communication role to play in the organisation. Information must be monitored so the manager can understand how the organisation operates and the influence of the environment.

7.4   The manager also acts as a *disseminator* of information, passing on information from the environment to the organisation and from senior management down to employees. The manager acts as a *spokesperson* communicating information to other departments or levels in the organisation, and outside the organisation to suppliers, etc.

Decisional roles

7.5   These involve the manager in making decisions about the future of the organisation and the department. In an entrepreneurial role the manager initiates and plans controlled change by solving problems and taking action to improve the existing situation. The manager can also act as a *disturbance handler*, reacting to involuntary situations and unpredictable events. The *resource allocator role* involves the manager in using formal authority to decide where effort will be expended and making noises about allocation of resources. The *negotiator role* involves the manager in negotiating activities with other individuals or organisations, e.g. a new agreement with a supplier.

7.6   These roles are illustrated by Mintzberg as shown in diagram on the next page.

Student Activity 5

This unit has given a general explanation of the manager's roles according to Mintzberg. Take each of the roles and give a *specific* example of when a manager might be seen to be observably taking the role.

7.7   Mintzberg suggests that this is an arbitrary division of a manager's role and that the manager's work does not divide itself neatly into these categories.

7.8   It is merely one of many ways of trying to categorise the manager's duties in

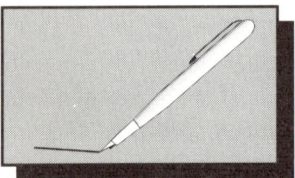

Managers' formal
authority and
status
|
Interpersonal roles:
Figurehead
Leader
Liaison
|
Informational roles:
Monitor
Disseminator
Spokesperson
|
Decisional roles:
Entrepreneur
Disturbance handler
Resource allocator
Negotiator

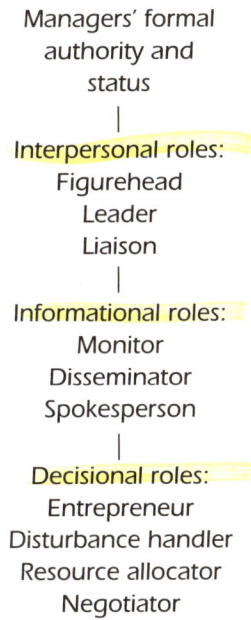

the organisation. Although there are a variety of managers of many differing levels and types, writers have maintained that certain common features can be found in many manager's jobs.

7.9   Braddick suggests the common features are:

- Paperwork;

- Telephone calls;

- Meetings;

- Contacts;

- Content: junior management deals with operational problems and senior management deals with fewer problems over a wider basis.

7.10   Rosemary Stewart developed a model for understanding managerial behaviour and work. The common features of a manager's job are:

- Demands: what the person *has* to do, *not* what the person *ought* to do.

- Constraints: the internal or external factors that limit what a manager can do (resource limitations, legal or other constraints).

- Choices: the activities the manager is free to do but does not have to do.

7.11   Stewart argues that the model provides a framework for thinking about the nature of managerial jobs and the manner in which managers undertake them. To understand the role of management you must be aware of their flexibility and the variations in behaviour and the different nature of the work. It is this very flexibility that makes for satisfying job design, but also makes job evaluation and in some instances linking pay to targets (performance related pay) difficult.

7.12   As well as similarities in the jobs of managers Stewart claims that there are also significant differences. There are 'hub-group' managers who interact with superiors, subordinates and peers; 'peer dependent' managers who work with managers of a similar level; managers who control and supervise the work of subordinates; and finally those specialist managers whose role is technical and have few contracts with staff.

8 The job of manager and subordinate

8.1 All individuals come to work with certain expectations about what they can gain from the organisation:

- Safe working conditions;
- Job security;
- Challenging and interesting jobs;
- Equitable personnel policies;
- Respect, etc.

8.2 But what distinguishes management from the individual? It is the responsibility of management to manage, i.e. get things done through others. It is through the process of managing that the efforts of all the individuals are co-ordinated and directed. Management is concerned with carrying out organisational processes and the execution of work. Individuals in the organisation should direct their activities towards the goals management has indicated. Their primary responsibility is for their own actions, whereas management is responsible for all subordinates. 'Management reconciles the needs of the individuals with the requirements of the organisation,' states Mullins. It is the integrating activity of management that permeates every aspect of the operations of the organisation.

8.3 There have been various attempts to study the behaviours which make a manager more effective. Boyatzis (1982) classified five key performance areas where assessment and development programmes could be focused. These are:

- Goal and action management;
- Directing subordinates;
- Human resource management;
- Leadership;
- Specialist knowledge.

Summary

Having studied this unit carefully you should now:

- understand the role of the modern manager;

- be able to discuss the main findings of:

- scientific management

- the classical school of management

- the human relations school

- systems thinking

- the contingency approach;

- know about modern management thought on the role of the manager;

- be able to reproduce Mintzberg's model;

- be capable of critical analysis of managerial performance.

Self-assessment questions

1. The Classical approach to the study of organisations considers:
   (a) social aspects of organisations;
   (b) the purpose and structure of organisations;
   (c) the history of the organisation;
   (d) management as the most important element.

2. Frederick W Taylor was most interested in:
   (a) methods of working;
   (b) the role management played;
   (c) how employees should be recruited;
   (d) the engineering process.

3. Taylor believed the principle objective of management should be:
   (a) docile workforce;
   (b) maximum prosperity for each employee;
   (c) to dismiss trade unions;
   (d) good organisational structure.

4. The work of Henri Fayol concentrated on:
   (a) methods of working;
   (b) the role of trade unions;
   (c) the role and principles of good management;
   (d) bureaucracy as a form of structure.

5. Henri Fayol believed maximum prosperity could be achieved through:
   (a) a careful division of work;
   (b) use of work study techniques;
   (c) bureaucracy;
   (d) following 14 principles for effective organisation.

6. Who led the Hawthorne experiments, and where?

7. What are the major elements of a system?

8. What did Child suggest were the problems with contingency?

9. What are Mintzberg's 10 roles of the manager?.

10. What did Rosemary Stewart say were the main features of a manager's job?

Unit 13

Leadership and Management Style

Objectives

After having studied this unit, you should be able to:

- understand several ways of approaching leadership;

- understand models of management style;

- understand how the concept of contingency applies;

- use the idea of power to understand leadership.

1   Leadership defined

1.1   Leadership can be defined in very basic terms as 'getting others to do things'; or more specifically as, 'the use of authority in decision-making'. Mullins (1989) defines it as, 'a relationship through which one person influences the behaviour of other people'. Feldman and Arnold (1983) state: 'Leadership involves one person (the leader) consciously trying to get other people (the followers) to do something the leader wants them to do'. It seems that it is impossible to separate (as Mullins states), 'the process of leadership from the activities of groups'.

1.2   The job of manager normally involves some leadership ability – but not all leaders are managers. The difference between leadership and management (although sometimes they may be synonymous) is that management involves co-ordinating activities to achieve organisational goals, whereas leadership is more generally concerned with acting as a guide and motivator for others.

Leadership effectiveness

1.3   An issue which has concerned organisational theorists is why some leaders are effective and others ineffective? Three are major approaches to leadership effectiveness, corresponding broadly to historical phases, the:

- Trait approach;
- Style approach;
- Contingency approach.

2   Trait approach

2.1   This approach is the earliest attempt at explaining why some people are successful as leaders and others are not. It focuses on the individual occupying the post not on the job itself.

2.2 The approach suggests that leaders have certain qualities or traits, which are innate and not easily developed or acquired, and this distinguishes them from their followers. Attention should therefore be directed to selecting as leaders those people who possess these qualities since the characteristics cannot be developed or encouraged through training.

2.3 Researchers have found it difficult to identify the traits likely to lead to leadership effectiveness. Among the many that have been suggested are: size, energy, integrity, decisiveness, knowledge, wisdom, imagination. Certain studies have cited 'significant correlations' between some traits and leadership effectiveness. Ghiselli (1971) found intelligence, ability, initiative, self-assurance and individuality important. Stogdill (1948) found intelligence, scholarship, dependability, responsibility, originality, social improvement and socio-economic status important in distinguishing leaders from non-leaders.

2.4 The problems with this approach are several:

- It may be that effective leaders learned to develop these qualities after becoming leaders and the ability to respond to the situation is the key trait.

- There is not much agreement among researchers as to which characteristics are important.

- This approach does not help in the development and training of future leaders.

Student Activity 1

Think of a leader in sport, in politics and in business. Do they have any traits in common? And are they in any way quite different in character?

3 Style approach

3.1 The style approach introduced the concept that managers adopt very different methods when motivating staff and completing a task. These styles range from the authoritarian to democratic. McGregor summed up these two extremes in his Theory X (the authoritarian) and his Theory Y (the democratic). McGregor believed Theory Y was more appropriate for today's manager.

Theory X

3.2 This traditional approach to motivation and encouraging a satisfactory level of employee involvement and effort is expressed in McGregor's Theory X:

- The average person has an inherent dislike of work.
- Because of this most people must be coerced, controlled, or threatened with punishment to get them to put forward adequate effort toward the achievement of organisational goals.
- The average person prefers to be directed, wishes to avoid responsibility, has relatively little ambition and wants security above all.

3.3 Fortunately, according to Theory X, not all employees are like this. There are some superior people, who can assume authority and control (those destined to be managers).

3.4 This approach can be summarised: 'Control them and lick them into shape.' A theorist belonging to this group is Frederick W Taylor with his view of man as a purely rational economic being. He assumes employees are motivated purely by economic reward and will work harder if they believe there is to be more money. These views can also be summarised as the 'carrot and stick' approach to management, with incentives and sanctions combined.

Theory Y

3.5 A modern approach to management is expressed in McGregor's Theory Y:

- Work is as natural as play or rest.
- The average person not only accepts but seeks responsibility.
- In modern industrial life people's potential is only partially utilised.
- External control and the threat of punishment are not the only means of bringing about effort towards organisational objectives.

3.6 The 'style approach' suggested that certain leaders were effective because of the style they adopted. There are a number of theorists who could be said to support this approach.

White and Lippitt Iowa Studies (1953)

3.7 Their research was carried out in a boys' summer camp. The group leaders adopted and changed leadership styles, from authoritarian to democratic and laissez-faire.

- *Authoritarian.* All policies were determined by the leader. The leader dictated the jobs to be done by each member and he was personal in his praise and criticism.
- *Democratic.* All policies were determined by joint discussion between the leader and the group. The division of tasks were determined by the group and the leader was objective in his praise and criticism.
- *Laissez-faire.* The group alone decided the policies, if any, and the way tasks were to be divided. The leader gave only occasional comments on performance.

3.8 Overall, the democratic style proved to be most effective in terms of group morale and productivity.

Tannenbaum and Schmidt

3.9 Tannenbaum and Schmidt developed a continuum of leadership styles ranging from boss-centred leadership (authoritarian) to employee-centred leadership (democratic). The continuum also includes the degree of authority used by a manager and the degree of freedom for subordinates. (See the diagram on the next page.)

3.10 This continuum could also be summarised as: 'tells, sells, consults'.

3.11 Tannenbaum and Schmidt suggest that there are certain factors which will help to determine what type of leadership style is most appropriate. These are:

Figure 13.1 Tannenbaum's and Schmidt's Continuum of Leadership Styles

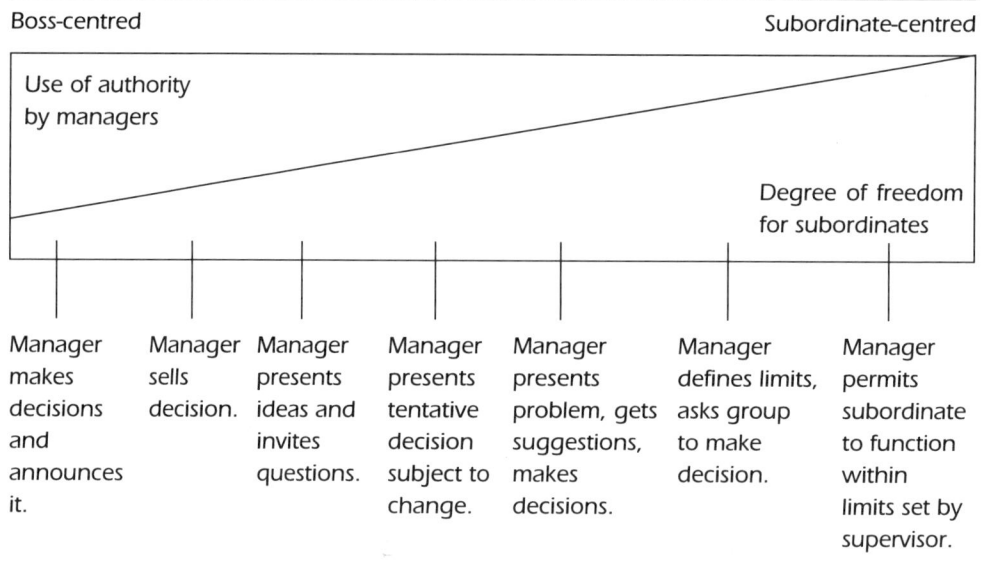

Boss-centred   Subordinate-centred

Use of authority by managers

Degree of freedom for subordinates

| Manager makes decisions and announces it. | Manager sells decision. | Manager presents ideas and invites questions. | Manager presents tentative decision subject to change. | Manager presents problem, gets suggestions, makes decisions. | Manager defines limits, asks group to make decision. | Manager permits subordinate to function within limits set by supervisor. |

- The manager:
  - security
  - leadership
  - confidence in subordinates
  - value systems;
- The subordinates:
  - necessary knowledge and experience
  - understanding of the organisation
  - willingness to accept responsibility
  - need for independence
  - interest.

3.12 The most successful managers are those who can assess the situation and respond to it.

Student Activity 2

Look at the Tannenbaum and Schmidt continuum. Think about your manager and carefully locate where that manager usually manages. Write notes to support your suggestion, and critically evaluate the style selected; then add some notes on how flexible the manager is: do they alter their style to fit the occasion?

Blake and Mouton Managerial Grid (1964)

3.13 Rather than seeing the authoritarian and democratic styles at opposite ends of a spectrum, Blake and Mouton see leadership as being two-dimensional, and so place the styles on a grid.

3.14 The most effective leaders are those who rate highly on both dimensions: concern for production and people. Blake and Mouton found evidence that

Figure 13.2 Blake and Mouton Managerial Grid (from *The Managerial Grid* (1984), R Blake and J Mouton, Houston Gulf Publishing)

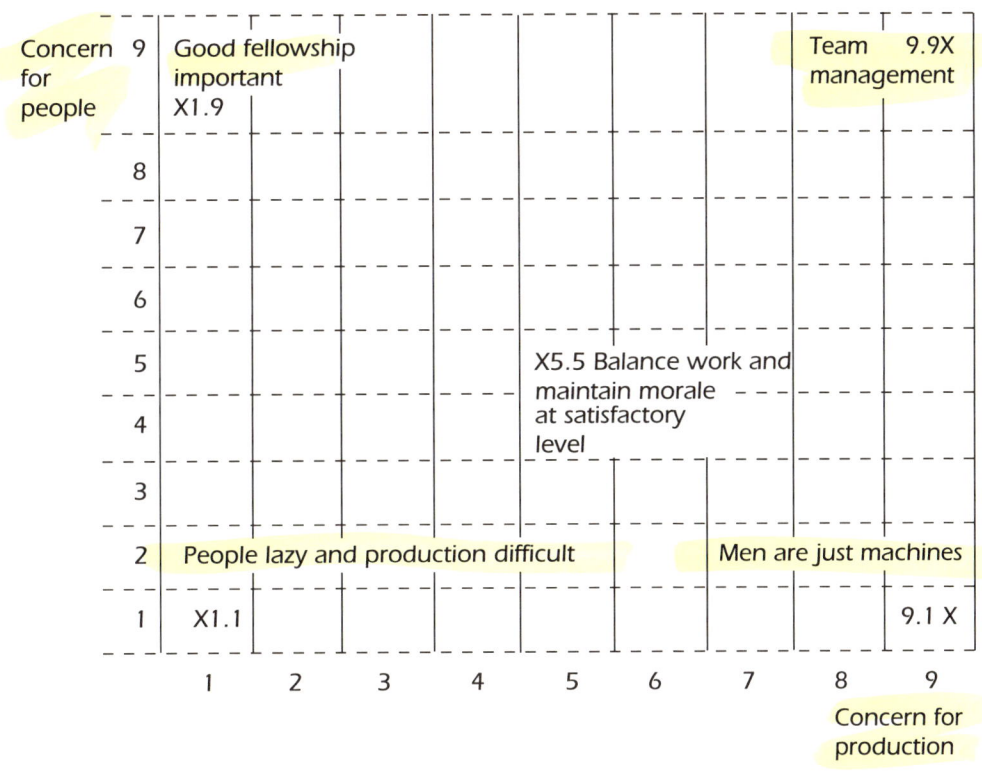

the supportive styles, i.e. concern for people scoring five or more, were related to lower labour turnover, less intergroup conflict and high group satisfaction.

3.15   A development from this research is the Reddin 3D model of leadership behaviour. By adding a third dimension of managerial effectiveness to the two of product and people orientation there are eight possible styles of behaviour. According to Reddin, the management must be adaptable in selecting the correct style.

3.16   The four styles, which can be used either effectively or ineffectively depending on the situation, are: related, separated, integrated and dedicated. Unlike Blake and Mouton who suggest there is one style which is most effective, Reddin indicates that there is no style that is better or worse than any other. It is the situation which will determine the appropriate and, therefore, effective style.

Ashridge Studies

3.17   A series of studies at Ashridge College in the 1960s and 1970s identified four styles of management:

- The tells style: the manager makes decisions and announces them.

- The sells style: the manager makes the decision, but rather than announce it to the subordinates, tries to persuade them to accept it.

- The consults style: the manager does not make the decision until the problem is presented to the group and their advice and suggestions are heard.

- The joins style: the manager delegates to a group the right to make decisions. The manager indicates the limits within which the decision must be made.

171

3.18 A survey was made of style in a large multinational business. It revealed that the consultative type was most often preferred, although this varied according to the different categories of employee.

3.19 Unlike Blake, McGregor, and Likert, the Ashridge researchers do not suggest an ideal style. It depends on circumstances.

4 Contingency School

4.1 The latest thoughts on effective leadership belong to the Contingency School and are developed from the concept that the most effective leaders have the ability to adapt their style according to the situation.

Fiedler's Contingency Theory

4.2 Fiedler (1967) classifies leaders' orientations in terms of whether they enjoy working with others (a high Least Preferred Co-worker score (LPC)); or whether they are more production oriented (a low Least Preferred Co-worker score). A questionnaire is issued to potential and existing leaders which when completed indicates whether they enjoy working with others – a high LPC score – or whether they dislike working with others – a low LPC score. Fielder also attempts to identify key features in the situation.

- *Leader-member relations:* Is the relationship between a leader and followers good (see (iii) in Fig. 13.3)?

- *Task structure*: A high degree of task structure gives a more favourable situation for the leader as it means subordinates' behaviour can be more easily monitored and influenced (see (ii) in Fig. 13.3).

- *Position of power*: The more formal the leader's position, the greater the range of rewards and punishments available (the power is judged as weak or strong: see (i) in Fig. 13.3).

4.3 All these factors are combined in Fiedler's Contingency Model indicating which situations are favourable to a particular type of leader.

General pattern of results of research on Fiedler's Contingency Theory

4.4 When the situation is very favourable (good leader-member relations, structured task, a strong position of power) or very unfavourable (poor leader-member relations, unstructured task, weak position of power), then a task-oriented leader (low LPC score) with a directive, controlling style will be more effective. When the situation is moderately favourable then a participative approach (a high LPC score) will be more effective. Fiedler concludes that leadership style will vary according to the situation and that leadership effectiveness may be improved by changing the leadership situation. The position of power, task structure and leader-member relations can all be changed to make it compatible with the characteristics of the leader.

Figure 13.3 Fiedler's Contingency Model from *Theory of Leadership Effectiveness* (1967), FEA Fiedler, McGraw Hill

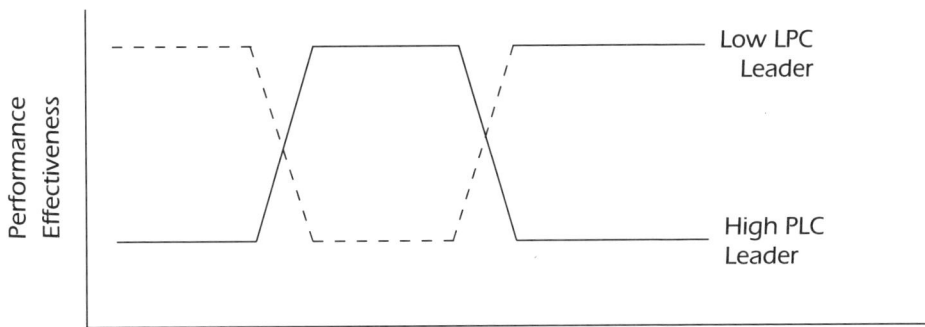

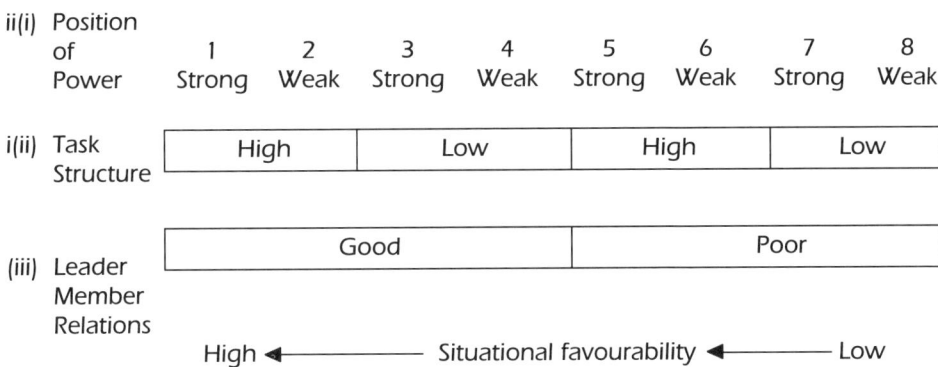

ii(i)	Position of Power	1 Strong	2 Weak	3 Strong	4 Weak	5 Strong	6 Weak	7 Strong	8 Weak

i(ii)	Task Structure	High		Low		High		Low	

(iii)	Leader Member Relations	Good				Poor			

High ◄——————— Situational favourability ◄——————— Low

Student Activity 3

Write a mini-essay, approximately one side of A4 in length, on what good management style 'depends on'.

Hersey and Blanchard's model of supportive and directive behaviour

4.5   These two writers suggested that managers engage in:

- *Supportive behaviour*, looking after the developmental needs of their employees; and

- *Directive behaviour*, giving general steering and direction and allowing the subordinate to perform independently.

4.6   Their model is represented in the diagram on next page:

4.7   This diagram indicates that, from the *right*, at the start of the subordinate's career there is growing supportive and reducing directive behaviour; but as the subordinate develops, the line moves *leftwards*, and eventually supportive and directive behaviour is reduced so that the subordinate stands more firmly independent. Thus the management style is contingent on the state of development of the employee, or rather, the readiness for the task or set of tasks being undertaken and managed.

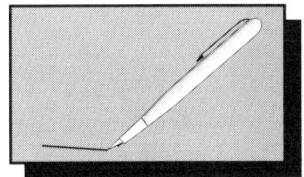

Figure 13.4 Supportive and directive behaviour

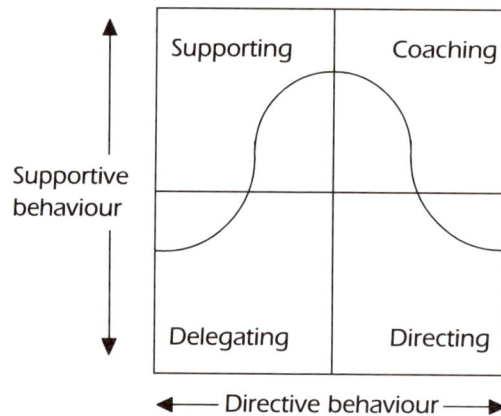

(Freely adapted from Hersey, P and Blanchard, K: Management of Organisational Behaviour, 6th ed, Prentice-Hall, 1993)

5   Action-centred leadership

5.1   John Adair uses a similar approach in training leaders in what is known as 'action-centred leadership'. The effectiveness of the leader is dependent on meeting three areas of need within the work group:

● The need to achieve the common task;

● Team maintenance in maintaining morale and building a team spirit;

● Meeting the needs of individual members of the group.

5.2   The action by a leader in any one area of need will affect one or both of the other areas. The most effective leader will be the one who can meet all these needs and maintain a balance between them.

5.3   The approach to effective leadership today stresses that no one style is best, but rather the successful leader is the one who can assess the situation and choose the most appropriate style, paying attention to the needs of the individual, the group and the organisation.

Student Activity 4

Using Adair's three-circle model, write a list of three observable actions that a leader can take to satisfy each of the three sets of group needs.

6 The leadership/interpersonal relationship

6.1 A leader can be appointed, selected or chosen informally. Attempted leadership occurs when one in the group tries to exert influence over others. Successful leadership occurs when influence brings about the behaviour and results intended by the leader. Effective leadership occurs when it results in functional behaviour and the achievement of group goals.

6.2 Within an organisation the leadership influence will be dependent on the type of power the leader can exercise over others. The exercise of power is a social process and it explains how different people can influence the behaviour of others. It enables managers to get things done.

6.3 There are four main sources of power as identified by French and Raven (see Unit 19).

- *Reward power,* based on the fact, and the subordinate's perception that the leader has the ability and resources to obtain rewards for those who comply, e.g. pay, promotion, etc.

- *Coercive power,* based on the fact and the subordinate's perception that the leader has the ability to punish those who do not comply.

- *Referent power,* based on subordinate's identification with the leader. The leader exercises influence because of perceived attractiveness or charisma. A manager may not be able to reward subordinates, but can still command respect.

- *Expert power,* based on subordinates' perception of the leader as someone who is competent and has special knowledge.

- *Legitimate power,* based on the leader's position of authority in the organisation.

6.4 Another category of power defined by other writers is *political power* which is derived from knowing 'how things work', the politics of the organisation.

6.5 The sources of power are based on the subordinates' perception of the leader. If suppliers believe a manager has the power to withdraw an order, *then* the manager can exercise considerable influence even though the individual may not have this power in reality. Leadership is dynamic behaviour because it is constantly changing and depends on the:

- Characteristics of each leader (behaviour analysis tools like the lifestyle questionnaire have tried to link style and personality);

- Attitude, needs and characteristics of the followers;

- Nature of the organisation – its purpose and structure bases;

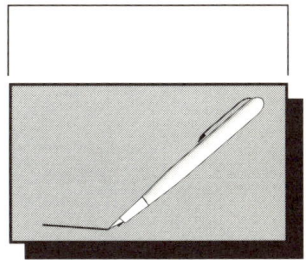

- Environment.

175

6.6   McGregor, who cites these variables, says leadership is not dependent on just the individual, but rather links many factors.

6.7   A leader can also act as a model for subordinates: attitude, energy, etc, can set a pattern for others to follow. The leader is also a representative of the group in the eyes of others. The leader is the link in the organisation between subordinates and others. Group members rely on their leader to act as the mouthpiece and occupy a representative role to other parties.

Summary

Having studied this unit carefully you should now:

- **know that there are several ways of approaching leadership;**

- **be able critically to analyse trait theories of management;**

- **be familiar with established models of management style;**

- **understand and be able to discuss contingency approaches;**

- **know what Action Centred leadership is;**

- **be able to use the idea of power to explain leadership.**

Self-assessment questions

1. Which phrase best describes a democratic style?

   (a) The manager makes the decision, helped by the group.

   (b) The manager makes the decision.

   (c) The manager allows the group to make all the decisions.

   (d) Decisions are made by the group with help from the manager.

2. Why are leadership theories based on traits difficult to accept?

   (a) No major theorist has developed it.

   (b) Other theories appear to make better sense.

   (c) There is little agreement on the significant qualities.

   (d) It is the earliest of the theories.

3. Style leadership is:

   (a) selecting the right leader for the post;

   (b) training someone to lead;

   (c) adopting a particular style of leadership;

   (d) changing style according to situation.

4. What are the styles of leadership quoted by Lippitt and Whyte?

5. What are the two dimensions of Tannenbaum and Schmidt's continuum?

6. What are the axes on Blake and Mouton's grid?

7. How did the Ashridge studies characterise management styles?

8. By what other name are the research studies of White and Lippitt known?

9. What are the four behaviours named by Hersey and Blanchard?

10. What, according to Adair, are the three sets of group need?

Unit 14

Organisational Communication; and Running Meetings

Objectives

After studying this chapter, you should be able to:

- **understand the communication process;**

- **have examined barriers to communication;**

- **be able to plan effective communication;**

- **understand the nature of meetings;**

- **be able to discuss the advantages and drawbacks of committees.**

1 The importance of communication in organisations

1.1 All organisations are dependent upon communications in order to meet three basic needs:

- Allocation of duties;

- Co-ordination and integration of tasks;

- Decision making and adapting to change.

1.2 Effective communication is, therefore, an essential prerequisite for an effective organisation, but it is important to realise that improved communication alone will not solve all management and organisational problems. The main criteria used to judge the effectiveness of communications has been accuracy and the use of time, energy and other resources.

2 The process of communication

2.1 Williamson (1981) defined communication as:

The process whereby messages are transmitted from one person to another.

Although it is a complex process it is possible to show it in a fairly simple diagrammatic form (see fig. 14.1).

2.2 Within an organisation communication is frequently defined as formal or informal. *Formal* is that given out by and approved by the organisation along established lines of communication and relationships, e.g:

Figure 14.1 The process of communication

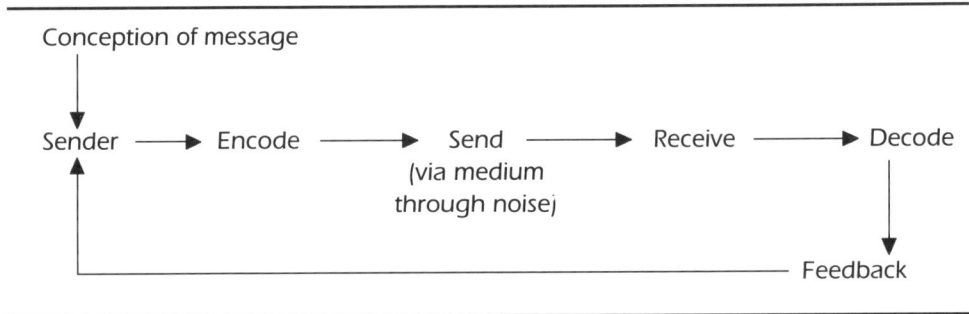

Conception of message

Sender ⟶ Encode ⟶ Send ⟶ Receive ⟶ Decode
(via medium
through noise)

Feedback

- Instructions;
- Circulars;
- Letters;
- Reports;
- Meetings;
- House journals;
- Interviews;
- Questionnaires;
- Induction programmes;
- contracts of employment.

2.3   *Informal* are those communications not transmitted along established paths and are unofficial, often unplanned and spontaneous. They include:

- Casual conversations;
- Personal contacts;
- Rumours and grapevine;
- Ignoring people (sending them to Coventry);
- Use of body language (signs and signals).

Student Activity 1

Take the model of communication given in the section above, and apply it to a recent Head Office circular. In what ways might that circular be an imperfect piece of communication, according to the model?

3   Problems in the communication process

3.1   Problems can occur in transmitting a message, whether formal or informal.

The sender

3.2   The first difficulty is in translating ideas (which can be vague and hazy) into a form that can be understood by someone else, either in speech or writing. How these ideas are encoded will depend, to a great extent, on what the sender is trying to communicate. The 'language' can vary in complexity.

The message

3.3 The message element of the communication process involves three aspects:

- Content;
- Code;
- Channel.

3.4 The *content* of the message is the meaning of what is being transmitted. This is the very substance of the message and needs to be clear in the mind before an attempt is made to express it in any form. Difficulties can arise because of technical language used or because the meaning is unclear.

3.5 The *code* of transmission is the 'how' of the communication process. There are many ways by which the same message can be communicated, e.g. diagram, written, sign language, verbal. The most appropriate method needs to be chosen if effective communication is to occur.

3.6 Finally, the *channel* of communication needs to be considered. There are many media channels available in the business organisation: face to face, telephone, memos, mass meetings, etc. There can be problems because an inappropriate method of transmission is chosen or the message loses its impact because of limitations in using the different media available.

Receiver

3.7 Before the message reaches the receiver there can be problems in the communication process termed 'noise'. Even if the message is clear, and the choice of media effective, the message can still be lost because of interference. This interference can be either internal or external. For instance, the receiver may be tired, preoccupied, angry or disinterested, and so the message may not be received at all. The interference can be external, in that the message is blocked by external noise from machinery, or traffic. The reception of the message can also be affected by the receiver's selectivity, picking out only the parts of the message the receiver wishes to hear, e.g. listen to all the praise and ignore the criticism, or alternatively jumping to conclusions about the message.

3.8 It can be difficult to achieve open communication when an employee is used to an authoritarian or dictatorial style of management.

Barriers to communication

3.9 These include:

- Translating ideas into a form of communication;
- Keeping the substance of the message clear;
- Use of technical language or jargon;
- Misuse of the form of communication, e.g. using a telephone to transmit accounts when written communication is more suitable;
- 'Noise' interference (physical noise, emotions, tiredness, disinterest);
- Receiver's selectivity, e.g. imposing stereotypes or hearing only portions of the message;
- Status of either sender or receiver.

Feedback

3.10 Feedback can aid communication. Research has demonstrated the need for feedback if communication is to be effective. It is not enough to pass orders or instructions down, you must ensure that the message is understood and that others are allowed to make a contribution if effective communication is to occur. What is termed 'active listening' is the ideal approach. It encourages contributions from the receiver indicating understanding of the message. Participation is one way of encouraging active listening because it keeps people involved and allows decisions and their effect to be discussed.

3.11 Some British banks have a structure of consultative committees or staff communication meetings, whereby directives from head office can be discussed at a local level and feedback given on their reception. Effective communication and participation means discussing management decisions before they are implemented and allowing responses from those involved.

3.12 However, 'open door' policy by managers is not necessarily the answer. It is time-consuming for managerial staff as well as creating hostility among supervisory staff who feel they are being bypassed. An alternative is either restricting the time a manager is available to employees or using a system of 'Management By Walking About' (MBWA). This gives employees the opportunity to communicate with managers, whilst at the same time indicating to employees that the managers are interested and approachable.

4   Effective communication

4.1 To ensure that effective communication is more likely to be achieved the manager can embark on a number of steps.

Attention

4.2 Before communication can occur communicators must gain the attention of those with whom they wish to communicate. The methods used to gain 'attention' in organisations are formal and familiar (notice boards, telephones, etc) and informal and perhaps less familiar (personal contact, body language, etc). Body language as a mode of communication can replace or support speech, indicating attitudes and emotions. It includes gestures, eye contact, physical distance from one another and emphasis or tone of voice and silence. However, body language is vague – most people use it instinctively rather than deliberately and it is a temporary mode of communication (unless preserved on video).

Figure 14.2 Stages of effective communication

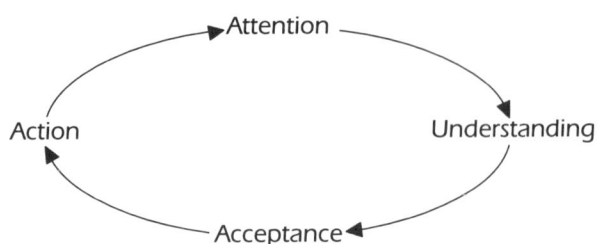

Understanding

4.3 This is having a clear idea of what to convey and encoding the communication by putting it into a meaningful form. Choosing words that fit into the understanding and vocabulary of the receiver; selecting the most appropriate medium for transmission and ensuring that the message gets to the receiver are all important. Checking the message is understood can be done by using questions, demonstration, giving a report of project, or examinations.

Acceptance

4.4 This is ensuring the communication is decoded so the intended message is conveyed and accepted, through the use of power, authority, participation, involvement, sanctions and rewards.

Action/behaviour

4.5 If the receiver has to take a course of action or change attitudes as a result of the communication, check this is done and elicit feedback on the communication and resulting action.

Student Activity 2

Suppose that you had to address a number of junior staff to introduce a new procedure in your office. You have decided to make a short presentation after the close of the day's work. How will you plan to communicate effectively via *the four stages suggested in the section above?* Write notes on each stage, including the possible problems and how you would overcome them.

Other points to remember

4.6 Other points to remember for effective communication are:

- *Frequency.* The more often the message is repeated the better it is remembered.

- *Intensity.* The more vivid, enthusiastic and personalised the communication, the better it is remembered.

- *Duration.* Short, pointed messages are more likely to get attention, understanding and the retention needed for effective communication.

- *Structure and communication.* The effectiveness of communication can also be affected by the organisational structure. Each of the structures below indicates the different path to be followed.

4.7 The wheel is the most centralised structure with just one co-ordinator. The circle and all-channel structures rely on decentralised channels with shared leadership, whilst the 'Chain' and 'Y' structures are most likely to be found in mechanistic/bureaucratic organisations. The all-channel structure will be found in organic organisations.

5 Communication techniques

5.1 The most commonly used techniques for down*ward communications* are:

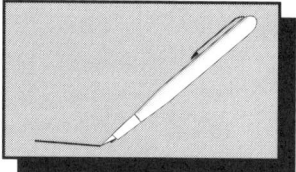

- Briefing groups;

Figure 14.3 Structures of communication

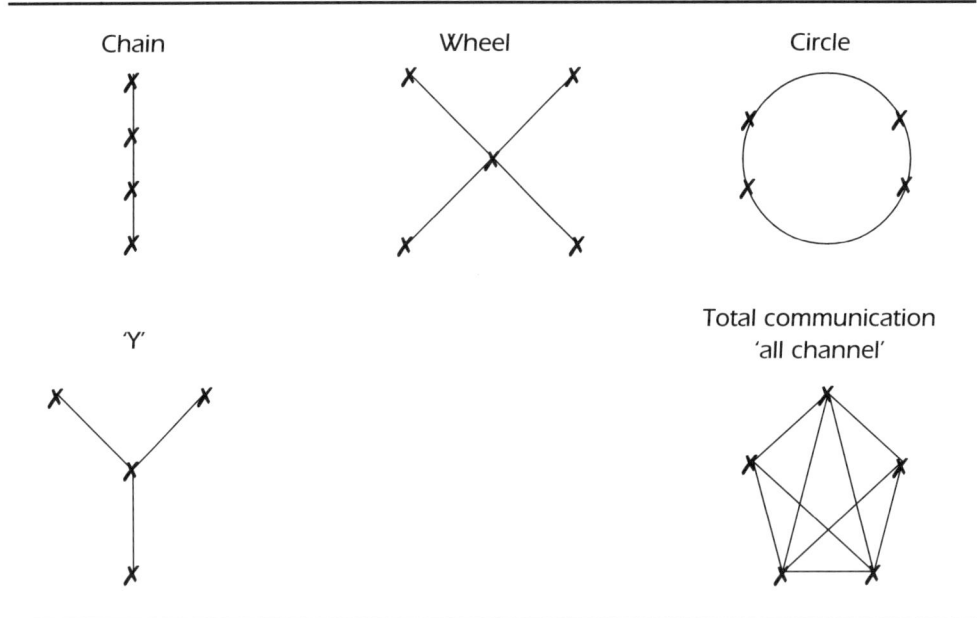

- Staff meetings;
- Bulletins, notices, circulars.

5.2   Techniques for *upward communication* include:
- Joint consultation;
- Suggestion schemes;
- Trade union channels;
- Grievance procedure.

5.3   The techniques used for *lateral communication* are:
- Interdepartmental committees;
- Special project groups;
- Co-ordinating committees.

Perception and communication

5.4   Frequently perceptual problems are referred to as communication problems. People communicate according to how they perceive their role and the role of others in the organisation.

5.5   The Durham Business School has devised the Expectations Approach in this context. Members of the group write down their expectations of group members, thus identifying the things others are expected to do. Managers write down the expectations they perceive the group has of them, identifying the things others expect them to do. This analysis enables the manager to see where communication channels have broken down.

Other perceptual problems

5.6   Other perceptual problems that can be experienced in communication include how we perceive others.

- *Implicit personality. We use a set of concepts to describe, compare and understand people. The set of concepts used by each person varies and differences are especially noticeable between people of different cultures.*

- We also assume *certain traits* are found together, and just one word or feature creates by inference a whole series of traits in the other person.

- *Halo effect.* We perceive people in terms of broad concepts – either good or bad – and all good qualities are possessed by the former and all bad by the latter.

- *Stereotyping.* 'Scottish people are thrifty,' etc. Stereotyping occurs because the world is so complex. It enables us to cope with all the information that bombards us.

- *Non-verbal communication.* 'Body language' is an important part of our communication process. There are a variety of modes, gestures and the use of hands and eye contact (people are encouraged to talk if you look at them). Distance between people is also an important means of communicating a relationship. Up to 18 inches is usual if you know someone well, but this is too close for an interview. Silence can also be important as it provides thinking time.

5.7   All these features influence and to some extent direct the way we communicate with others, frequently acting as a distortion rather than aid to communication.

Student Activity 3

Consider your colleagues at work, and apply the considerations listed above to one or another of them. Write a sentence or two on how these perceptual problems might apply to people trying to communicate with them.

6   Processes of running and participating in meetings

6.1   Much of the success of meetings depends on planning and having respect for established procedures. The rules which govern the conduct of meetings exist to facilitate business. The three fundamental requirements of an effective meeting are that it must be properly

- Convened by dispatch of notice to everybody entitled to receive it;

- Constituted with the right person in the chair and a quorum, i.e. the specified minimum number to constitute a meeting;

- Conducted with the regulations, rules and standing orders of the organisation which apply.

6.2   There are some legal regulations relating to meetings which are found in statutes such as the Public Order Acts and Companies Act, but the larger part of law relating to meetings consists of general rules and customary procedures held by courts to be fair and reasonable.

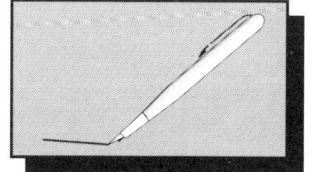

The role of the chairperson

6.3 The chairperson is the one who can contribute most to the effectiveness of the meeting, arranging before the meeting the preparation of an agenda, circulation of previous minutes, arrangement of the business and facilities for the meeting.

6.4 After the meeting has opened the chairperson should encourage active participation by members, yet at the same time ensure time limits are observed.

6.5 The opening address should:

- State the purpose of the meeting;
- Welcome people;
- Outline business;
- Suggest time limits for speakers;
- Suggest the amount of time available for discussion;
- Suggest the time of closure of the meeting.

6.6 The chairperson should be impartial and listen to all contributions attentively. He or she has a duty to preserve order and ensure proceedings are correct, and that the opinion of the meeting is correctly ascertained. The chairperson only has a second or casting vote if regulations grant it. Voting of any sort may even contradict the objectives of a meeting, e.g. in a joint consultative meeting. A chairperson should guide discussion by asking neutral questions, summarise contributions by members and at the end establish a final conclusion.

6.7 A chairperson must also know and apply the conventional rules of debate and any special orders adopted by the meeting:

- The subject of debate is expressed in the form of a motion.
- The opener and opposer each speak for a specified time, e.g. up to 15 minutes.
- One or two supporters of each side speak for a lesser time than the principals.
- The debate is thrown open for, say, 30–45 minutes. A member wishing to speak may do so for up to three minutes, but no member may speak more than once.
- The opener has a right of reply for, say, five minutes.
- All speakers must address the chair and the chairperson's ruling is final.

Contributions by others

6.8 The chairperson is not the only person who has a duty at a meeting. Everybody who attends has a duty to assist the chairperson in getting the business transacted in the best interests of the meeting. The members should:

- Be prepared: read the agenda and think about the points you wish to make, making sure they are relevant.
- Send any relevant documentation you wish to present to the secretary so other members may see it in advance.
- Inform the chairperson of 'any other business'.

- Arrive promptly.
- Do not interrupt others.
- Respect the chairperson and any rulings made.
- Do not make long unproductive speeches.
- Report back to those who need the information.
- Carry out any action you were requested to do.

Student Activity 4

Call to mind a time at which you were at a badly-run meeting. In what ways does what you have studied so far in this unit explain why it was a poor meeting? Were there any other reasons? Write a mini-essay, not more than a side of A4, on badly-run meetings.

7   Committees

7.1   Committees are present in all larger organisations and appear to be an integral part of most enterprises. They are formal groups with an agenda, chairperson and rules of conduct.

Features of a committee

7.2   The main ones are that:

- They normally have a specific task to fulfil, usually associated with decision making. This can be either temporary or permanent.
- They can meet regularly, e.g. quarterly planning committees, or for *ad hoc* purposes.
- There is a chairperson responsible for ensuring the committee's meetings are conducted in accordance with the rules and supplied with whatever resources it needs (this is usually information).
- There is often a secretary appointed to take minutes, send out agendas and act as an administrative link.
- The agenda sets out the agreed subject matter for the meeting and the committee members approve the agenda in advance so they can prepare adequately for the meeting.
- The minutes of the meeting are the official record of what has occurred. They remind members of important issues and decisions and act as a reliable source of information for non-committee members.
- Committee papers and reports provide information for decisions as well as giving ideas and suggestions.
- The rules of procedure promote the smooth running of the meeting. The meeting is conducted as a debate with a proposal motion and then a vote. The rules of debate enable both sides to state their case.

Advantages of a committee

7.3   These include:

- Because it is an organised group, committees are able to undertake a larger volume of work than individuals or small groups.

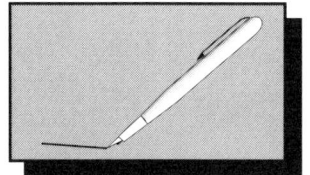

- Decisions or proposals are based on the *group's* assessment of facts and ideas.

- Committees encourage a pooling of information.

- They achieve co-ordination between groups.

- Committees provide a focal point for information.

- Decisions taken by committees are less prone to problems, rather than decisions taken at speed. The committee may consider them for longer, but action later is much quicker.

Problems of a committee

7.4   These include:

- Decision making is slower.

- Compromise decisions are taken.

- Managers can abdicate personal responsibility for the decision.

- Procedural restrictions.

- Certain skills are required. Some members feel unable to contribute because they do not possess those skills.

- They do not exist between meetings and so cannot respond to a situation quickly.

Summary

Having studied this unit carefully you should now:

- **be able to reproduce the communication model and discuss it;**

- **have examined barriers to communication;**

- **be able to plan events for effective communication;**

- **have examined a variety of communication structures;**

- **understand the role of perception in communication;**

- **know how to plan, run and participate in effective meetings;**

- **understand the contribution of committees to organisational success.**

Self-assessment questions

1. Which is not a formal communication:
   (a) interview;
   (b) report;
   (c) meeting;
   (d) rumour?

2. What does the term 'noise' mean within the communication process:
   (a) interference;
   (b) loud sounds;
   (c) machinery;
   (d) problems in receiving the message?

3. What is *not* the result of active participation:
   (a) lack of interest;
   (b) allowing the effect of decisions to be discussed;
   (c) more relaxed employee relations;
   (d) indicating understanding of the message?

4. Draw the communications model.

5. What are the features of the 'total communication' structure?

6. What are the four stages of effective communication?

7. Why do people engage in stereotyping?

8. A chairman always has the right to:
   (a) give a casting vote;
   (b) overrule a quorum requirement;
   (c) call a meeting to vote;
   (d) move the discussion on.

9. Minutes should:
   (a) provide a detailed summary of a meeting;
   (b) alert absent members to events;
   (c) provide an accurate summary of decisions taken;
   (d) be kept by each member.

10. What are the main duties of a chairperson?

Unit 15

Quality Management

Objectives

After studying this unit, you should be able to:

- understand the concept of quality;

- know how quality is measured;

- see how quality must be part of strategic management;

- understand the place of customer care in quality.

1   The importance of quality

1.1   Over the last decade service quality has emerged as a key strategic issue for financial service providers. Quality of service is becoming the area where competition will be won or lost. There are two major reasons for this:

- Competition on price is difficult, so it is better to compete on quality.

- The recession of the 1980s and 1990s has damaged the image of the financial services industry. Poor quality service and the appearance of putting depositors and shareholders before other customers has led to criticism of the service provided.

1.2   Following a quality strategy in the organisation has implications for management on a number of different levels encompassing systems, structure and products, underpinned by having competent and motivated staff. Quality impinges on all aspects of management, for example:

- Management structure

- Organisation of work

- Training

- Communication

- Appraisal and reward

- Recruitment and selection

- Development and promotion.

2   What is quality?

2.1   The term quality expresses a general, almost abstract, characteristic of 'excellence' and appears to be an intangible measure. Many definitions have been provided to describe quality, for example, quality is:

- Conforming to requirements;
- Getting it right first time;
- Meeting the requirements of the customer.

2.2   In the service industry it is the customer who should define quality rather than the organisation providing it. Two useful definitions of service quality are:

- A measure of how well the service level delivered matches or exceeds customer expectations;
- Delivering what the customer wants in the most efficient way, or better, exceeding customer expectations.

2.3   At the centre of any quality programme there has to be an effective system for measuring quality. Research has identified certain key components consumers use in forming expectations and perceptions of service quality. These dimensions provide a useful framework for measuring service quality performance.

Student Activity 1

Find by research some quotation from your organisation which states or implies what it means by quality. You may find it in any documentation which relates to customer care, or to the mission statement.

Think carefully about what you really offer your customer. Does it meet the criteria implied in the quality definition? Write a paragraph on where your service, or one of them, does or does not do so.

3   Measuring techniques for service quality

Measurement	Example
Tangibles	The physical evidence such as quality of fixtures and fittings (are they in keeping with the company image?), well-designed branches, a professional image.
Reliability	Consistency of quality and getting it right first time with each customer.
Responsiveness	Willingness of staff to deal with customer queries.
Communication	Ability to communicate so the customer can understand. Keeping customers informed.
Courtesy	All staff seen by customers as friendly and polite.
Competence	All service staff should understand the product range and needs of customers.
Understanding customer needs	Customer data bases can help in finding appropriate services or products for each individual.
Security	Free from risk and doubt. Give the customer a feeling of privacy and confidentiality, as well as feeling the bank is financially secure, honest and trustworthy.
Access	Minimising queues and a fair queuing system with speedier, accurate service.

Student Activity 2

Effective customer care systems include some way of measuring success. In your organisation, what are those measures?

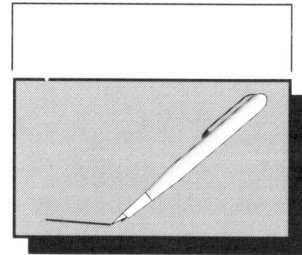

4   Quality as a key strategic issue

4.1   An organisation's ability to stay in business is a function of its competitiveness and its ability to retain existing customers and win new customers from the competition. Consumers in today's competitive climate will switch financial service suppliers if they receive inferior service. Furthermore, research has indicated that quality of service captures greater market share than lower prices.

4.2   Intense competition, compressed industry margins, an expanded array of financial providers and product options, combined with increased customer sophistication, are all significant factors which place quality in a strategic position for the financial services industry. In a market place where product features can be quickly copied, it will be quality which will give an organisation a competitive advantage that is likely to last and is, consequently, worth striving for. Quality of service, will be, for many consumers, the differentiating factor between financial service providers.

4.3   Therefore quality must be recognised at a strategic level, as a competitive strategy and one which has implications for the whole organisation. Many organisations who fail to deliver quality do so because they view it as a short-term programme and for some it is merely a cosmetic exercise, e.g. 'smile at the customer' campaigns. True quality of service is continuing and ongoing. It is a platform for sustainable and profitable growth.

4.4   There are many benefits to be derived from increased quality service:

● Enhanced customer retention rates and increased loyalty;

● Attraction of new customers from personal recommendation;

● Higher market share;

● Improved employee morale, lower employee turnover, fewer mistakes/errors (zero defects) and so lower operating costs;

● Insulation from price competition;

● Improved company image;

● Lower advertising/marketing costs;

● Increased productivity.

4.5   All of these can contribute to increased efficiency and profitability. Therefore, quality should be viewed as a profit strategy not a cost strategy. However, quality can be difficult to sustain because it relies on individuals continuing to achieve high standards.

5 A quality culture

5.1 Research suggests that to achieve quality it must be integrated into the corporate culture of an organisation. For financial services organisations with histories of long entrenched work processes it will involve a complete change of corporate culture.

5.2 A quality culture is driven by:
- An outward looking stance (focus on the customer);
- Top management commitment;
- Clarity of quality goals;
- Effective communication, training and involvement of staff.

5.3 Whilst there is no single formula for service excellence, the essentials of building a quality culture are committed leadership with a clear vision, solid information, committed employees and technology to support their effort.

6 How to create a quality organisation

6.1 Whilst there is no panacea for achieving service quality there are fundamental requirements. Fig. 15.1 provides a framework for building a quality organisation.

6.2 In order to create such an organisation, it is possible that there will need to be changes not only in the attitude of the staff but also in the structure of the organisation and even the nature of the product or the make-up of the service.

6.3 A conscious attempt to make these changes is often referred to as (business) re-engineering. This does not consist of making minor changes, nor slight philosophical vector-changes: a team of managers and staff drastically alter the way in which an organisation's business, its processes, its systems, its internal and external relationships operate. It relies on expertise in the present processes but also deep knowledge of state-of-the art technologies, including information and communication systems.

6.4 The results can be dramatic changes in structure, in the collapsing of hierarchical levels, of functions in the removal of whole departments and sections, and in process, changing, shortening or eliminating unnecessary steps. However, experience indicates that not all attempts to re-engineer processes and organisations work successfully. They can cause resentment, morale problems and non-cooperation, and the enthusiasm for cutting can result in mortal wounds to reasonably successful existing business. Successful re-engineering, though, can result in very large increases in return.

7 Total quality management (TQM)

7.1 TQM is an approach to improved organisation effectiveness developed in the 1980s by two management scientists, Deming and Juran, and first adopted

Figure 15.1 Creating a quality organisation

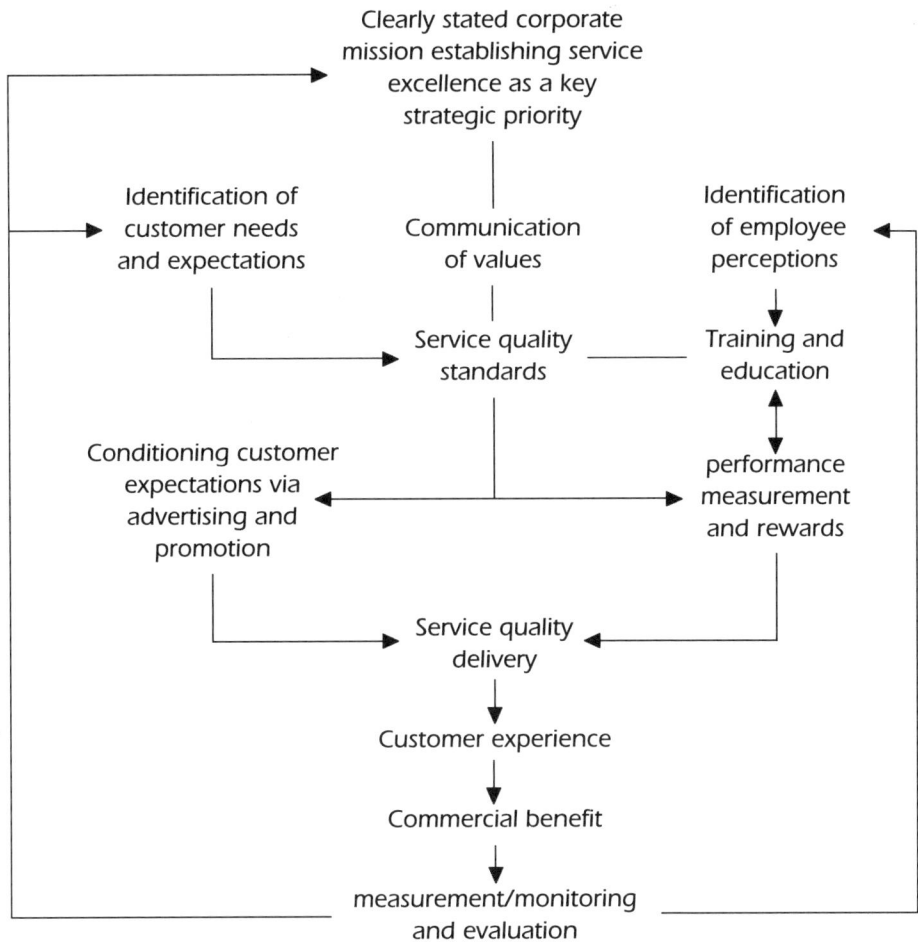

(Model provided courtesy of Ann Norton.)
Adapted from A Strategic Framework for Quality and Setting the Service Quality Agenda,
Berry LL, Bennet DR and Carter WB; Service Quality – A Profit Strategy for Financial
Institutions, *Dow Jones Irwin, 1989; and PA Consulting Group,* Quality in Financial Services,
The Economist Publications, October 1989.

by Japanese companies. It is concerned with developing a long-term quality culture in the organisation. It is based on the principle that to achieve maximum profitability an organisation must not only do things 'right' but focus on prevention of errors rather than correction of errors. Deming and Juran advocated the abolition of inspection departments, since these underpinned the rejection of substandard products. The emphasis was developed in terms of 'Right First Time'. Also the policies procedures and practices must be focused on the customer, i.e. 'the customer is king'.

7.2   This philosophy means quality is perceived as a company-wide issue, involving all levels of employee. It is a way of life for the organisation as a whole, giving commitment to total customer satisfaction through a continuous process of improvement using the contribution and involvement of people.

7.3 To achieve TQM, participation from everyone in the organisation is required. It emphasises the importance of people as the key to quality and thus it is a key issue for 'human resource management'. However, this involvement of people also means quality of service depends on the interpersonal skills of the individuals charged with delivery. Quality can only come from empowering employees and this dual philosophy has led to the development of quality circles and TQM.

Student Activity 3

Take your organisation carefully through the above diagram. Write brief critical notes about the way you see it taking observable actions at each point, or failing to do so.

8   Quality Standard BS 5750

8.1 BS 5750 is a British quality standard which gives details of quality management within the service industry. It sets out quality assurance guidelines in the areas of commitment by management to train staff, provide material resources and review the quality of service given. To achieve registration for this standard an organisation has to be independently audited. Those seeking accreditation have to look not only to their own quality systems but also those of their suppliers, thus ensuring consistency.

8.2 First, the foundation for creating a quality organisation requires the right culture, along with a clearly stated mission and genuine commitment of senior management to lead by example.

8.3 Understanding customer expectations and requirements of service along with the setting, communicating and measuring of customer-defined standards will ensure an organisation is on the right track.

8.4 A quality strategy must involve everyone in the organisation – staff involvement is crucial. This is especially important in the financial services industry where staff represent and personify the organisation in delivering the products.

8.5 The key issues to gain commitment from staff to quality include:
- Communication – awareness of the 'quality vision' and how that translates into action for individual members of staff;
- Education/training;
- Reinforcement and encouragement;
- Rewards;
- Seeing quality in the way the organisation treats them as individuals.

9   Quality for the external and internal customer

9.1 The quality of service reaching a customer is often determined by the quality of service staff provide for each other internally. It is important to remember that the various functions of an organisation have their own internal customers. Therefore, staff in departments or sections need to treat other employees as internal customers, because they are providing a service, e.g. training department, payroll and personnel.

9.2   By satisfying internal customers the organisation should be better placed to satisfy the needs of external customers and thereby maintain and generate new business. Managers must be seen to be part of the quality service process by encouraging and providing support to employees who have direct contact with customers.

10   Managing quality at branch level: quality circles and quality action teams

10.1   Quality circles and quality action teams seek to involve employees throughout the organisation in satisfying the requirements of the customer. The benefits of such a programme are that they:

- Focus on customer needs;
- Encourage ownership of quality across all the business ;
- Allow for consistent quality performance;
- Identify the costs of quality so wastage in time and error is eliminated;
- Allow employees to identify improvements in quality as and when they occur;
- Encourage a team approach to problem solving;
- Encourage ongoing improvement.

10.2   Within quality teams there should be a good balance of individual roles:

- Enabler;
- Executive;
- Controller;
- Planner;
- Driver.

10.3   They usually involve four to 10 volunteers working in a related area who meet on a regular basis in working hours to identify, analyse and solve problems related to service quality. Their purpose is to improve quality, reduce costs, raise productivity and increase involvement. The quality teams recognise that the people doing the job know most about it and employees are motivated when they are put in a position to make a contribution and dialogue is encouraged, so giving common ownership of quality goals.

10.4   Quality improvement teams have the same principles as quality teams but are cross-functional and work at problems occurring at the interrelationship of departments.

10.5   Branch quality programmes should be directed at providing customers with a high quality of service. Within the branch environment quality of service standards must be set. To reinforce the quality momentum customer, research should be undertaken on a continuous basis to monitor attainment or short-fall of achieving the quality standards.

10.6   The dimensions of service quality at a branch level could include factors such as:

● Queuing time;

● Speed and efficiency of cashier;

● Friendliness of cashiers;

● Branch appearance and image;

● Enquiry response time and quality of information and advice provided;

● Cash dispenser reliability;

● Branch privacy.

Student Activity 4

Wherever you are in your organisation, partially evaluate the success of your customer care at branch level. Take at least one improvement it has demanded in service, and make written observations about how it has made the customer experience better. Do this either by observation from your workplace if you are in a branch, or from the customer side if you are a non-branch customer.

11   Barriers to quality

11.1   The key to achieving quality is to meet or exceed what customers expect from the service on a consistent basis. However, the main barriers to achieving quality can be identified in terms of a lack of what is required to build quality into the organisation, i.e. top management commitment, quality culture, committed staff, effective communication system.

11.2   Most organisations have run quality programmes since the mid-1980s, focusing on raising the awareness of staff as to the importance of customers to the organisation and enhancing interpersonal skills.

11.3   Commitment to quality should be displayed throughout the organisation and the message of quality needs to be delivered by senior executives. This is normally done using a corporate video, raising the profile of quality as an issue or delivering personal messages to staff.

Summary

Having studied this unit carefully you should now:

- **understand the concept of quality and its importance;**

- **know about standards and how quality is measured;**

- **see how quality is integrated in strategic management;**

- **be able to discuss TQM and re-engineering;**

- **have examined the place of customer care in quality in your organisation;**

- **have analysed quality circles and action teams.**

Self-assessment questions

1. Which of the following best describes the concept of quality in the financial services industry:
   (a) making no mistakes;
   (b) conforming to standards;
   (c) matching customer expectations;
   (d) fitness for purpose?

2. What is TQM?

3. The management scientists who introduced TQM are:
   (a) Denning and Jennings;
   (b) Deming and Juran;
   (c) Dimmer and Juran;
   (d) Deming and Jones.

4. What is BS 5750?

5. What are quality circles?

6. What is an internal customer?

7. What is re-engineering?

8. What is a quality circle?

Unit 16

Decision Making, Problem Solving, and Project Management.

Objectives

After studying this unit, you should be able to:

- **understand the decision making process;**

- **know about the factors affecting decisions;**

- **understand a leader's need for a decision style;**

- **gain knowledge on project management.**

1   Introduction

1.1   Decision making is an important element in leadership and therefore a factor in successful management. It may be described as, 'a resolution to adopt a particular course of action in preference to alternative policies' (according to Vroom and Yetton (1973)). It is a judgment based on available information; a judgment that must always involve some element of risk, since any one outcome is never wholly certain. There are close links between decision making and problem solving. A situation needing a decision arises because a problem has been identified, and the first stage in decision making therefore involves problem identification.

2   Factors that indicate the need for a decision

2.1   A situation which calls for a decision to be made only arises because a problem has been noticed. The individual will probably notice a problem exists because:

- The performance of the branch or section is falling;

- There is negative customer reaction to service;

- There are environmental changes in terms of competition, technology and economy;

- There are other adverse comments by staff or customers.

2.2   The evidence that a problem exists reaches a point where it cannot be ignored and the manager is then in a position to embark on a problem solving and decision making process.

3 Levels of decision making

3.1   In the same way as there are three levels of management in the organisation, so there are three levels at which decisions can be made.

Figure 16.1 Levels of decision making

3.2   *Strategic decisions are* concerned with the long-term future of the organisation, e.g. deciding on new growth areas or deciding on new services, products and payment systems. This is primarily the responsibility of very senior management.

3.3   *Administrative/managerial decisions* are concerned with the routine decisions of business. Most organisations provide procedures, rules and systems which offer guidance on, for example, handling grievances and recruitment. Banks are frequently referred to as bureaucratic organisations because they have so many rules and procedures for managers to follow. However, the rapidly changing environment is creating a need for banks to be more flexible in their approach.

3.4   *Operational decisions* are concerned with ensuring the day-to-day operations proceed smoothly, e.g. decisions about a breakdown in equipment, reorganising staff when there is an absentee, amending a plan which is not working.

3.5   It is also possible to divide decisions into two types, either programmed (administrative) or unprogrammed (operational) decisions. Programmed decisions can be described as following procedures and precedents, whilst unprogrammed decisions are those for which no guidance is available, e.g. adjusting work allocation because of sudden illness. The difficulty with unprogrammed decisions is that each situation is unique and what is right in one is not necessarily correct in another. There is a trend towards more programmed decision making in certain areas, e.g. lending with credit scoring.

3.6   It is useful to distinguish between different levels of discretion particularly for unprogrammed decision-making.

- Authorise: power has been delegated to an individual to make a decision.
- Ratify: the boss agrees with a decision already made by a subordinate who has not been given the power to make the decision.

- The individual possesses the power to make the decision.
- The subordinate is in a position to recommend a decision to the boss.

Figure 16.2 Key steps in the decision making process

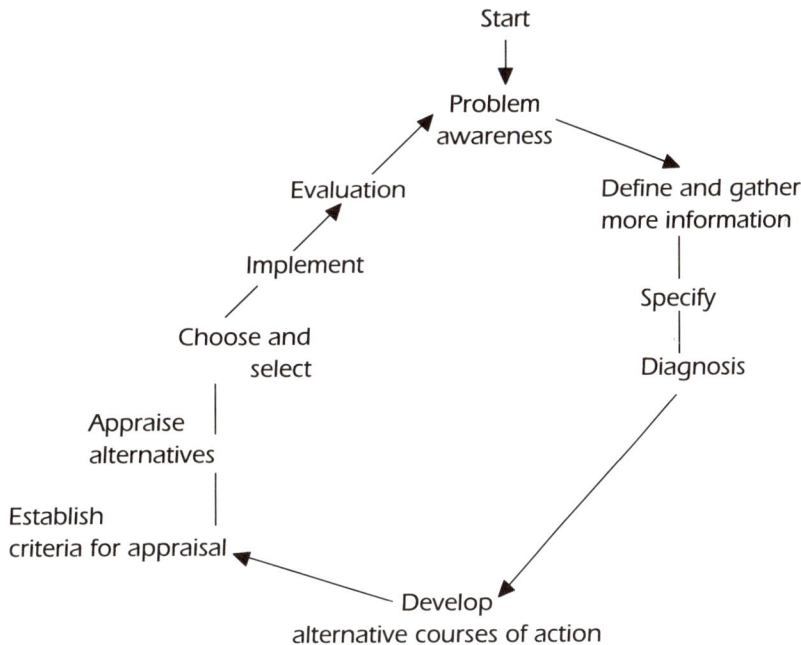

4 Key steps in the decision making and problem solving process

4.1   It seems that if a manager or employee is to make successful decisions, a similar pattern of stages should be followed. Archer, in a study of 1980, found that most managers follow and find helpful a 10-step process.

- *Problem awareness.* The environment, both external and internal, should be constantly monitored to obtain feedback. The decision maker monitors the environment to detect deviations from plans, and therefore is aware of problems.

- *Define and gather more information.* The problem or situation facing the employee needs to be precisely defined. The information that has been picked up through monitoring could be the symptoms, not the cause. Further information may be required. The monitoring and defining stages are in fact problem solving processes.

- *Specify.* The decision objectives have to be specified with the key result areas and clearly defined standards of performance. The likely risks and constraints need to be identified. What the decision makers hope to achieve should be clarified.

- *Diagnosis.* The problem must be analysed and the causes scrutinised before action can be taken.

- *Develop alternative courses of action.* The options open to the employee are considered, and if necessary or appropriate, discussed at length. The critical options can then be listed.

- *Establish criteria for appraisal.* The methods or criteria to be used in the appraisal of different options need to be established.

- *Appraisal.* Alternative solutions or courses of action must be appraised. Each is evaluated in terms of the quantity and quality of information that can be provided and the costs of implementation of the various alternatives are also explored. Costs and benefits can be expressed in both quantitative and qualitative terms.

- *Choose.* The best alternative is then selected by an individual or a committee.

- *Implement.* The one option chosen is implemented.

- *Evaluation.* This involves the assessment of the consequences of the decision and leads to monitoring for new problems. This is an important stage because it is a way of ensuring that action is carried out in accordance with the plans.

5   Alternative models

5.1   There are several other different decision making models available. Each contains key steps which could be summarised as:

- Deciding on the issue;
- Using the options;
- Considering the consequences;
- Making the decision;
- Evaluation or follow up.

Student Activity 1

Suppose that your organisation has found itself in possession of a seaside hotel in lieu of repayment for a debt, which it can:

- Dispose of for cash;
- Convert into holiday accommodation for staff;
- Convert into training premises; or
- Run as a going concern.

Go through and make notes on each of the steps of the decision-making process detailed in the Unit, making some imaginative assumptions; and make a decision on behalf of the organisation.

6   Factors in decision making

Risk

6.1   Any decision involves a certain amount of risk that may affect the outcome of the decision.

6.2   There are a number of types of risk in lending in the financial services industry:

- *Country risk.* Risk associated with lending to countries in political or economic difficulties.

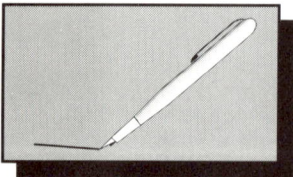

Figure 16.3 Factors influencing decision making

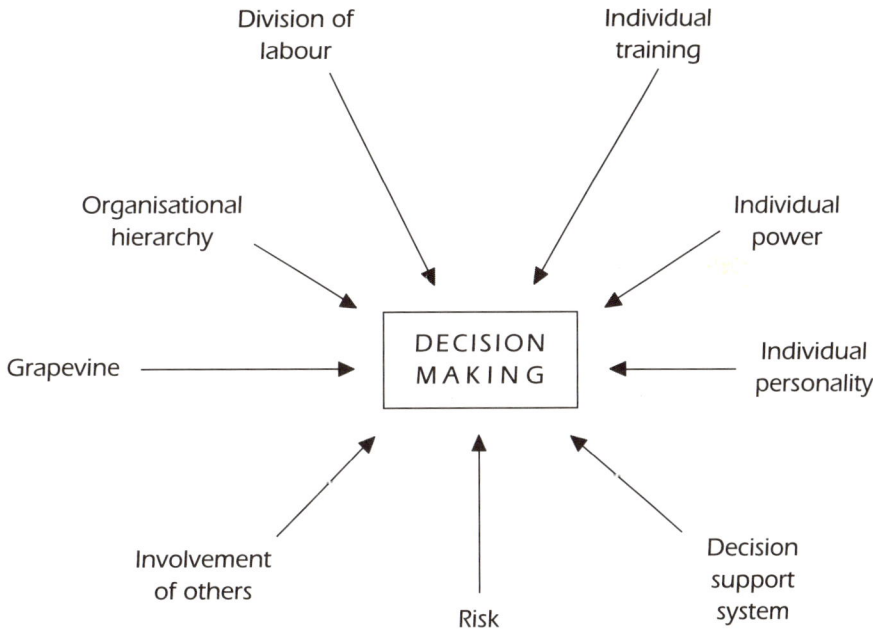

- *Settlement/delivery risk.* The risk that the other party will fail to pay over funds due to the bank.
- *Product risk.* The risk associated with a product, e.g. swaps or options.
- *Industry risk.* The risk that an industry will hit problems and put lending at risk.
- *Portfolio risk.* The risk of a category of lending as a whole.
- *Credit risk.* The risk a borrower will be unable to repay.

6.3   The risk must be assessed or analysed before it can be accepted. Risk analysis involves not only examining the impact and probability of an event occurring, but also studying the relationships between impact, probability and costs as well as impact, probability and reward.

6.4   The advantages of risk management are:
- Better decisions before the activity starts;
- Better decisions during the course of activity;
- Careful documentation to improve future risk analysis;
- Assessment of the risk/reward ratio of future activities;
- Unacceptable risk identified and eliminated;
- Acceptable risks receive managerial attention.

6.5   Financial service organisations take a number of steps to manage risk:
- Credit scoring;
- Greater use of information technology to limit subjectivity in risk decisions;
- Applying portfolio management techniques limiting exposures to categories in accordance with the risk/reward ratio;

- Training initiatives for lower/middle management to enhance the lending decisions;

- Separate business development from the management of risk at central and local level;

- Sensitive pricing policy to maximise funds.

6.6 Risk can be minimised by:

- Reducing to a minimum the time scale between the point of decision and emergence of results;

- Identifying correctly the nature of the problem;

- Allowing the decision process to follow a logical sequence;

- Analysing correctly the ramifications of the decision;

- Ensuring that the information available is adequate for the decision.

Risk management

6.7 Most business activity involves some risk. The more successful the business then the more likely it is that the business has been able accurately to assess risk and rewards.

6.8 Banking, like all businesses, involves taking risks. There are a series of established stages according to Whyte and Plenderleith (1994) in risk management:

- Analysis of risk.

- Quantifying the risk.

- Recording the objective data in the decision.

- Monitoring the effects of the decision.

- Feedback and adjustment of risk analysis.

- Risk analysis involves measuring:

  o the probability an event will occur;

  o the impact of it, if it does occur.

6.9 So a rise in interest rates of 5% can be regarded as probable or improbable, on a sliding scale and the impact of the rise can also be considered. Investment in a new project, for example a tunnel linking England and the Isle of Man, if viable as a physical exercise can then be assessed as a risk exercise by anticipating the length of time capital would be tied up, the amount of capital required, the ability of the tunnel to generate income, the date of return on capital and the ability of the borrowers to manage the cash flow.

6.10 Credit scoring is the assessment of loan applications against a set of criteria. Standardised criteria enable an organisation to manage risk.

Student Activity 2

Consider the possibility of your deciding whether or not to apply for a job in a different organisation, i.e. changing your employment. Go through the risk-management steps in the section above, analysing the risk in the decision.

Decision support system

6.11 This provides information to supplement rather than replace managerial decision making. Normally it consists of a database which can then be analysed and rearranged using a computer model. An expert system is one example of a computer-based decision making model which is used to make lending decisions on small businesses. Another example is the computer-based credit scoring system for credit card applications.

6.12 The higher the risk the greater the reward for the organisation. Good lending decisions can become poor ones because of changes in circumstances. However, these decisions were not a mistake and whilst correct at the time are inappropriate now.

Individual influences

6.13 An individual may influence the way in which information is acquired, processed and used. Research reveals that dogmatic or authoritarian personalities show a lack of tolerance for ambiguity and uncertainty and are less likely to search for information. They are also less capable of dealing with inconsistent information, and are less flexible in approach. Those who regard power as important can use information as a tool for achieving personal objectives, resulting in the withholding of information in order to maintain control or win favours. This can be detrimental to decision making, which relies on co-operative or combined efforts.

6.14 Sometimes the training provided by an organisation results in an interference with the decision process. This can arise when the decision rules or procedures do not fit the decision. Rigidity can result and impair the capacity to react to circumstances.

Organisational influences

6.15 The division of labour in organisations allows for specialisation in decision making, but also provides restrictions in the form of specialised language and terminology.

Organisational hierarchy

6.16 This is the organisation of tasks in hierarchical form. It can lead to problems in the processing and transfer of information. The organisation filters information by providing less detail to the top of the organisation. Technology has aided this process because senior managers can have direct access to certain information. Nearly all organisations possess a grapevine (the informal communication system). The grapevine can ease the burden of overloaded communication channels, but sometimes it is inaccurate and the quality of information received from this source can have an effect on decision making.

When to refer a decision

6.17 Decision making not only involves what to do but also how to do it. Sometimes decisions have to be passed up to the next organisational level. One factor may be whether the decision is programmed or unprogrammed. Questions which help to identify this are:

- Is this an isolated incident – a unique problem – or will there be others affecting other sections?

- Does the problem affect other areas?

- Is there a need for long-term change?

6.18 Vroom and Yetton developed a decision making model which indicates to the manager the most suitable style (democratic or authoritarian) to use in particular circumstances. This use of style obviously has links with leadership (see Unit 13).

Vroom and Yetton Normative Model

6.19 This assumes decision making is a key factor which determines the success or failure of a manager. There are three critical components that influence the overall effectiveness of the decision.

- *Decision quality.* The extent to which the decision meets the objective demands and requirements of the problem.

- *Decision acceptance.* The extent to which subordinates understand, accept and commit themselves to the decision.

- *Timeliness.* The extent to which decisions are made according to schedule.

6.20 Vroom and Yetton believe that the managers can adjust their decision style to the situation, and again they provide a model which guides a leader towards effective behaviour. At certain key points in the decision process, the manager has to ask key questions. For example, at Point A: does the problem possess a quality requirement? The answer Yes or No will determine the decision path taken. The manager then moves on to the question at Point B, etc. At the end of the path a particular leadership style is recommended. A description of those styles is given below.

- AI: You solve the problem or make the decision yourself using the information available to you at the present time.

- AII: You obtain any necessary information from subordinates, then decide on a solution to the problem yourself. You may or may not tell subordinates the purpose of your questions or give information about the problem or decision you are working on. The input provided by them is clearly in response to your request for specific information. They do not play a role in the definition of the problem or in generating or evaluating alternative solutions.

- CI: You share the problem with the relevant subordinates individually, getting their ideas and suggestions without bringing them together as a group. Then you make the decision. This decision may or may not reflect your subordinates' influence.

- CII: You share the problem with your subordinates in a group meeting. In this meeting you obtain their ideas and suggestions. Then you make the decision, which may or may not reflect your subordinates' influence.

- GII: You share the problem with your subordinates as a group. Together you generate and evaluate alternatives and attempt to reach agreement (consensus) on a solution. Your role is much like that of chairman, coordinating the discussion, keeping it focused on the problem, and making sure that the critical issues are discussed. You can provide the group with information or ideas that you have, but you do not try to press them to adopt your solution, and are willing to accept and implement any solution that has the support of the entire group.

6.21 As well as a range of styles suggested by Vroom and Yetton, there are certain factors used to identify the type of decision and therefore fit style and decision together.

**Figure 16.4 Vroom and Yetton Decision Process
Flowchart (1976), AMACOM**

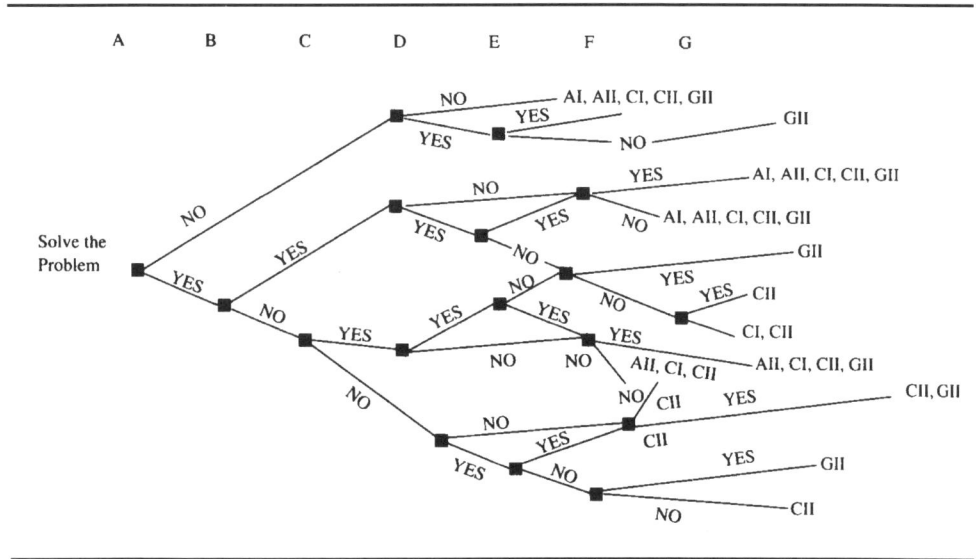

(A) Does the problem possess a quality requirement?

(B) Do I have sufficient information to make a high-quality decision?

(C) Is the problem structured?

(D) Is acceptance of the decision by subordinates important for effective implementation?

(E) If I were to make the decision by myself, am I reasonably certain that it would be accepted by my subordinates?

(F) Do subordinates share the organisational goals to be attained in solving the problem?

(G) Is conflict among subordinates likely in preferred solutions?

Student Activity 3

Suppose you are a manager who has just been made responsible for the complete redecoration of your office. Using the Vroom and Yetton model, decide on the leadership/decision style you might make to decide on the decor.

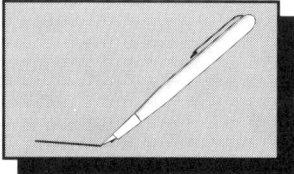

7   Problems in decision making

7.1 There are several things that can go wrong in the decision making process. The decision maker:

- Is risk aversive: he or she makes the decision that is the easy option and largely trouble free. However, this is not always the *best* decision.

- Hesitates about the decision and the optimum time for making the decision has gone. This is sometimes referred to as 'transcendental hesitation'.

- Hurries the decision, and does not wait for all the relevant information. The decision is not therefore necessarily the best one.

8 Project planning

8.1 The use of project teams or groups within organisations has become increasingly popular. These teams can deal with a variety of tasks from the strategic level (reorganising structure by, say, establishing a new branch network) to specialist managerial groups (a team to look after the interests of new business), to lower level branch teams (to examine the possibilities for a branch customer care programme). The thing all projects have in common is that they introduce change as opposed to 'Business As Usual' (BAU) management. BAU caters for efficient organisation within a stable environment. Whatever the level of the organisation the team is involved in, there must be certain features if the project group is to be successful.

Student Activity 4

Think of an example of a project in your bank, preferably one you have been involved in. Write notes on

(a) What the aims of the project were?

(b) How was it planned?

(c) Was it directed efficiently?

(d) What was done well and less well?

(e) How could it be improved?

9 Features of successful project management

9.1 These include:

- Clear aims and objectives to follow;
- Clear planning of events with timetable, concluding date and budget;
- A sponsor or director of the project;
- Carefully chosen team with particular skills and expertise;
- Evaluation of project;
- Communication policy.

Clear aims and objectives to follow

9.2 The manager of the project should ensure that there are clear aims for the group to follow with initial costings. Tasks and deadlines can therefore be allocated to the group. It is not always easy to set clear aims at the outset of a project because situations change. However some aims should be established and clear issues can be defined and incorporated into the aims.

Clear planning of events

9.3 Every project needs a clear timetable of events. It is likely that activities may be proceeding concurrently. Network analysis can be a useful planning tech-

Figure 16.5 Network analysis for the development of a new banking service (courtesy R Mercer)

Project General Stages	Concept Development 1	Development of new Systems 2	Prepare Literature Pre-Production Run 3	Promotion 4	Introduction 5	Volume Production 6
Specific New Banking Service	Customer Research	Develop Proto-type of New System	Prepare Service Literature – Customer and Internal. Develop and Test Customised Software (In Parallel)	Press Review	Launch 1 month	From Small To Large Scale 'Take-up' 6 months
	6 months	6 months	4 months	2 months	Run Out Old Service in Parallel (7 months)	

nique. It breaks down the programme of implementation for the project into its constituent parts by resource area, so events can occur simultaneously. It also helps to identify priorities because it highlights activities on which others involved with the project depend. The network therefore represents a plan of action enabling the co-ordinator to examine implications of changes in the plan or deviations from the plan.

Sponsor or director of project

9.4 Every project needs a sponsor, director or supervisor. This is an individual in the organisation who fully supports the project and wants to see it happen, and can influence and exert power to see it introduced. Projects are concerned with change and people resist this. Someone with power and influence is needed to make sure it happens. A large project will need a director or even a team of directors to ensure it achieves its goals. Similarly, even a quarterly charges printout or an irregular advances return requires someone to organise a team working away from the normal office and monitoring its progress.

A carefully chosen team and management structure

9.5 The project team must be carefully selected. This selection should be based on expertise and potential contribution rather than status. The ability to work as a member of a group is clearly important. They should have clearly defined tasks and have the correct training and motivation. This is required for research and development problems like marketing initiatives for specific services.

9.6 The team needs a management structure so it is aware who is in charge and how responsibility is allocated. With a large project there is usually a steering committee in charge. The committee is made up of not only key members of the project team but also the sponsor and representatives from the final users. There is also a project director who liaises with the steering committee and has overall responsibility for the project with the allocation of resources. There are, in addition, project and sub-project managers who have specific areas of responsibility. The structure is usually a matrix one so the team members have two bases.

Evaluation

9.7 A project needs constant evaluation so adjustments in costing and timing can be made as appropriate. An initial evaluation will also be needed to ensure benefits outweigh costs.

Communication policy

9.8 A communications policy should be decided not only within the group, but also to operate between the group and the rest of the organisation.

Owner

9.9 This is the person or section of the organisation that will benefit from the changes proposed by the project. The owner should be informed throughout the life of the project of developments as they happen.

Summary

9.10 The successful management of a project not only involves technical expertise but also a knowledge of people: how they communicate and operate in groups. You should therefore ensure you relate the information contained in Units 6 and 14 to this section.

9.11 It could be said the key to successful project management lies in good control, that is:

- Establishing standards for evaluation;
- Establishing feedback systems so performance can be compared with standards;
- Taking appropriate action to ensure any deviations are improved and standards met in the future.

Summary

Having studied this unit carefully you should now:

- **be able to trace all the steps of the decision making process;**

- **line up decision making and problem solving;**

- **understand the factors affecting decisions;**

- **be able to use techniques of risk management in making decisions;**

- **be able to use Vroom and Yetton's model to choose a leadership/ decision style;**

- **discuss project management, and design a project plan.**

Self-assessment questions

1. Diagnosis in the decision making process involves:
   (a) planning;
   (b) controlling;
   (c) analysing;
   (d) solving.

2. When you have decided on a solution to a problem you must:
   (a) find more problems;
   (b) advise supervisors of your success;
   (c) give responsibility to another;
   (d) implement your solution.

3. Before solving a problem you must as a first step:
   (a) determine who is responsible;
   (b) recognise that there is a problem;
   (c) suggest alternative solutions;
   (d) gather information.

4. Give examples of three internal factors which can have an effect on the decision making process.

5. What types of risk are suggested in the Unit concerning lending?

6. Briefly summarise Vroom & Yetton's five styles of leadership/decision.

7. What might be the problems associated with the actions of a decision maker?

8. Which of the following is not a feature of successful project management:
   (a) clear aims;
   (b) clear plans;
   (c) clear rules for meetings;
   (d) evaluation of project?

9. A project need a sponsor, to:
   (a) Give it financial support;
   (b) Exert influence for its recommendations to be introduced;
   (c) Check on its progress;
   (d) Evaluate its costs and benefits?

10. How can network analysis aid project planning?

Unit 17

Career, Time and Stress Management

<table>
<tr><td>

Objectives

After studying this unit, you should be able to:

- understand the concept of career management;

- be familiar with the causes and symptoms of stress;

- know about some stress-relieving techniques;

- learn about time management.

</td></tr>
</table>

1 Career management

1.1 Whilst organisations do exert influence over career progression, much of the responsibility for managing careers rests with the employees themselves.

1.2 The term career has widened in scope over the last 25 years to include, not only those in highly paid positions, but many different levels within the organisation. Career progression does not necessarily mean just vertical moves but can also incorporate horizontal positions and may involve two or three different fields within the organisation.

1.3 Indeed it is increasingly the case, even in such a relatively stable industry as finance and banking, that the 'career-for-life' is a thing of the past. Major technological changes, competition and profit-based influences have caused employers, and staff, to settle for the prospect of having to move at some time. It is no longer out of the question that staff are either made to leave by way of redundancy, or move voluntarily for promotion in an industry with fewer and fewer middle and senior management positions.

2 Stages in career management

Early career stages

2.1 *Join up process* – people are motivated to accept a job in so far as they:

- See themselves in the job;

- Value its rewards;

- Expect to perform successfully.

They have already decided that they want to work and also that they want to work in an organisation.

215

2.2 In these early stages there are several actions new recruits can follow to develop their own career, suggest Feldman and Arnold (1983). These entail being pro-active rather than reactive.

- *Obtaining a challenging job.* Challenge and potential for career growth should weigh more heavily than shorter-term considerations, such as marginal pay differences in making job choices. The growth which occurs in that first job can lead to even wider choices of better jobs later. However there is a need to be realistic and flexible in the goals set, adjusting them as circumstances change.

- *Be an outstanding performer.* The evidence is strong and consistent that more rewarding opportunities open up to the more outstanding performers. Learning the job as quickly as possible and training a replacement makes it easier to move on to more broadening assignments. Take the opportunity to raise your profile.

- *Actively manage your own career.* It is important that new recruits be active in influencing decisions being made about their careers higher up the hierarchy. New recruits should be prepared to practice self-nomination, to make it known to superiors that they want a particular job and are prepared to work to qualify for it. Plan career moves three or four jobs ahead.

- *Seek out a mentor*: someone whose attitudes and development you can identify with and model yourself on. Learn the politics of the organisation and social skills so you can gain from relationships within and outside the organisation.

- *Take training and development opportunities*, but be realistic in your self-assessment.

Student Activity 1

Look at your own career development to date. Of the activities suggested by Feldman and Arnold, being entirely realistic, make notes on those which are:

- Genuinely within your power and control: and of those

- The extent to which you have or have not taken action under each heading

Middle and later career issues

2.3 At this stage the employee is likely to experience slower transfers and promotions, and the criteria for which they were selected is not the same as that for which they are being moved through the organisation, i.e. the emphasis is on resource management rather than looking at, say, numerical skills, etc. The work environment may seem more threatening with a sense of obsolescence, as people realise their age is against them.

2.4 Progression is still important to people today, but with rapid changes now occurring in organisations uncertainty arises. This is because employees may have to change not only their career during their working life but also their technical knowledge. Middle age is significant, because as career progress slows down with fewer new job opportunities, it can lead employees to dwell on fears, disappointment, isolation, their knowledge obsolescence and result in a fall in energy, and increase in stress. Competition from younger employees can create insecurity and subordinates can become a boss.

2.5   However, the middle career manager still has much to offer organisations. In terms of Mintzberg's analysis, many interpersonal and decisional skills are possessed, which may be lacking in the younger manager. Although updating informational and technical skills may be needed, many banks provide mid-career assessment programmes with specially developed training courses to give this knowledge.

2.6   The middle managers who will eventually become senior managers are broadening their work and experience during this phase. Good middle managers will be consolidating their roles and developing contacts, within and outside the organisation.

2.7   Steps can still be taken to manage careers by keeping up to date, and even broadening knowledge, and ensuring their superiors realise they are still looking for personal and career development.

3   Definition of stress

3.1   The definition of stress given in physics is that it arises from the impact of an environmental force on a physical object. The object undergoes strain and this reaction can result in a temporary or permanent distortion. Any situation that is tiresome, burdensome or pressures individuals beyond their capacity to cope is likely to induce stress. Pressure can also arise because the individual is expected to perform a task or job in a particular way which causes discomfort or anxiety.

3.2   However people respond differently to stress. For example, on retirement (a stressful situation) some individuals are deeply depressed or sad, while others are contented. Stress can result in a reduced quality of work, increased absenteeism, labour turnover and lateness.

4   The relationship between occupation and stress

4.1   From the various studies of occupation and stress a number of factors have been identified as significant in creating stress at work.

From within the organisation

4.2   If too much work is carried out (overload), in excess of 70 or 80 hours a week, it can give rise to a number of symptoms of stress: excessive drinking, lower motivation, low estimation of one's abilities and unwillingness to suggest improvements in work practices and procedures (Margolis, Kroes and Quinn, 'Research in Job Stress', *Journal of Occupational Medicine*, No 16, 1974).

4.3   If there is role ambiguity in the organisation and the requirements of a job are unclear, it can lead to similar symptoms (Shirom, Eden, Silberwasser and Kellerman, 'Job Stress in Kibbutzim', *Social Science and Medicine*, No 7, 1973).

4.4   Stress incidence can also be related to organisational level. According to Cooper, top managers show a tendency to be more outgoing and enjoy managing others. The pressure arises from the substantial amount of communication

Figure 17.1 Factors causing stress to the individual at work

From within organisation	From within individual	From outside organisation
Role overload/ excessive responsibility or role underload	Inbuilt inability to cope with stress situations	Conflict between domestic life and work
Role complexity		
Role ambiguity	Dissatisfaction with career development	Fear of change, redundancy, early retirement
Role conflict		
Difficult boundary roles	Aversion to shouldering responsibility for people	Family crises: marriage, children, health, finance
Position in hierarchy/ organisational structure leadership, monotony of job	Feelings of unease in relating to others	

and consultation, bureaucratic rules and regulations, and from the pressure from conflicts between home and work. Middle managers found personnel matters more of a strain, and using new systems or methods also created stress. They also felt pressure from bureaucracy and the conflict of home and work. Middle managers are also more likely to experience stress as a result of trying to attain new positions and promotion (CL Cooper, Th*e Executive Gypsy – the Quality of Manager Life*, 1979).

4.5   A participative leadership style is said to lead to less stress. However, it means that a manager has to use an open approach successfully, otherwise managers may feel anxious and resentful because their actual power falls short of their formal power (Donaldson and Gowler, *Prerogatives, Participation and Managerial Stress*, 1975).

Student Activity 2

Managers can cause or relieve the stress of their staff. Make observations for one working week, and make notes of:

● Occasions when your manager's actions either causes or relieves stress; and

● The reasons why those actions had that effect; and

● The extent to which the manager seemed conscious of the stress caused.

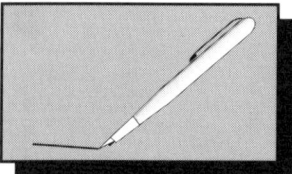

From within the individual

4.6   In considering the effects of stress on people, some account should be taken of the individual's capabilities to withstand stress. Research by Friedman and Rosenman (*A Predictive Study of Coronary Heart Disease*, 1964), indicates a relationship between personality factors and heart disease. Those more prone to disease were described as: extremely competitive, high achievers, aggressive, hasty, impatient, restless, with a tenseness of facial muscles, inclining to time pressures and keen to assume responsibility.

Outside the organisation

4.7   It is accepted that certain events can have a dramatic impact on stress levels and hence affect work performance. Dr Holmes and his colleagues developed a stress scale measure in life change units (LCU) and predicted that people who exceed 300 LCU points run the risk of becoming seriously ill in the next two years.

Figure 17.2 Holmes Stress Scale

Events	Scale of impact	Events	Scale of impact
Death of spouse	100	Change in responsibilities at work	29
Divorce	73	Son or daughter leaving home	29
Marital separation	65	Trouble with in-laws	29
Jail term	63	Outstanding personal achievement	28
Death of close family member	63	Spouse begins or stops work	26
		Begin or end school	26
Personal injury or illness	53	Change in living conditions	25
Marriage	50	Revision of personal habits	24
Fired at work	47	Trouble with boss	23
Marital reconciliation	45	Change in work hours or conditions	20
Retirement	45		
Change in health of family member	44	Change in residence	20
		Change in schools	20
Pregnancy	40	Change in recreation	19
Sex difficulties	39	Change in church activities	19
Gain of new family member	39	Change in social activities	18
		Mortgage or loan less than £10,000	17
Business readjustment	39		
Change in financial state	38	Change in sleeping habits	16
Death of close friend	37	Change in number of family get-togethers	15
Change in number of arguments with spouse	35	Change in eating habits	15
Mortgage over £100,000	31	Vacation	13
Foreclosure of mortgage or loan	30	Christmas	12
		Minor violations of the law	11

Source: TS Holmes, TH Holmes, Journal of Psychosomatic Research, Vol.14, June 1970.

Student Activity 3

Consider a stressful time in your life. Work out your stress score on the previous table.

The benefit of stress

4.8 It should not be denied that a certain amount of stress and pressure can be beneficial. The butterflies felt before a public appearance can be utilised to add colour to the performance; the excitement of apprehension before examinations sharpens most people's ability to do well; doing some tasks under the pressure of imminent deadlines stimulates some people to a much better piece of work. It is only when stress becomes excessive for the individual in question that it impedes performance. Fig. 17.3 sums this up.

Figure 17.3 Performance and stress

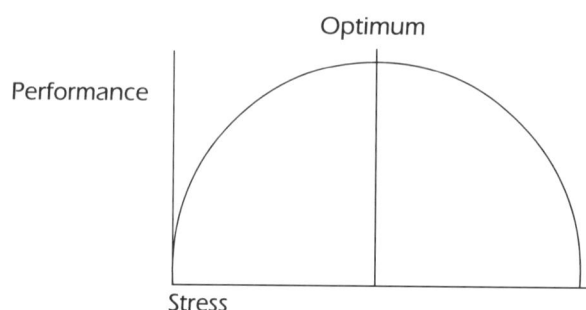

5 Symptoms of stress

5.1 When you perceive an element in the environment to be threatening, the brain sends instructions to be ready for an emergency. Hormones trigger a series of responses to release energy so individuals can have greater speed, strength and sharper concentration. If the stressor is not eliminated and the stress continues for a long time then it can become a problem because any of the symptoms given below can persist for a long period of time.

5.2 A stressful situation can be improved by being aware of the stressors (what stresses an individual personally) and recognising the signals to indicate over-stress. The signals can be mental, physical, emotional or behavioural. There are several steps an individual can take to avoid stress:

- *Healthy diet.* Most dietary experts are agreed that it is beneficial to eat less saturated fats, less salt and sugar, less cholesterol and more high fibre food and products which contain starch. They also agree that excess caffeine and nicotine in the body can increase stress levels. Alcohol consumption should be reduced or avoided.

- *Fitness.* Keeping fit can lengthen life, have a positive effect on the brain and increase capacity to cope with stress. To get fit and stay fit regular exercise is needed. For example a guide is to exercise three times a week for at least 20 minutes so you are out of breath.

- *Balance of work and personal life.* Most people lead complex lives having to

Diagram 17.4 Checklist of symptoms of stress

Symptom	Describes poorly	Describes well
Constant fatigue		
Low energy level		
Recurring headaches		
Gastrointestinal disorders		
Chronically bad breath		
Sweaty hands or feet		
Dizziness		
High blood pressure		
Pounding heart		
Constant inner tension		
Inability to sleep		
Temper outbursts		
Hyperventilation		
Moodiness		
Irritability and restlessness		
Inability to concentrate		
Increased aggression		
Compulsive eating		
Chronic worrying		
Anxiety or apprehensiveness		
Inability to relax		
Growing feelings of inadequacy		
Increase in defensiveness		
Dependence upon tranquilisers		
Excessive use of alcohol		
Excessive smoking		

Source: Williams and Huber, Behaviour in Organisations *(1978), South-Western Publishing Co*

balance work, family commitments and social/leisure activities. It is important to get a balance between these different areas, otherwise they can be a cause of stress.

● *Support.* It is important to have people around to share problems. Talking to people even if they cannot solve the problem helps in managing stress.

6 Remedies for stress

6.1 Obviously, one way of reducing stress and tension is to take tranquillisers or other drugs. However, this remedy helps the person deal with the immediate condition without helping to face future stressful situations, and deal with them alone.

6.2 Therapeutic stress therapy and skilled stress counselling emphasise rebuilding the thinking process about issues and thereby helping people who overreact to stress by giving them responsibility to examine their own faulty reactions. The emphasis is on helping individuals relax, through relaxation techniques, e.g. breathing exercises. It also aims to take steps to control and manage the environment, being realistic about what can be achieved, being assertive and allowing time so one is not rushed. Remember, it is not hard work that creates stress, but a person's reaction to failure or inadequate performance, e.g. exam stress can often be avoided by continuous hard work through the year.

6.3 *Note:* It is the responsibility of managers to be alert to the symptoms of stress in others and act to relieve it. This can involve professional counsellors or reallocation of work and training in assertiveness.

Short case study on stress

6.4 After a period of five years with the bank, Linda Hilton was promoted to supervisor. In this capacity she supervised two men and three women, some of whom had also hoped for promotion. Except for her lack of previous supervisory experience, she was well qualified for the job and her performance was excellent. However she was subject to a high level of stress. Although the additional responsibility was a stressor, so was Linda's inability to accept the fact that two of her subordinates resented her promotion and would negatively influence the attitudes of the other staff toward her.

6.5 Linda's stress began to diminish when she started to see the problem in a different way. 'I don't have to be liked by everyone to be effective. I am not in a popularity contest. It is enough I do my job well and am respected. I do not have to be liked by people whose attitudes are biased by jealousy. Their hostility is not directed to me, but anyone who might be in my position. Part of my job is to absorb this hostility.'

6.6 Another technique Linda used was from an insight. 'I have been under pressure because I have worked in a hostile environment, but I created part of this environment by being promoted and part of it by *my* perception of other's reaction to the event. I have expected everyone to be resentful and so seen hostility where it did not exist.' Her solution was to say, 'I am going to be the most effective, likeable, considerate supervisor in the organisation. Although being liked is not crucial, I would expect everyone will grow to like me and I am going to act as if they do.'

6.7 Linda's situation improved, her stress reduced and interpersonal relations were much better.

6.8 The approach adopted by Linda is known as *perceptual adaptation*, interpreting a situation in a positive way, thereby reducing stress.

Physical and mental techniques of stress relief

6.9 Since a good deal of short-term stress has physical effects to some extent based on the release of adrenaline into the bloodstream, it can be relieved by taking up the physical exertion which this hormone demands of the body.

- In the short term, a piece of exercise such as a good run, a game of squash, a work-out in a gymnasium can relieve the pressure by obeying the body's flight-fight demands.

- In the slightly longer term, adopting breathing techniques or Yoga-style exercises or meditational mental/physical techniques like Tai-Chi can relieve the mind and body of some stress, by displacing the concentration.

- Spare-time activities which make their own intellectual demands, from games through music to fishing or chess, shift the attention away from the sources of stress.

- Proper control of diet, sleep and even social life can also be a source of defence against the worst ravages of excessive stress.

7 Time management

7.1 Time for every manager is limited. Once wasted it cannot be regained. Time-management is not something that happens accidentally, nor does it arise out of a manager's innate skill or talent. It is to a very large extent under the control of the manager, and is largely an act of will. Of course there are always mishaps, and the unexpected may change plans; but those who decide that they will manage their time usually succeed in doing so better than those who believe that serendipity will take care of them.

Student Activity 4

Using your observation of good and poor managers you have known, write a half-page mini-essay giving advice to a junior manager on *one* technique for managing time in a busy office in a financial institution.

Establish priorities
7.2 Managers must ensure they cover the tasks they are supposed to. This will involve:

- Assessing tasks as to their urgency and to their importance (there is a difference between urgent and important items);

- Relating the importance of items to key result areas;

- Giving more time to the important items;

- Dealing swiftly with minor, urgent items;

- If necessary, scheduling a time to deal with the important items.

Retain a balance
7.3 Managers through time management must retain balance to their working life in several respects:

- *Ensure that they have a leisure time*, so maintaining a balance between work and home. People need to relax so that they return to work refreshed.

- Make sure that their time at work is balanced. This may involve them keeping a 'time diary' for a period, so they can check how long different items are taking and try to reallocate time according to priorities. On a longer term basis they may decide to use a diary or time management system to schedule and allocate time to all activities.

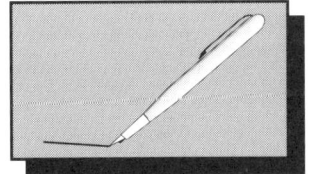

- If they operate an 'open door' policy for staff and customers, ensure it is not too disruptive. It may be better to agree times to be available to see staff and ensure they stick to this time (sometimes termed 'BBC' or Better Bandit Control), or alternatively Manage by Walking Around (MBWA), so staff can approach them then.

- *Keep a balance* between work that may be delegated to you, your own work and work delegated to others. As a manager certain tasks should be achieved and this is a priority. Additional work should be fitted around these tasks, not replace them. Similarly specialist work should be tackled by specialists.

Effective team management

7.4   Effective team management, delegating work where appropriate, can be a great aid to the manager. It frees time, allowing the manager to concentrate on key tasks whilst offering subordinates a chance to broaden and develop their work experience. The advantages and problems of delegation are discussed in Units 12 and 18, and you should note that certain types of leadership style would be more prone to delegate tasks than others, e.g. the democratic or consultative style would be more likely to delegate than the authoritarian. Some jobs or functions are also more easily delegated than others. Personnel and strategic work can by its nature be highly confidential and therefore not suitable for delegation.

Paper management techniques

7.5   Careful paper management techniques are useful, ensuring each piece of paper is handled only once. This entails either:

- Dealing with it.

- Delegating it.

- Diarising it (detailing the time when it will be dealt with in the diary).

- Dumping it.

Key features of successful time management

7.6   There are three key features of successful time management:

- Effective integration of long-term goals, both personal and organisational, with short-term priorities.

- Key tasks once identified, should be prioritised on a scale of vital to relatively trivial. The aim is to concentrate time and activity on the prime tasks first.

- Record systems established to:

   ○   track discretionary and non-discretionary time;

   ○   record commitments given and received;

   ○   aid retrieval of information when required.

Summary

Having studied this unit carefully you should now:

- understand the concept of career management;

- know the extent to which it is under the employee's control;

- be familiar with the causes of stress;

- be able to recognise the symptoms of stress;

- be familiar with some stress-relieving techniques;

- be able to apply some techniques of time management.

Self-assessment questions

1. Briefly, what are Feldman and Arnold's five pieces of advice for recruits to manage their career?

2. Which of the following is not a stage in career development:
   (a) join up process;
   (b) career identity;
   (c) career training;
   (d) middle career?

3. Which one of the following personality characteristics is not linked with being more prone to stress:
   (a) extremely competitive;
   (b) poor at managing time;
   (c) impatient;
   (d) aggressive?

4. Which of the following techniques is not normally associated with reducing stress:
   (a) management of time;
   (b) relaxation technique;
   (c) more exercise;
   (d) increased delegation?

5. Which of the following is not a symptom of stress:
   (a) constant tiredness;
   (b) recurring headaches;
   (c) sudden changes in moods;
   (d) ability to concentrate?

6. What is regarded as an excessively stressful weekly workload?

7. Name one physical technique used to relieve stress

8. Which of the following is given the greater value according to the Holmes life stressor scale:
   (a) change in responsibilities at work;
   (b) divorce;
   (c) business readjustment;
   (d) death of a close family member?

9. What are the four 'D's' of paper management?

10. What are the three key features of time management?

Unit 18

Organisational Design and Organisational Culture

Objectives

After studying this unit, you should be able to:

- understand how organisations chart their structure;

- understand the foundations on which organisational structures stand;

- know how organisations deal with spans of control, and delegation;

- become familiar with the concept of organisational culture;

- be able to classify different types of organisational culture.

Student Activity 1

Before you start to read this unit it is essential you complete the following exercises:

1 Find out/draw an organisational chart which summarises your organisation's entire structure.

2 Find out/draw an organisational chart for your section/branch/department. Indicate your own position with an asterisk.

1 Organisational structure

1.1 If an organisation is to achieve the goals and objectives it has established for itself, then its work must be divided between various departments and individuals. This in turn means that a structure must be imposed on the organisation to ensure the effective performance of key activities. There appears to be little doubt amongst organisational writers that the structure is a key element in determining whether an organisation will achieve its objectives.

1.2 According to Drucker:

> ... good organisational structure does not itself produce good performance. But a poor organisational structure makes good performance impossible, no matter how good an individual manager may be.

1.3 Structural design has an effect on people, for instance, merging departments at a branch into local area or head office activities, and creating or withdrawing a managerial level in the organisation.

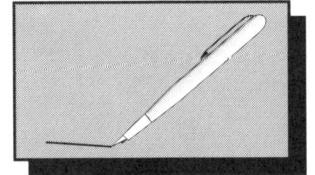

227

2   Terms connected with organisational structure

Organisational charts

2.1   The formal structure of an organisation is most often represented in a chart or diagram. There are certain advantages in doing this:

- It helps to clarify the objectives of the organisation and the methods used to achieve them. It indicates, for instance, whether an organisation specialises in providing services or is essentially a manufacturer.

- It *provides flexibility*, so structural adjustments created by the influence of changes in policy or the environment can occur, e.g. the current trend towards specialisation of services in banking.

- It clearly *defines responsibility* by illustrating each post, indicating authority, responsibility and span of control (the number of individuals reporting to one supervisor). It will also ensure *unity of command* (that each individual only reports to *one* superior).

- The chart indicates where and how *delegation* may occur.

2.2   There are several different types of structures available for an organisation. In considering the design of an organisational structure, Mintzberg gives nine essential design parameters which he maintains should be considered. Mintzberg's design parameters are:

- How many given tasks should a position contain and how specialised should each task be?

- To what extent should the work content of each position be standardised?

- What skills and knowledge are necessary for each position?

- On what basis should positions be grouped into units?

- How large should each unit be within the span of control?

- To what extent should the output of each position be standardised?

- What mechanisms should be established to facilitate mutual adjustments among positions?

- How much decision making power should be delegated?

- How much decision making should pass from line managers to staff specialists and operators?

2.3   The other factors which influence structure are:

- The nature of the business;

- History of the business, ownership and control;

- Size of the business;

- Management philosophy and personality of top management;

- Location;

- Availability of skills;

- Costs associated with a geographic area;

- Technology;

- Relationship with customers.

Span of control

2.4 This describes the number of subordinates reporting to one superior. The number should be limited because of the number of relationships and responsibility the supervisor then has to deal with. The complexity and structure of a job will determine the span. The more complex the task, the fewer the number of people that can be successfully supervised. Graicunas found that with six subordinates a supervisor had 222 relationships to contend with. An equation was produced to illustrate this:

$$R = n \left(\frac{2^n}{2} + n - 1 \right)$$

R = number of interrelationships

n = number of subordinates

2.5 The larger the span of control the flatter the organisational form, whereas the smaller the span the larger the hierarchy and the taller the organisation:

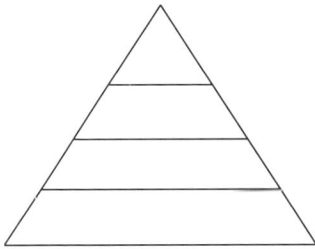 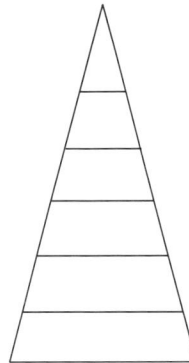

Wider span gives fewer levels   Smaller span gives more levels

2.6 However, recent research indicates successful spans can range from two to 18, depending on the process or type of work involved.

Student Activity 2

What is/are the span(s) of control in your office or section? Write a short paragraph to describe them, and then go on to write a second paragraph to:

- Justify the number; *or*
- State why it is too large and what problems this might cause; *or*
- State what problems might be caused because it is too small.

Centralisation or decentralisation

2.7 Centralisation implies that control is retained in one central place by the organisation, rather than being delegated to geographical areas.

2.8 The *advantages* of retaining control centrally are:

- Easy and quick access to data.
- Access to specialised knowledge.

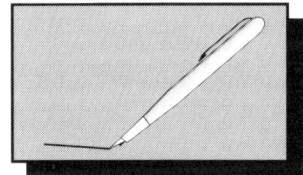

- Standing pressure better, e.g. complaints from a demanding customer are easier to deal with when removed from personal contact.
- Consistent standards.

2.9   The *disadvantages* of centralisation are:
- Decisions are taken away from the point of operation.
- It is difficult to monitor action.
- It can be de-motivating.
- Slower decision making.
- No sensitivity to local market needs.
- No opportunity for individuals to develop and grow in responsibility.

Delegation

2.10   Many authors argue that although centralisation or retaining control has many advantages, there is far more to be gained from delegating duties. A manager is thus developing his subordinates, increasing their motivation and skill, giving responsibility and encouraging specialisation. Managers are thereby freed from routine tasks and able to make best use of their time. Decisions are taken closer to the action, improving cost efficiency and giving better cover for jobs.

2.11   Delegation is founded on the principles of *authority* (the right to take action or make the decisions the manager would have done), and *responsibility* (the obligation by a subordinate to perform duties and make decisions or accept reprimands for performance). One without the other leads to an abuse of delegation.

2.12   Delegation can also occur upwards in the organisation when a manager may temporarily take over the work of an absent or hard-pressed subordinate. However much is delegated, the manager still remains accountable for the actions of the subordinate and has ultimate responsibility. It is therefore in the manager's own interests to ensure staff are fully briefed and trained and left to complete the work within time limits with some monitoring.

2.13   Managers appear to show a reluctance to delegate work. Newman, in his research, indicated why (*Management Review*, 1976):
- I can do it better myself;
- Lack of ability to direct;
- Lack of confidence in subordinates;
- Absence of selective controls;
- Not encouraged by the organisation or by one's supervisors.

2.14   Subordinates also tended to avoid it:
- Easier for boss to do it;
- Fear of criticism;
- Lack of information and resources;
- Too much work;
- Lack of self-confidence;
- No incentives to do delegated work.

2.15 Before a decision to delegate work can be made, several points should be considered.

- What will be the benefits of this delegation to the employee?
- Is the employee able to take on this additional work?
- What training does the employee need?
- How much time needs to be spent training and briefing?
- What control mechanisms need to be set up to ensure acceptable work?
- What arrangements need to be made in cases of absenteeism, resignation or promotion?
- Who should now be told that the subordinate is completing the work?

Student Activity 3

Write a mini-essay of approximately half a page to describe an instance when you observed *either* a piece of delegation which was well implemented in your office *or* a piece of delegation which was badly implemented in your office. Include your reasons for describing it as a good or a poor piece of delegation, based on the pointers given in the text.

Line and staff

2.16 The line relationship is that existing between senior and subordinate (usually a linear or vertical relationship). The staff relationship is lateral, offering specialist advice to another, e.g. premises department offering advice to a manager on refurbishment. A line person could therefore be said to be directly involved in providing financial services. A staff person is one who assists line.

Committees

2.17 A committee is a group of people committed to reaching a joint decision. They are established when one individual alone may not effectively administer a position or the expertise of a group is needed.

2.18 There are policy-making and operating committees. Both need:

- objectives;
- authority;
- membership; and
- decisions.

2.19 The advantages of the committee form of structure is that actions and ideas are co-ordinated, communications should be improved, judgment and responsibilities are pooled. Because ideas and action are collectively accepted, implementation is more rapid. However, they can be time-wasting and costly because of the manpower absorbed and can mean that individuals avoid accepting responsibility for decisions. (The management and administration of meetings is covered in Unit 16.)

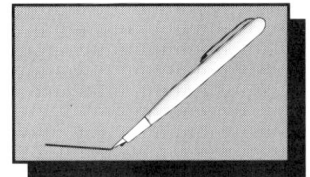

3   Symptoms of inappropriate structure

3.1   Having explored various aspects of organisational structure and examined the implications of adopting various types of structure, it is perhaps appropriate to examine the symptoms associated with an inappropriate structure.

3.2   Some symptoms of inappropriate structure are:

- Low motivation;
- Arbitrary and inconsistent decisions;
- Insufficient delegation;
- Lack of clarity in job definition;
- Lack of clarity in performance assessment;
- Undue amount of competition between parts of the organisation;
- Inadequate support systems;
- Inappropriate decisions;
- Conflict;
- Lack of co-ordination;
- Poor response to opportunities and external change;
- Rising administrative costs;
- Poor flexibility;
- Poor adaptability to change (both internal and external change).

4   Different types of structure

By function

4.1   This is the most commonly used format. It entails the use of the same set of resources or expertise by members of staff. Once a functional format has been decided upon, the designer then has to decide which activities are important enough to be given a separate department. In manufacturing organisations the usual functional areas are research and development, marketing, production, finance and personnel.

Figure 18.1 Example of functional structure at branch level

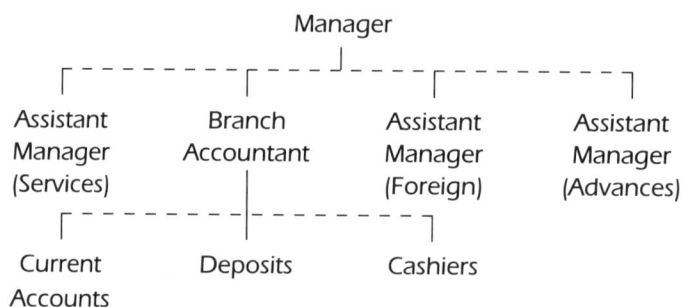

4.2   The *advantages* of the functional structure are the:

- High degree of specialisation.

- Clear promotion paths through departments.
- Free and supportive exchange of information.

4.3   The *disadvantages* are that:

- It is a narrow structure that is often lacking in lateral communication.
- There is no general management stream.
- It is less adaptive to change.

By product or service

4.4   This is where the contribution of specialists are integrated into semi-autonomous units with collective responsibility for a major part of the business process or for a complete cycle of work. An example is the food industry where marketing, production, technical and financial staff have responsibility for only one product in a range, say, baked beans. Another example would be a hospital where medical and support staff are located in different units dealing with particular treatments: surgery, maternity, etc.

Figure 18.2 Example of structure defined by specialist services

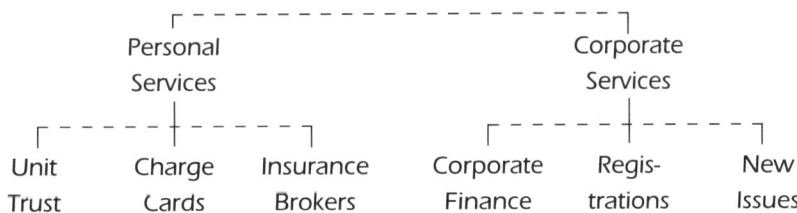

```
           ┌ ─ ─ ─ ─ ─ ─ ─ ─ ─ ─ ─ ─ ─ ─ ─ ─ ─ ┐
        Personal                          Corporate
        Services                           Services
    ┌ ─ ─ ─ ─ ┼ ─ ─ ─ ─ ┐        ┌ ─ ─ ─ ─ ─ ┼ ─ ─ ─ ─ ┐
  Unit      Charge    Insurance   Corporate   Regis-      New
  Trust      Cards     Brokers     Finance    trations    Issues
```

4.5   This product structure affords the *advantages* of:

- Specialised skills, experience and machinery available.
- Increased co-ordination of responsibility for one service.
- Easily assignable praise or criticism for a success or failure.

By location

4.6   This is the structural format when different services are provided by area or geographical boundaries, according to particular needs or demands, e.g. the sales territories of organisations or the grouping of retail shops under one regional manager. An example of such a structure would be an international bank.

Figure 18.3 Example of structure defined by location

```
        ┌ ─ ─ ─ ─ ─ ─ ─ ─ ─ Bank ─ ─ ─ ─ ─ ─ ─ ─ ─ ┐
     Regional            Regional            Regional
     Manager             Manager             Manager
     America              United              South
                         Kingdom             America
```

4.7   A geographical structure provides the opportunity for widely-based training with lower and more tightly controlled operating costs, local knowledge of consumer tastes and increased motivation for staff who can feel an important part of a smaller organisation.

4.8 However, there is an obvious loss of control by head office with a consequent 'us and them' situation. The geographic unit may feel that their needs and difficulties are not understood by head office. There can also be inconsistencies in treatment and the standard of service provided by the different geographic units.

By project

4.9 Individuals or departments are brought together to work on one specific project. This is sometimes termed a *matrix structure*. An example of its use would be, say, in a proposed merger between two companies when legal experts, accountants and management consultants may be employed to bring the project to a successful end.

Figure 18.4 Example of a matrix structure

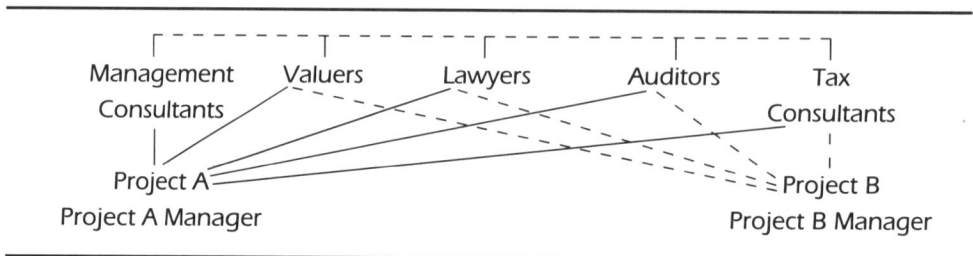

4.10 The *advantages* of using matrix structures are that they give:

● Better control of the project.

● Better customer relations because of this.

● Lower costs and tighter control.

● Shorter project development time because of the intensive team work; and they

● Act as an aid to training.

4.11 The *disadvantages* of using matrix structures are that they:

● Are complex to manage.

● Give lower staff utilisation.

● Give inconsistent policy application.

● Mean the functional areas often opt out of responsibility.

● Mean that the shifting teamwork lacks stability.

Other types of structures

4.12 The other type of structures which can be found in business organisations although less commonly seen in banking are:

● *By nature of the work performed.* This is where there is a need for a special common feature of work, e.g. confidentiality, knowledge, local conditions, speedy decisions.

● *By common time scales.* An example would be shift working and the extent to which different tasks are taken on by different shift groups.

- *By common processes.* This method of structuring is similar to the division by function. It includes for instance the decision as to whether to have a centralised word-processing pool for all departments or to allow each department to have its own service. Services using expensive equipment, e.g. mainframe computers, may need to be grouped together for efficiency and economy. There is a move towards structuring some bank departments according to a common process, e.g. security departments, who deal with security work from a collection of branches, or the provision of 'sheds' to process the day's work from a collection of branches.

- *By staff employed.* This is when the allocation of duties may be according to experience, or skill, for instance, the division of work between barristers, solicitors, and legal executives. Work may also be planned deliberately to give people a variety of tasks and responsibilities.

- *By type of customer to be served.* Some organisations establish different departments to deal with differing consumer needs, for example, personal and corporate customers, or catering services (restaurant or self-service), etc. In banking there has been a move to establish departments to deal with, say, mid to major corporate customers and marketing to identified targets.

4.13 Most organisations tend to use a mix of structures. Head office is often on a functional or product base. Then the regions are structured geographically with branches again on a functional basis.

Student Activity 4

Write notes to describe the structure of your organisation in the terms used in the foregoing sections. Note that it can be a mix of such structures. Include in your notes the reasons why your bank adopts the structure(s) described.

5 Trends in structure

5.1 In the past, banks have tended to be structured on a geographic basis. They offered a range of general banking services to a wide market. The advantages of having this type of structure meant attention could be paid to local conditions, which at that time were more important than the broad product characteristics. However, this structure started to come under strain, according to Livy (1985), when consumers started to demand rather different services, e.g. project finance and leasing, acquisition advice, medium-term lending to companies. These activities could not be handled by the generalist managers that the structure produced. The need was for specialist advice that could not be provided by the geographic structure. Although some form of product specialisation was obviously needed, it was difficult at first for the banks to adjust to this type of structure. The bank was providing the specialist services through completely separated managements (merchant banks, leasing, credit cards).

5.2 There is no doubt that the geographic structure created many problems, a conflict of marketing priorities, fragmentation in customer contact and a lack of expertise. In recent years there has been a move towards product

235

management in the leading banks with separate divisions for consumer credit, corporate lending and international businesses.

5.3   However, it should not be thought that such a move is straightforward or easy. For instance, do consumer credit card services become part of consumer lending or part of money transmission service management? It must be decided to what extent the product management crosses geographical frontiers. Does it make sense to have the cash management department in London to control cash management in Canada? To ensure smooth operations and consistency of treatment the answer must be yes, *but* with local conditions and personalities it would make better sense for the local department to have control. All these are difficulties that need to be decided by an organisational designer.

5.4   It is normal to find that in an international bank there are subsidiaries and holding companies, so a group works through a board of directors responsible to the holding company. The holding company can then request certain control data. Reportable matters would be:

- Liquidity;
- Capital investment;
- Risk exposure;
- Public relations;
- Social responsibility;
- Personnel policy;
- Managerial control systems;
- Advertising that may affect the group.

5.5   The day-to-day management is at a local level.

5.6   There have been other changes in structure with the introduction of new services, e.g. First Direct telephone banking and new processing systems. There are now separate retail units for private and small business accounts.

5.7   Many of the changes have been cost driven. Branch networks were established when high street premises were cheap and communication difficult. The branch network has now become an extensive, costly and unwieldy series of outlets which put banks at a disadvantage to building societies in terms of costs. Networks are being reorganised to make better use of expensive space, termed the 'hub and spoke' structure. There is centralised processing in cheaper out-of-town sites, a reduction in the number of outlets, increased selling and public space and greater use of ATMs. It is also expected that regional offices will decline in number as branches reduce and communication becomes easier.

6   Organisational culture

6.1   As a country or region has a culture of its own, so does an organisation with differing procedures, differing amounts of individual freedom and different atmospheres or climate. The culture of an organisation may determine its structure or can indeed be determined by its structure. The two have a very close and at times indistinguishable relationship.

6.2   Schein, Hofstede and others have suggested that culture can be examined in three layers:

- At the *lowest, or base level*, there are the *basic assumptions* that people in the culture make about the facts of the world about them. In many European societies, for example, it is seen as incontrovertible that sickness has a physical source; in other societies it is firmly believed that sickness comes from being cursed by someone.

- At an *intermediate level* are the *norms and values* that the society bases on the beliefs. For example, if it is believed that sickness has a physical source, then society may develop the right to access to medicines which will cure the sickness; or if it is believed that sickness comes from being cursed by someone, society may press the cursed to believe it socially necessary to take actions to lift the curse.

- At a *surface level* are the *artefacts* that society creates, the visible manifestations which show the existence of an aspect of culture, such as a national health service, a medical centre, pharmacists, consultant witch-doctors, ritual cleansing procedures, or amulets to ward off curses and so on.

6.3   The *reasons* behind different organisations developing different cultures are:

- History;
- Economy;
- The nature of the people in the organisation;
- Organisational policies and values;
- Structure, whether centralised or decentralised;
- Nature of employees;
- Nature of the business;
- The life stage of the organisation: whether it is in its youth, maturity or decline.

6.4   There are many *signs* as to the culture of the organisation, some more obvious and visible than others:

- The setting: design, reception area, building and layout;
- Corporate image in brochures, literature, etc.;
- Customer relations;
- History;
- What sort of person does the organisation reward?
- Methods of communication;
- Freedom for staff;
- What the company stresses, e.g. Marks and Spencer plc stress their high-quality goods.

6.5   McKinsey and Co developed a model to try to explain how the culture of an organisation is exhibited, the 7 's's. The most important one is shared values, the others are structure, systems, style, staff, skills and strategy.

Figure 18.5 McKinsey's model

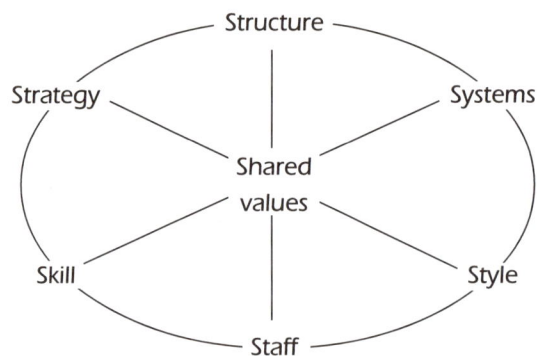

7 Types of organisational culture

7.1 Organisational writers have tried to classify the different types of organisational cultures available. Deal and Kennedy in their book *Corporate Culture* identify four major types:

- *The Hard 'Macho' Culture.* The organisation is made up of people working as individuals, who take high risks and receive quick feedback on whether the actions were right, e.g. entertainment, management consultancy, advertising.

- *The 'Work Hard/Play Hard' Culture.* The team is all important and the customer is the key to success, e.g. retailing, Marks and Spencer, McDonalds.

- *The 'Bet-Your-Company' Culture.* Slow feedback culture with decision cycles taking years, e.g. oil companies, architectural firms, public utilities.

- *The 'Process' Culture.* Low risk, slow feedback culture. Technical perfection of importance with calculation of risks. Emphasis on *how* to do something, e.g. insurance, banking, financial services.

7.2 Handy in his book *Understanding Organisations* (1985) also discusses and categorises four different types of culture:

- *Power Culture.* Found in small entrepreneurial organisations. The structure is best depicted as a web – all authority and power emanating from one individual. There is little bureaucracy but they rely heavily on the central figure and the successor provides the key to continued success or failure. It is a competitive atmosphere, closely controlled from the centre.

- *Role Culture.* A bureaucracy: the organisation's strength lies in its rational formal procedures and functional specialities. The role of a job is more important than the individual and the structure is best illustrated by a Greek temple. It functions best in a stable environment because it is slow to change and react. It is virtually the opposite of the power culture. Communication functions well from top to bottom, but poorly from bottom to top or across the organisation.

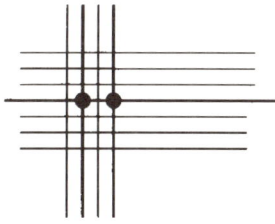

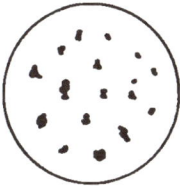

- *Task Culture.* This is job- or project-oriented. It is the equivalent of a matrix structure and can be represented by a net. The power and influence tends to lie at the intersections. This culture brings together all the resources necessary to complete a project. Influence is based on specialist knowledge, not position or individual characteristics. Appropriate where flexibility and adaptability are needed. People tend to work for two bosses.

- *Person Culture.* This is where the organisation is geared to satisfying individual member needs, e.g. barristers' chambers, etc. The organisation is made up of a number of individuals without any real structure. A commune or kibbutz are perhaps other examples. Professionals joining this structure have the benefit of economies of scale, and there are few rules.

Student Activity 5

Write a one-page essay, in note or bulleted form, describing your organisation's culture using (a) McKinsey, Deal and Kennedy, *and* Handy's models of culture, and (b) illustrating each point by specific observations of the beliefs, norms, values, practices, and symbols you have observed.

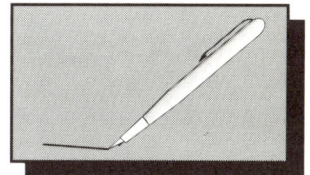

8   Signs of failing culture

8.1   As time passes organisations may need to change and adapt their culture. Braddick believes that there are signs that a culture is in trouble. The symptoms as he sees them are:

- No clear vision of the future.
- No widely shared beliefs or values.
- Strong contrasting values held in different parts of the organisation.
- Leaders encourage 'divide and rule' by providing disagreement and division within the business.
- No central drive.
- Internal focus.
- Short-term focus.
- High labour turnover, absenteeism and complaints.
- Subcultures flourish.
- Lack of emotional discipline; outbursts of anger and frustration.

8.2   To handle these cultural problems, Braddick believes the organisation needs:

- A manager with a vision of the right type of culture.
- A manager who can communicate this vision to others.
- The setting of high standards and insistence on achievement.
- Publication of successes.
- Reward of those who make important contributions.

239

8.3   Although an organisation can possess a culture, the type of atmosphere or culture in different departments may well vary. So, for instance, the organisation as a whole may reflect a role culture, but at regional office a power culture may well be apparent. Those departments or sections concerned with quality as an issue may exhibit a task subculture.

Summary

Having studied this unit carefully you should now:

- **understand how organisations chart their structure;**

- **have become very familiar with your own organisation's structure;**

- **understand the foundations on which your organisational structure stands;**

- **have thought out your own experience of spans of control, and delegation;**

- **be able to discuss the concept of organisational culture at a sophisticated level;**

- **be able to classify different types of culture, with relation to your own organisation.**

Self-assessment questions

1. Line and staff is a term used to describe:
   (a) The way of doing a job;
   (b) The manual workers in an organisation and management;
   (c) The behavioural aspects of structure;
   (d) Those involved in producing services and those who assist them.

2. A functional structure is one where:
   (a) There is no waste;
   (b) It is organised so the same resources or expertise are together;
   (c) Everything revolves around the manager;
   (d) It is arranged according to geographical location.

3. What is the 'span of control'?.

4. What is the informal organisation?

5. Why use a chart to depict the formal structure of an organisation?

6. On what two major principles is delegation founded?

7. What are the three levels at which culture can be examined?

8. What is the central element in the McKinsey model of organisational culture?

9. What are Deal and Kennedy's four types of culture?

10. What are Charles Handy's four types of culture?

Unit 19

Organisational Development, Management of Change and Power, and Inter-Departmental Co-operation

Objectives

After studying this unit, you should be able to:

- **understand why organisations change;**

- **have an overview of what causes change;**

- **have considered the management of change;**

- **understand power in an organisation;**

- **be able to analyse the sources of power;**

- **see how power relates to structure.**

1 Organisational change and development

1.1 A failing organisational culture, or indeed any sign of problems in the organisation, indicates the need for change. Corporate planning by its very nature makes the demand that the organisation should change and adapt to meet the challenges of the environment (see Unit 3). It is logical, therefore, to examine the process of organisational change and development after learning about corporate planning, organisational structure and culture.

1.2 Organisational development is the term used to describe the conscious process of helping organisations evolve new systems, procedures, or methods, or organising ways of working to cope with new situations. This often means changing managerial values, beliefs, motivations or attitudes that might support the existing organisational system. It refers to the process of devising new kinds of organisation to achieve an effective mix of individual, organisation and task.

1.3 Major industrial changes have created a society with several key features:
- The trend towards large organisations;
- Mobility among the population;
- Urbanisation;
- Affluence – consumer society;
- Small family units;
- State intervention in the areas of education, transport, energy, health care, housing.

1.4   It is difficult objectively to study change in our society because most people are involved in change on a daily basis. Things are never static.

1.5   Change can be studied at several different levels:

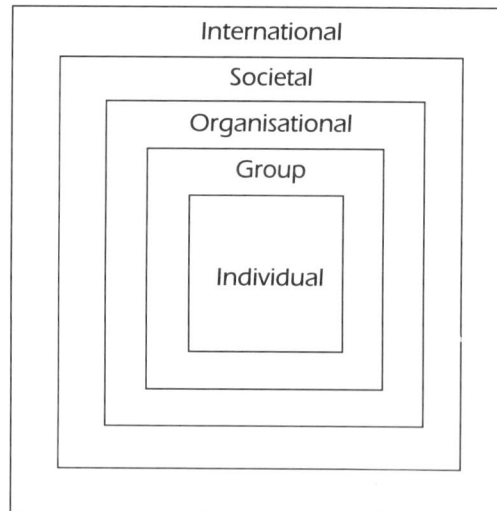

```
┌─────────────────────────────────────────────┐
│                International                  │
│  ┌─────────────────────────────────────────┐ │
│  │               Societal                    │ │
│  │  ┌─────────────────────────────────────┐ │ │
│  │  │           Organisational             │ │ │
│  │  │  ┌───────────────────────────────┐  │ │ │
│  │  │  │             Group              │  │ │ │
│  │  │  │  ┌─────────────────────────┐  │  │ │ │
│  │  │  │  │                          │  │  │ │ │
│  │  │  │  │        Individual        │  │  │ │ │
│  │  │  │  │                          │  │  │ │ │
│  │  │  │  └─────────────────────────┘  │  │ │ │
│  │  │  └───────────────────────────────┘  │ │ │
│  │  └─────────────────────────────────────┘ │ │
│  └─────────────────────────────────────────┘ │
└─────────────────────────────────────────────┘
```

It is the first three levels – individual, group and organisational – that we are particularly concerned with in this course.

2   Features of organisational change

2.1   There are, according to Mullins (in *Management and Organisational Behaviour*), four features that are apparent in any type of organisational change;

- A trigger;
- Interdependencies;
- Conflicts and frustrations;
- Time lags.

Trigger

2.2   This is a factor either within or outside the organisation that creates pressure to change. It could be that machines become obsolete and a new manufacturing process is required or new legislation on safety procedures creates a need for change. There could be alterations in the goals or objectives of the organisation and individual.

2.3   Some triggers are:

- Technology;
- Consumer tastes;
- Competition;
- Materials;
- Legislation;
- Social values;
- Economic factors.

2.4   All these factors and more can create the need for internal modification in terms of:

- Job design;
- Product design;
- Office layout;
- Alterations in responsibilities;
- Alterations in technology.

Student Activity 1

Look carefully at the elements of Leavitt's model. Write a mini-essay on change in your organisation, no more than one side of A4. Base it on a change in any one of the interdependent elements and show how that change affected all the other elements.

Interdependencies

2.5   A change in one aspect or feature of the organisation creates pressures for adjustment in other areas, e.g. the introduction of word processors creates the need to alter the style and presentation of letters.

2.6   HJ Leavitt (1975) presented this interdependency in a diagrammatic form.

Figure 6.1 Leavitt's model of interdependency

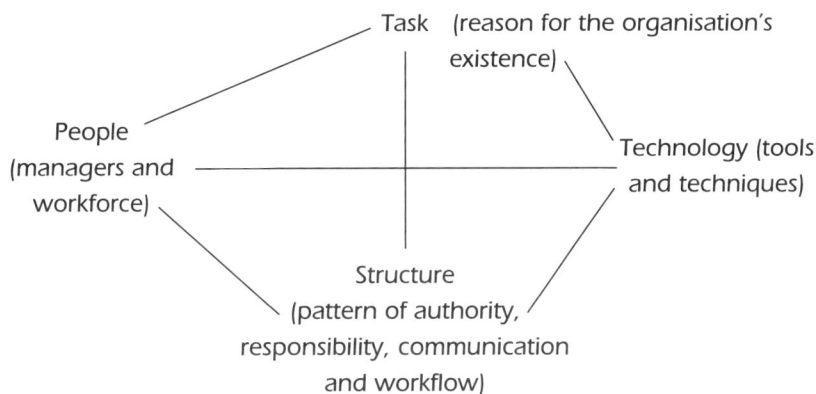

2.7   Leavitt maintained that a change in any one of these factors inevitably affected other features. Any one variable that is altered may lead to undesirable changes in others.

Conflicts and frustrations

2.8   The technical and economic objectives of employers may well conflict with those of the employees and lead to a conflict situation which can create pressures for or resistance to change.

Time lags

2.9   The whole process of organisational change is not a smoothly running affair, but can often occur in an untidy fashion, with some features changing in rapid succession, others slowly altering over many years. The key to successful organisational development is learning to manage these changes.

3 How to manage a programme of organisational development

3.1 Organisational writers have declared that merely to *respond* to change is dangerous and that organisations should take a pro-active stance, planning what changes are needed and putting them into force (see Unit 3). The corporate appraisal will indicate what changes are necessary in the organisation. This unit concentrates on how to introduce these changes.

3.2 There are five key steps in planning and administering organisational change.

Figure 6.2 Managing a programme of organisation development

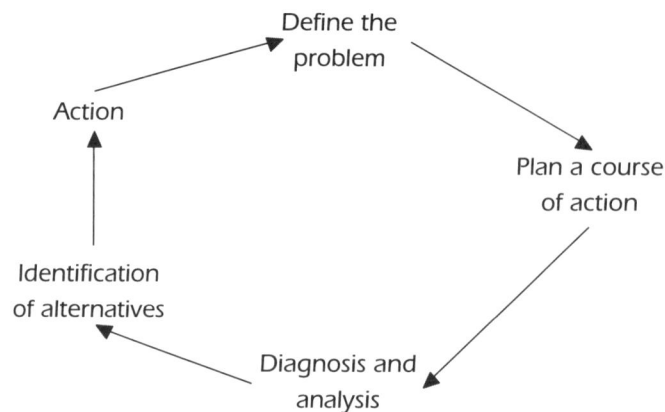

Step 1: Define the problem

3.3 Try to establish the true cause of the problem and get the people responsible for the introduction of change to clarify their role, who they are working for, what the outcome will be and the degree of confidentiality required. Failure to do this can result in ambiguity and mistrust. Ensure realistic and clear goals are set within the limitations of time-scale and costing. Ensure that progress is reported.

Step 2: Plan a course of action

3.4 Ensure the politics of the situation are known: who is likely to resist change, etc. The key people should be identified and involved, the culture understood and the communication should be effective.

Step 3: Diagnosis and analysis

3.5 People's feelings and perceptions should be taken into account and notice taken of any previous investigations.

Step 4: Identification of alternatives

3.6 Each alternative should be weighed and the implications for organisational change that follow from it.

Step 5: Getting action

3.7 There is a theory that the only way to get successful action for change is to gain co-operation. This is known as Planned Change Theory.

Student Activity 2

Imagine that you are to be given a free hand to change one thing about the space or accommodation in your office. Consider managing that change, and write brief notes under the headings of each step suggested in the previous section.

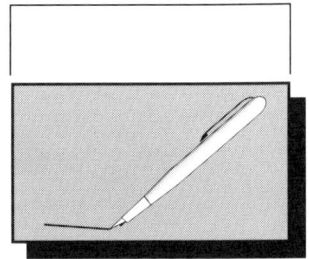

4   Planned Change Theory

4.1   This theory provides a series of assumptions and steps the organisation can adopt in order to change. It explains how to initiate change, manage the change process and stabilise the change outcomes. It makes several assumptions.

- Any change not only involves learning something, but also *unlearning* something already present. Changes should be well-integrated with personal and social relationships in the organisation.

- No change occurs unless there is some motivation to change, and if there is no motivation present then this must be induced as part of the change process.

- Organisational changes such as new structures and reward systems only occur through individual changes in key members, so organisational changes are mediated through individual changes.

- Most adult change involves attitudes, values, self-images and the unlearning of present responses, so it is both threatening and painful to people.

- Change is a multi-stage cycle and all stages have to be negotiated before stable change can be introduced or be said to have occurred.

4.2   Kurt Lewin (1952) suggested that three key phases should occur in this change process:

- Unfreeze;
- Change;
- Refreeze.

Stage 1: Unfreeze: the creation of motivation to change

4.3   The creation of motivation to change involves three specific mechanisms, so the individual *wants* to unlearn present behaviour and attitudes:

- *Mechanism 1.* The present behaviour or attitudes are discontinued. Then it is legitimate to introduce discomfort or dissatisfaction with these feelings.

- *Mechanism 2.* Disconfirmation of current attitudes has established sufficient guilt or anxiety to motivate change.

- *Mechanism 3.* The creation of psychological safety by reducing the barriers to change.

4.4   The change agent, i.e. the person introducing the change, makes people feel secure and capable of changing without reducing their power. Once they have accepted the disconfirming message, they are motivated to change and some new learning can occur, e.g. before a word processor can be successfully introduced, people must be convinced that it will be an improvement in terms of doing the job and improving their task.

Stage 2: Changing

4.5   This involves developing new attitudes and behaviours on the basis of new information. If the motivation to change is created then a person will be open to new sources of information, concepts or ways of looking at old information. This can occur through:

- *Identification with a role model, mentor, friend or other person* and seeing things from their point of view. Often consultants are seen as targets of identification and so it is important they act as role models.

- *Scanning the environment for information* relevant to a particular problem and the selection of information from multiple sources. This can be difficult, but it can produce more valid change, as the appropriate information for the individual is selected.

Stage 3: Refreeze: Stabilise the changes

4.6   The individual may not show new behaviours when placed back in the familiar situation. The manager may learn a new attitude towards the team, but boss and subordinates are more comfortable with the old attitudes and so disconfirm the new. Then the cycle of change reverts back to its original state. For example, people go away on a course and learn a new approach, but this may not always be used when they return to the workplace. There is therefore a need for integration of behaviours which can be achieved through two mechanisms.

- *Mechanism 1.* The person has the opportunity to test whether the new attitudes or behaviours really fit existing ideas and behaviour.

- *Mechanism 2.* This provides the opportunity to test whether others will accept and confirm the new attitudes and behaviour patterns. The change programme can be targeted at a group of people. Team training may be more effective because it gives the opportunity to reinforce behaviours. Although initially slower in being introduced, they will last longer.

4.7   Lewin's process can be summarised as:

Unfreeze   ⟶   Changing   ⟶   Refreeze

4.8   An example of Lewin's theory in practice would be when introducing a new electronic mail system. Employees would need to be shown the benefits of the change – its flexibility and speed. Once training has been carried out they should be provided with a reward for achieving certain targets, e.g. 80% of communication by EMS systems within two months.

4.9   Current writers suggest the most effective manager of change is one who first spends time studying and understanding the organisation before introducing change.

5   How do we know if an organisation has been successful in responding to change?

5.1   The first issue is: how do we measure if an organisation has been effective in responding to organisational change? Do we look for just one dimension, e.g.

return on investment, or a multiple of dimensions. If we are using several, should they be weighted according to their importance? Can we just consider the attainment of specified goals or do we consider the extent to which the personal goals of individuals within the organisation are achieved?

5.2 Most writers take the view that organisations should be assessed on multiple criteria, namely the capacity to:

● Attract resources;

● Integrate resources more effectively;

● Adapt to change.

5.3 However, it is not merely enough to assess how well an organisation achieves its goals. It should also consider whether it chose the correct goals in the first place. Schein feels that the effectiveness of an organisation should be assessed as, 'the capacity to survive, adapt, maintain itself and grow'.

5.4 A successful organisation requires the ability to:

● Take in information, communicating it reliably and validly;

● Develop the internal flexibility and creativity to make changes which are demanded by the information obtained;

● Integrate the multiple goals of the organisation, and from this develop a willingness to change if necessary.

● Establish an internal climate of support and freedom from threat – when an organisation is threatened, it undermines good communication, reduces flexibility and stimulates self-protection rather than concern for the total system;

● Redesign continuously the organisation's structure to be congruent with the goals and tasks of the organisation. This can be achieved through:

   ○ recruitment and selection processes;

   ○ utilisation of employees: using payment by results, linking rewards to the achievement of goals;

   ○ groups and intergroup relations;

   ○ design of the organisation: introducing participation by employees through quality circles, etc;

   ○ leadership.

6 Why organisations fail

6.1 As might be expected, not all organisations are successful in introducing change or adapting to change. The key reasons for failure according to Schein (1979), appear to be:

● *Failure to sense changes* in the environment or misperceive what is happening. Many organisations adjust to new circumstances, provided they can sense the time is appropriate: the changing needs of a consumer, etc.

● *Failure to transmit relevant information* to different parts of the organisation so they can act on it. It is difficult to get people to change attitudes or opinions. To get information imported or digested may involve a lengthy programme of influencing attitudes, self-images and working procedures, and must be based on a realistic change model.

This can lead to the use of an external consultant as a change agent, because the consultant has prestige which can be used to impart information into the system.

- *Failure to influence the conversion* or production system to make the necessary changes. This results from a lack of recognition that such changes are necessary and from resistance to change. Although organisational planners may announce the need for change and give orders to change, *resistance* to change is still the norm.

6.2 There are several major reasons for resistance to change:

- *Self-interest*: the fear of loss of power, prestige, money or respect that the change may bring.

- *Contradictory assessments*: there are different analyses given of the reasons for change.

- *Misunderstanding* of the reasons for change: its nature and consequences, and the way it is introduced.

- *Low tolerance* of change: individuals differ in their ability to cope with and face the unknown. It can reveal itself in resentment, frustration, anxiety, dissatisfaction with status, fear of incompetence and insecurity at the loss of order.

- *Failure to export the new results from the change*. The sales and marketing sections fail to communicate to the environment or world outside the changes that have occurred.

- *Failure to obtain feedback on the success of the change*, thus not winning the necessary support for further changes and developments.

6.3 The way to overcome this resistance is now thought to be through full involvement, feedback, communication, and rewarding those who contribute to a successful introduction.

7 Ways of encouraging change

7.1 Braddick believes the ways of encouraging change are:

- *Training.* Upgrade the skills and awareness of individuals.

- *Organisation and job redesign.* Increasing the fit between the technical and task requirements of the organisation.

- *Team development.* Get the team to work better together by sharing objectives, the weaknesses and strengths of the group, defining desirable leader behaviour, understanding different roles in the group and awareness of communication.

- *Intergroup problem-solving.* Sharing group perceptions of each other to enable intergroup misunderstandings and conflicts to be handled constructively.

- *Sensing meetings.* To speed up the flow of relevant information, groups of 10 to 12 people come together to discuss the strengths and weaknesses of the company.

- *Organisational restructuring.* The whole organisation can be redesigned to obtain the major benefits of some change.

7.2 Organisational change and development is a complex area where far more research is needed to give any definitive guidelines for action. However, it is certain that all organisations today face situations of change and uncertainty and the key to survival is learning to cope successfully with the demands made by the environment.

Student Activity 3

Think about a change which took place in your organisation while you have been employed, which directly affected your office. Under each of Braddick's headings, write brief notes to consider whether any action was taken, and whether it was effective or ineffective.

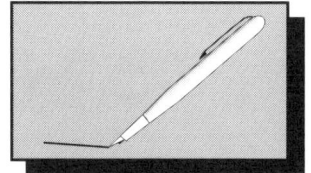

8 Power in organisations

8.1 As part of the corporate planning process, all organisations continuously review their performance, changing their activities and policies when deemed necessary. This in turn means that employees' performances must change in line with these requirements, and a system of rewards and penalties of both a formal and informal nature are established to ensure this compliance. The managerial levels in the organisation are usually the people placed to administer these rewards, and control, to some extent, the activities of others. This is seen by employees as possessing power in the organisation.

8.2 Power in organisations has been the subject of extensive research since the late 19th century when Max Weber carried out research into the topic. He stated that:

> Power is the probability that one actor within a social relationship will be in a position to carry out his own will, despite resistance and regardless of the basis on which this probability rests.

8.3 Although discussions on power in organisations have most often referred to individual power, they can equally well refer to the power of groups or sections of the organisation.

9 Sources and types of power

9.1 Within the organisation there are several sources of power for the individual:

- Administering financial and non-financial rewards;
- Administering punishment or restrictions;
- Physical coercion (although this is unlikely to be a formal means used by the organisation);
- Respect for authority from others;
- Interpersonal skills ('charisma');

- Technical expertise possessed by an individual or section;
- Possession of resources.

9.2   These sources of power come either from the individual (technical or physical), or from the organisation administering rewards.

Types of power

9.3   Different definitions of the types of power exhibited in the organisation are available. One of the best known has been that provided by Etzioni who categorised power into three types:

- *Coercion*: the ability to inflict punishment (using violence if necessary);
- *Remunerative*: the need of subordinates for money to satisfy wants;
- *Normative*: using prestige to gain compliance, like the Accounting Institute's role as professional body.

It is possible to find the three types of power coexisting within one organisation.

9.4   Weber talks of three types of *authority* (authority is, of course, closely linked with power, since it permits the exercise of power without the necessity for coercion):

- *Legal authority.* This rests on a belief in the right of those in high office to give orders and be obeyed, i.e. power *given* by the organisation.
- *Charismatic authority.* This rests on the personal influence of the individual, giving power over devoted followers.
- *Traditional authority.* This is based on a belief in the traditional order of things including respect for those in authority.

9.5   French and Raven have developed Weber's sources of authority into five types of *interpersonal power* as they affect power holders and recipients.

- *Reward*: the ability to give recognition;
- *Coercive*: the ability to punish;
- *Legitimate*: acknowledgement by the recipient of authority;
- *Referent*: the admiration the recipient has for the power holder;
- *Expert:* the special knowledge and expertise held by the power holder.

Student Activity 4

Select in your mind one of your managers. What kind of power in French and Raven's list does that person possess?

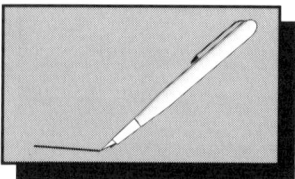

10 Departmental power

10.1 Some departments or sections in the organisation appear to possess more power than others, e.g. they get more resources and benefits. These departments are normally 'line' ones because they can be seen as crucial to the success or failure of the organisation.

10.2 Traditional organisations are hierarchical in structure and power can be seen in vertical terms, descending through the managerial levels by delegation. Within the structure, power can either be retained at the centre or decentralised to the operating units.

11 Organisational structure and power

11.1 Research, especially by the contingency theorists, has further developed work on power and organisational structure.

11.2 In a mechanistic structure Burns and Stalker found power and authority was retained at the top of the management hierarchy, whereas in an organic structure it was delegated to the different task groups.

11.3 Lawrence and Lorsch found in the more stable container industry, power was centred at the top of the organisation, whereas in the plastics industry, which was more dynamic and liable to change, power was divided between six levels of management.

11.4 Mintzberg views organisational behaviour as a power game in which players seek to control the organisation's decisions and actions. Structure is influenced by power and organisational design is not an exact science. The crucial issue is whose preferences and interests are to be served by the organisation and therefore influenced by power.

11.5 Within an organisation there are internal and external coalitions. The internal coalitions can be subdivided into five:

- *Personalised.* Simple structure with all power concentrated at the top in a charismatic leader.

- *Bureaucratic.* Dominated by rules and procedures. An impersonal organisation with weak expertise levels; highly political. (Some parts of banking organisations could perhaps resemble this).

- *Ideological.* Dominated by ideology and the goals of the organisation, not the leadership. Pockets of expert power are dispersed throughout the organisation.

- *Professional.* Dominated by professionals with a high degree of skill, with weak political and ideological systems and decentralised, e.g. an accountant's office with specialists in tax, insolvency, auditing.

- *Politicised.* Power rests with politics. There is a constant round of political games and it weakens alternative forms of power.

11.6   The most powerful coalition will make the key decisions. The external coalitions cover owners, external or non-executive directors, associates, employee associations, e.g. unions and the general public, consumer associations, etc. Their power will determine the influence they have on the organisation.

Internal coalitions	External coalitions
Personalised	Owners
Bureaucratic	Directors
Ideologic	Employee associations
Professional	Unions
Politicised	Public
	Consumer Association

11.7   The Power-Control Model from *Behavioural Sciences for Managers* (Cowling, Staniforth, Bennett, Curran, Lyons) discusses power in terms of decision making constraints.

Figure 19.3 The Power-Control Model for managers

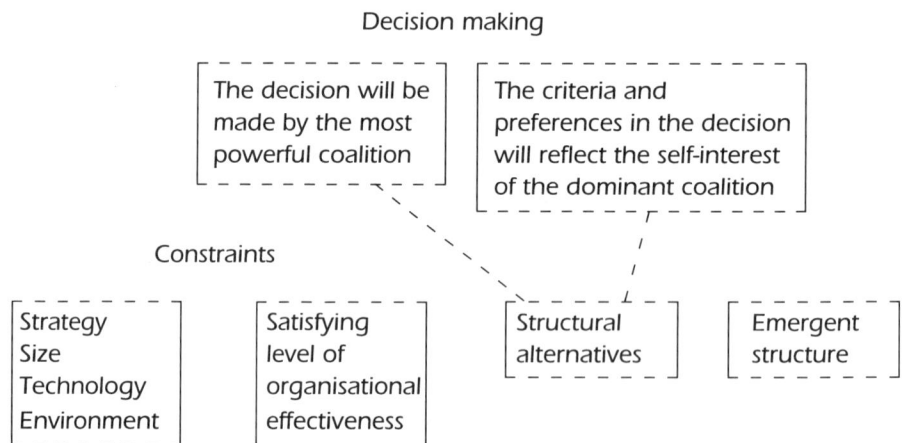

Decision making

The decision will be made by the most powerful coalition

The criteria and preferences in the decision will reflect the self-interest of the dominant coalition

Constraints

Strategy
Size
Technology
Environment

Satisfying level of organisational effectiveness

Structural alternatives

Emergent structure

11.8   Power is a concept which permeates all aspects of an organisation's life as it influences much of the behaviour, decisions and structure. (Further issues relating to power will be explored in Unit 15.)

Summary

Having studied this Unit carefully you should now:

- **understand why organisations have to engage in change;**

- **have an overview of what causes change, and what triggers it;**

- **have considered systems for the management of change;**

- **understand the vital role of power in an organisation;**

- **be able to analyse a variety of sources of power;**

- **see how power relates to structure;**

- **be able to think and write cogently about change and power.**

Self-assessment questions

1. The first stage in planned change theory is:

   (a) Preparation;

   (b) Collecting data;

   (c) Unlearning present behaviour;

   (d) Investigating problems.

2. Who talks about unfreeze-change-refreeze?

   (a) Lawrence;

   (b) Lorsch;

   (c) Newman;

   (d) Lewin.

3. Which is not a criterion to be used in assessing the success of organisational change?

   (a) Profitability;

   (b) Adapting to change;

   (c) Integrating resources effectively;

   (d) Attracting resources.

4. Which of the following is *not* given as a reason for organisations failing in the process of organisational change?

   (a) Failure to transmit relevant information;

   (b) Failure to control the change;

   (c) Failure to sense changes in the environment;

   (d) Failure to make the changes needed.

5. Organisational development is:

   (a) The slow alteration of an organisation over a period of time;

   (b) The expansion and enlargement of a firm's business;

   (c) The conscious process of causing an organisation to change;

   (d) Calling in consultants to advise on organisational design.

6. What are the elements of Leavitt's model of interdependencies in change?

7. What does the unit suggest are the reasons for resistance to change?

8. Name Weber's three kinds of power structure

9. List French and Raven's sources of power

10. Who believed that 'organisational behaviour is a power game in which players seek to control the organisation's decisions and actions'?

Unit 20

Examination Questions

We strongly recommend that you attempt these questions, writing out the answer. Answers are given in the Appendix. Remember that although there is no single correct answer (you may obtain a pass mark through several different answers), there is a core of subject matter that should be in all the answers. Each answer should deal thoroughly with the central subject matter and include all the issues raised by the question (see Introduction for detailed guidance on answering examination questions).

Business Environment

1. In 1991 the chairmen of the UK's major banks were summoned to account to the Chancellor of the Exchequer for their policy with regard to the support of 'small business'. This was an example of the interface between a bank and the complex environment in which it operates.

    (a) Explain the underlying factors which prompted or justified the Chancellor's intervention. (20)

    (b) Explain, in general terms, how the banks defended themselves to the Chancellor and responded to his comments. (5)

2. In recent years banks have become increasingly aware of the difficulties of taking action that satisfies all their stakeholders.

    Among the stakeholders in a large bank are the:

    - Shareholders;
    - Employees (both as individuals and as members of representative bodies);
    - Customers; and
    - State.

    (a) List the bank's main responsibilities to each of the stakeholders mentioned above. (9)

    (b) Choose TWO of the following pairs of the stakeholders. For each pair, identify conflicts between the interests of the two stakeholders and specify steps which can be taken by the bank, its directors and staff to manage these conflicts:

    - Shareholders and employees;
    - Employees and customers;
    - The state and shareholders. (16)

Corporate Appraisal and Strategic Management

3. Developments such as the Single European Market have caused banks to consider whether, and how, they should operate outside the home territory. As a result, a number of banks have made changes to their strategies, structures, staff, and systems.

   Briefly describe the organisational changes made by those banks which have chosen to operate globally. (25)

4. More and more businesses operate on a global basis. Banks are no exception. How well equipped are British banks to succeed in the international arena? (25)

Marketing Strategy and Competition

5. Many banks have taken initiatives to improve the quality of service offered to customers.

   Imagine you are the manager of a branch or office of the bank.

   (a) What steps would you take to initiate a 'customer care' programme? (10)

   (b) How would you ensure improvements in quality of service were maintained? (15)

6. During the late 1980s banks, in common with many organisations from other sectors of the economy, introduced programmes designed to ensure that they offered a high level of customer service.

   In December 1991 the UK's banking ombudsman reported that over the previous 12 months the level of complaints from the bank's customers had risen by approximately 65%.

   Discuss this apparent failure of the banks' Customer Service Programmes, taking into account the circumstances in which the banks operate and their position relative to other sectors. (25)

Organisation Culture and Power

7. Many organisations are described as having a product organisation structure; other organisations are described as having a functional organisation structure.

   (a) Briefly describe the product form of organisation structure. (3)

   (b) Briefly describe the functional form of organisation structure. (3)

   (c) What are the advantages of each of these forms of structure? (8)

   (d) What are the disadvantages of each of these forms of structure? (8)

   (e) Describe briefly how an organisation could be designed in order to combine the benefits of both of these forms of structure. (3)

8. (a) In the context of 'organisation cultures', explain the connection between 'culture' and 'shared values'. (9)

(b) Describe the following categories of culture:

(i) power; (8)

(ii) people. (8)

Information Systems, Budgetary and Financial Systems

9. Commercial organisations are concerned to manage costs.

(a) Identify the reasons why banks, in particular, have made stringent efforts to manage their costs. (5)

(b) Describe those strategic initiatives which banks have taken in the past five to 10 years in order to facilitate cost management. (15)

(c) List the steps which are essential to the management of costs through budgetary control. (5)

Information Technology and the Organisation

10. During his presidential address to The Chartered Institute of Bankers, entitled 'Information Technology in Banking', Sir John Quinton FCIB speculated on the future relationship between banking (as an industry) and Information Technology (IT). Amongst other things he mentioned:

- Price competition
- Infrastructure
- Oversupply
- Product development
- Strategies
- Globalisation
- Segmentation
- People
- Change

Discuss the future relationship between banks and IT. (You may include any, all or none, of the above topics in your answer; you may introduce other topics if you wish.) (25)

Organisational and Management Theory

11. What contributions did FW Taylor make to management thinking?

What contribution did Elton Mayo make to management thinking?

How relevant are their ideas to banking today?

12. Amongst the key activities of a manager within a 'business as usual' environment are:

(a) forecasting;

(b) planning;

(c) organising; and

(d) monitoring and controlling.

Briefly describe each of these activities.

Role of the Manager Today

13. It is generally agreed that delegation is advantageous for the manager who delegates, for the subordinate to whom work is delegated and for the organisation for which they work.

    (a) Describe more specifically the advantages of delegation. (6)

    (b) Some managers are reluctant to delegate. What possible reasons are there for this reluctance? (13)

    (c) What points would you consider in planning the delegation of part of your work? (6)

Managerial/Leadership Style

14. Six weeks ago, Martin Nicholls took over as head of a department of 34 people. Rebecca Stevens is in charge of one of his sections, providing technical information to customers and to other departments.

    The components of Rebecca's job are: technical – 60%; managerial – 30%; departmental – 10%.

    The departmental component comprises work done on behalf of the department as a whole, rather than that directly connected with the section.

    Rebecca has two staff in the section – Trevor Unwin and Ann Wickham. All three are very good workers in the sense that they have the ability to supply accurate and timely technical information.

    A recent internal audit has, however, thrown some doubt on the effectiveness of the section.

    The section has failed to implement a company-wide directive to plan to change its IT software in order to conform to a new organisational standard.

    The internal audit discovered that the section is not entirely well-regarded within the organisation – technical advice is sometimes sought from outside the organisation even though the section's advice is acknowledged to be sound.

    Trevor Unwin's sickness record is poor; he has had 50% more days off sick than the company average. Each day's sickness has been properly certificated and there is no reason to suppose that they are not genuine, but Trevor is known to be looking for other jobs.

    Although the section is well-organised, this tends to be along traditional lines, which means that its approach to an ever-increasing workload is somewhat inflexible.

    When he took over the department, Martin interviewed all members of staff; when questioned, Rebecca held to the view that it was not part of her job to 'sort the section out'.

Rebecca largely ignores the 'departmental' aspect of her job so that she can concentrate on technical matters.

She is not supportive of Martin in front of her own staff and cannot be regarded as a 'team player' as far as her other supervisory colleagues are concerned.

Martin's current feeling about her is that she may have been over-promoted and she is therefore very insecure in her position; however, her financial commitments are such that she would be unwilling to accept any job which required her to take a cut in salary.

Having regard to Rebecca's performance and behaviour, there is probably enough scope to justify invoking the company's disciplinary procedures, but this is likely to be a lengthy process and one which would be difficult within the culture of the company.

Martin has asked for your advice.

(a) Analyse the problem(s) Martin has as manager of Rebecca and her section. (18)

(b) Suggest how Martin should proceed. (7)

Leadership Style and Decisions

15. David Johnston is an experienced manager. He has been asked to take over the management of a project which is regarded as very important by his organisation. The project began eight months ago and is scheduled to finish one year from now. It is imperative that this deadline is met. David's predecessor as Project Manager was Sharon Nolan, who is taking a career break. Sharon worked hard and successfully to build a highly motivated Project Team.

David has reviewed the project file and discovered the following:

- Morale within the team is high.
- The quality of the work which the team has produced is very high.
- The work is one month behind schedule.
- Projections suggest that the project will overrun its budget by 10%.
- There has been no formal meeting with Ann Armstrong, the Project Director, for three months.
- Laura Carter, one of the key workers on the project, has for the past three months been in the habit of arriving late for work on about two mornings a week. No reason for this lateness has been ascertained.
- The team go out together for an extended lunch break every Friday.

(a) Analyse the situation in which David now finds himself, both as the person accountable for the work of the Project and as the leader of the Project Team. (10)

(b) Suggest how David should manage the situation. (15)

Communication in Organisations

16. There are many barriers to communication. What can the sender of a message do to make sure it is clearly conveyed? (15)

   What can the receiver do to grasp the meaning of the message as accurately as possible. (10)

Conduct of Meetings

17. That was the most effective meeting I have ever attended,' said Nigel Weston. 'We achieved everything we wanted. We fully discussed each item on the agenda and yet we finished on time. Sue Field did a marvellous job in the chair, everybody contributed positively, and Steve, as secretary, made sure that the administration was perfect.'

   What preparations and contribution by Sue, Steve and the other participants are likely to have made the meeting so efficient? (25)

Decision Making

18. (a) Define

   (i)   administrative decisions;

   (ii) operational decisions.

   Which of these two types of decision is the most difficult to make and why? (6)

   (b) Outline a structure for decision making. (6)

   (c) Explain the common faults which lead to poor decisions. (5)

   (d) In what circumstances should a manager:

   (i)   share a decision with his subordinates?

   (ii) refer a decision to his boss? (6)

Project Management

19. An increasingly popular method of ensuring co-ordinated effort towards the introduction of change is to apply the techniques of project management.

   (a) List the features (apart from those mentioned in (b) and (c) below) which distinguish project management from 'process' or 'business as usual' management. (5)

   (b) Amongst the key requirements for successful project management are:

   - Clear aims
   - An owner
   - A sponsor
   - A project team
   - A management structure

- A communication system

Briefly describe four of these key requirements. (12)

(c) A further key requirement of the project is the project plan. Briefly outline the process of planning. (8)

Time, Career and Stress Management

20. Some friends of your parents have recently asked you for information and advice about career prospects in bank management. They have a daughter, Kathryn, who is 16 and has recently completed her school examinations; she is now pondering whether to seek employment or to continue with her studies (she probably has the ability to proceed to college or university education).

    What would your advice to Kathryn be on the following:

    (a) Choosing a career generally; (6)

    (b) Career prospects in the banking industry? (7)

    If Kathryn is seriously interested in a career in bank management, what would your advice be on:

    (c) The level at which she should enter banking; (4)

    (d) The subjects she should study; (5)

    (e) The other activities she should pursue to enhance her career prospects? (3)

21. It was getting to the end of Harry Ibbotson's appraisal interview. He was pleased with it so far; his boss, Fiona Glencross, had been complimentary about his year's work.

    'Now for what I see as a problem area', said Fiona. 'Time management – not yours, Harry – but Julie Kent's.' (Julie was one of the supervisors in the department of which Harry was manager.)

    Fiona continued, 'Over the past three months I've noticed that:

    - Julie always seems to have a mound of paper in her in-tray;

    - Despite this she spends most of her time on the telephone or typing away at her electronic mail keyboard;

    - She submitted a report to me the other day – 14 pages of well researched work, very well presented. It must have taken her days to produce the report, but it concerned only a minor part of her job and I'd emphasised to her when briefing her that I only wanted a half-page opinion;

    - She's submitted annual appraisal reports on two of her staff which have been over a week late;

    - I've checked her holiday records – she's not taken a major holiday for 12 months, and did you notice that last week she struggled in every day despite being obviously ill?'

    'I know,' said Harry, 'I've already spoken to her about this. I confirm everything you say. I told her to sort herself out but she's made no effort. She says she has no way of knowing how much work will hit her desk on any one day. Do you think I should reprimand her?'

'Harry, is it you or Julie who's at fault?' said Fiona. 'You selected her, we both agreed she was the right person for the job. Have you identified what's wrong with her time management? Have you given her guidance or support or advice?'

'No,' said Harry.

(a) Explain what aspect of poor time management each of Julie's symptoms suggests. (13)

(b) What suggestions could Harry make to Julie to help her overcome her time management difficulties? (12)

22. Recent research suggests that stress as a cause of ill health is a matter of major concern to commercial organisations; for example, it is reckoned that the annual cost to British industry of stress related illness exceeds £1bn.

How can individuals minimise the risk of their suffering from such illnesses? (25)

Personnel Management

23. In Britain in 1992, the number of school-leavers will be approximately two-thirds of what it was in 1981. This will mean that major employers of school-leavers such as banks may be faced with a recruitment crisis.

(a) What actions can banks take to enhance their chances of recruiting suitable school leavers? (10)

(b) What else can banks do to ensure that they will fulfil their manpower needs after 1992? (15)

Manpower Planning

24. In common with many organisations, some banks have had to develop plans to bring about a reduction in their workforce.

(a) Outline the factors which should be taken into account in formulating such plans. (15)

(b) What should a manager take into account when a member of staff is about to leave the manager's area of responsibility for any reason? (10)

25. ABC bank generally aims to fill most of its key senior positions by promotion from its existing workforce.

(a) List steps which the bank should take to ensure that it has a sufficient pool of individuals capable of filling these positions for the foreseeable future. (12)

(b) List steps an employee of the bank should take in order to enhance the chance of advancing to a senior managerial position. (13)

Recruitment and Selection

26. Recruitment is the process by which human resources are brought into an organisation.

    (a) What are the basic objectives of an organisation's recruitment procedures? (3)

    (b) List the key features of a well-structured recruitment framework. (9)

    (c) Draft an advertisement for a job with which you are familiar, containing all the information you would expect to find in a well-drafted job advertisement. (13)

27. John Dart, your opposite number as supervisor in a neighbouring department, has been given his first opportunity to select staff. He has been given the responsibility for finding a replacement for a clerical worker who recently left, and he asks for your advice on how to tackle the task. Explain to him:

    (a) The process for selection and recruitment of staff. (15)

    (b) The particular features to be considered in interviewing potential recruits. (10)

Motivation and Reward

28. You have been studying the staff turnover rate in a region of the bank where you arc employed as a personnel manager. You notice that the turnover of clerical staff is much higher in the regional head office than it is in a busy branch in a suburb of the same town.

    What are likely to be the key factors which would explain the difference, and what might be done to lower the clerical staff turnover rate in the regional head office?

29. It is time for Pauline Radway's annual performance appraisal and Steve Taylor, her manager, has sought your advice on two problem areas which he has identified as 'motivation' and 'the organisation's systems'.

    The appraisal system has a six-point rating scale;

1 – Excellent	4 – Acceptable
2 – Outstanding	5 – Room for improvement
3 – Competent	6 – Unacceptable

    The annual pay increase is determined, in part, by the overall rating of the employee.

    Pauline was recruited into Steve's section 18 months ago. She took about five months to learn the job and achieve competence. Accordingly, at last year's appraisal she and Steve agreed that an overall rating of '4' was appropriate.

    Over the next six months Pauline worked hard and well and in effect developed her job so she was able to accept more responsibility and expand her range of activities into areas which were both interesting and demanding.

During the last six months the section has been 'rationalised' and the workforce has been reduced (although the workload has increased). Steve is under pressure to contain costs – particularly in the area of salary increases.

Steve now has to rely on Pauline performing her enriched job which, taking the past six months as a whole and given the increased pressure, she performs 'competently' rather than 'outstandingly'; there are aspects of her performance in this enriched job which she could improve.

When Steve met Pauline to agree the time for the appraisal interview she said – only half jokingly – 'I warn you, I'm looking forward to a respectable pay rise this year.'

(a) Outline the problems for Steve that arise from the above scenario:

(i) in relation to Pauline's motivation; (8)

(ii) in relation to the organisation's systems. (8)

(b) Suggest how Steve should proceed. (9)

Training

30. One year ago Keith Lamb came to the large branch of which you are manager. He joined on an internal promotion as the head of a section in a department managed by Gillian Hunter.

Within six months – despite turning in excellent performances – he was actively applying for other jobs within the organisation. Recently he secured a sideways move. He will be replaced by Ian Jones, who is currently working in another branch.

At his exit interview, Keith was sufficiently encouraged by your open approach to say:

'This whole appointment has been a disaster for me from beginning to end. Gillian hardly spoke to me for my first two weeks here; she left me to deduce what I was supposed to do from the files and from questioning staff.

'Later on she did tell me – in no uncertain terms – about my mistakes, but by that time I'd made them!

'I found it very difficult to sort out where the work of my section fitted into the work of the department and I couldn't see any evidence of a plan for how the work flowed between the sections.

'During the year there were only two meetings of section heads and at both of those Gillian simply lectured us about the topics on the agenda.

'Gillian did tell me, at my appraisal, that I'd done a good job, but she didn't give me much of a chance to say anything.

'Generally speaking, I feel that I've been left on my own too much.'

(a) What issues does this raise for you as manager both of the branch and of Gillian Hunter? (17)

(b) Describe how you would proceed. (8)

31. Bruce Collins (who already works for your bank) is about to join your staff. The following is an extract from his most recent appraisal report:

Bruce is meticulous in all he does. Although he learns thoroughly, he does not learn quickly, preferring to observe others in action before committing himself to any new activity. When he does start, he is every effective.

The work with which Bruce will be involved is entirely new to him. None of his colleagues does similar work. Off-the-job training is available; a suitable two-week course will start the week after Bruce joins your staff. The current job-holder, Fiona, from whom Bruce will be taking over, will leave one week after the end of the course; the next opportunity for Bruce to undertake this course will be in six months' time.

Having planned Bruce's induction, you now have to plan his training programme.

(a) What general considerations would you take into account when planning the training programme? (10)

(b) Discuss what other points you would consider in this particular situation. (15)

Job Design and Evaluation

32 (a) What are the advantages and drawbacks of a job evaluation system? (18)

(b) Describe two major types of job evaluation systems. (4)

(c) What steps should an organisation take in order to implement a job evaluation system? (3)

Appraisal, Discipline, Grievance

33. Jim Dixon, who supervises a section under your control, always ensures that his team are completely interchangeable in all the tasks which the section is required to perform. In consequence, his subordinates enjoy working for him, because they get a good training and a variety of work. They also get the opportunity to move on to other parts of the organisation quickly, because they are trained in a variety of tasks and compete well when promotion opportunities are available.

Jim manages in a casual way which might suggest a lack of discipline to the outsider. In fact, his staff achieve results because they enjoy the work and the atmosphere which Jim generates.

From Jim's point of view this means that he is constantly losing people, so that training is a never-ending task. Furthermore, he does not appear to be quite so productive as some of his colleagues, because he usually has at least one person under training in the section.

Charles Graves, another section head, trains newcomers to undertake two tasks at most. He is a strict disciplinarian and demands high output from his staff. He is respected as demanding but fair. He does not lose many staff on internal promotion, but after a time a number of staff leave the bank for another career. He tends to get a higher sickness rate than other groups but his output figures are maintained by his pressure on staff.

At the last appraisal review Charles was rated more highly than Jim.

What issues does this case raise?

Groups

34. You have recently been appointed to supervise a group of 10 people who have to co-operate to achieve the goals of their section. You have found disquieting evidence that all is not well. The output of the section is not as high as you feel it should be. Although overtime is regularly worked, there are substantial backlogs and targets are missed. Absenteeism in this section is higher than that of any other section. The same people seem to be absent regularly and often produce poor excuses or none at all. People fall out over trivial issues and the lack of co-operation impairs efficiency. You feel a general air of lethargy, if not hostility. What do you propose to do about it? How will you know when you are succeeding?

35. You have been appointed to supervise a section of your department. What are the factors you would consider to get your section to work effectively as a team?

Appendix

Answers to Student Activities and Self-Assessment Questions

Unit 1

Student activities

1. As you will see as this unit continues, among other things your definition should have suggested that organisations contain people, who are structured to co-operate, to pursue certain goals or objectives: working together to do something.

2. You might have mentioned the company which made your carpet, the manufacturers of soap and toothpaste, deodorant, razor, after-shave, the electricity company for your light, the water company, the clothes and shoe manufacturers, the makers of cereal, the baker, the coffee company, the publishers of your newspaper and the post office (to name but 15!), and many others.

3. You could have said ergonomics, operational research, piece-work systems, performance-related pay, work-study, or just-in-time warehousing systems, stock control and the like.

Self-assessment questions

1. Organisations have social mechanisms so that people can co-operate; they have aims, goals, targets or purposes that they try to achieve; and they have structure and hierarchy - are organised, in fact.

2. The bus-queue and the Wimbledon crowd lack the element of structure and hierarchy, and would not normally be regarded as organisations.

3. Your family co-operates (sometimes); its function is to protect and develop its individuals; there is a structure, usually in terms of father-mother-sibling relationships.

4. The church and other religious organisations; armies and local militias; farming co-operatives; governments and local authorities; theatres companies; small trading companies, and so on.

5. Classical, Human Relations, and Systems.

6. Financial organisations, for example, have stationery suppliers, deal with the central bank such as the Bank of England, have specific large and small corporate customers, deal with the Chartered Institute of Bankers and the banking press, and have some quite proper agreements with their competitors (via the Clearing House, for instance).

7. Because tools are made by people to perform tasks which would not be possible without them.

8. Because profit is only one of the purposes of any organisation, and because there are many organisations which have no intention of making profit at all.

9. Interpersonal, Informational, Decision.

10. Have you ever noticed any two departments not co-operating, because of lack of communication or because of politics? Have you seen the hierarchy not functioning properly, where there is confusion about whose orders we are supposed to obey? Have you ever seen people confused or unclear about aims, targets or objectives, or notice people doing things which clearly does the organisation no good? Any such examples would have answered this question satisfactorily.

Unit 2

Student activities

2. Conservatives encourage free enterprise and market forces to determine the price, even the survival, of anything, including formerly state-owned enterprises which they have been eager to privatise, i.e. place in the hands of private shareholders. They claim to want to reduce taxes, and are in favour of private health-care and education.

   Labour also encourage free enterprise, but support the idea of social ownership, which means governmental (part) ownership of shares in organisations. They are in favour of simultaneous strong welfare arrangements, such as free health-care and education. They believe in fair taxation, bearing particularly on high earners, to fund social care.

3. You will realise that the positions suggested are in fact extremes, with a range of positions in between. Most organisations, in western commercial society, have regard for the profits of their shareholders but strongly believe that they make an important social contribution both directly and indirectly. Even so-called 'ethical' organisations wishing to make a high level of social contribution still have to give a return to their shareholders/stakeholders sufficient to keep them investing.

4. Remembering that serving the customer, paying the staff, paying local and national taxes are not 'socially responsible' but simply required, your list should not include these.

   You will be seeking such items as honestly telling *customers* when they have been over-paying fees, or have money in a less-lucrative account than is available to them; providing time out for *staff* to engage in school governorships or charitable or important sporting events; sending staff into volunteer activities to help regional charities or local events; and providing facilities for collection for, or making substantial donations to, national charitable appeals, or the like.

Self-assessment questions

1. The traditional/classical view, as opposed to the accountability/mutual shareholder view.

2. The classical viewpoint.

3. • Competitive recruitment for school-leavers (increased salaries, perks, etc).

   • More use of part-time employees.

   • More use of returning female employees after a break.

   • More automation for mundane jobs.

4. Banks have to consider stakeholder responsibilities in the areas of:

   (a) Shareholders:

   - Fair return on investment;
   - Honesty by management.

   (b) Consumers:

   - A good and reliable service;
   - Politeness.

   (c) Suppliers:

   - Adequate notice of requirements for goods and any changes; prompt payment within terms.

   (d) Employees:

   - Working conditions;
   - Health and safety;
   - Job interest;
   - Information disclosure.

   (e) Community:

   - Economic efficiency;
   - Good commercial practices.

5. You might have given such examples as the Co-op Bank's advertising about ethical organisations, or Midland's National Trust card, or NatWest's young saver's scheme linked with animal welfare; then of recycling schemes, restrictions on smoking, vegetarian provision in canteens and so on.

6. Ethical, political (including legal), economic, social, technological and competition.

7. The responsibility of business to all those with whom they come into contact, customers, shareholders, employees, suppliers, the community.

8. The environment is constantly changing and exerting influences on business. The skill of management lies in taking advantages of the beneficial factors and counteracting the harmful ones.

9. In its mission statement, at least; then in pledges to customers, in the annual report, and in some staff reports.

10. Your examples are probably accurate: but you might, for example, have suggested such ethical systems as depend on the honesty of staff to survive, like handling personal expenses; economic factors like how frequently the organisation can afford to re-decorate your office; and technological factors like how up-to-date your IT facilities are.

Unit 3

Student activities

1. At some point in your studies you will find such a summary useful. The objectives should be objectively *measurable*; and they should state clearly *what* should be achieved, *how* it is to be achieved, *who* is supposed to contribute, and, most importantly, by *when*. Check yours to see if they comply with this.

2. Since this exercise is so dependent on *current* circumstances, and on inter-organisational differences, we cannot give you feedback. Trust your judgement; and when you have time, expand the analysis to a full SWOT.

3. Corporate strategy and planning can be located in any of the places suggested in the question; and it can sometimes be hard for ordinary members of staff to find out where it is done, never mind how, or what the plans are: they are obviously highly confidential and very useful to competitors. You comments on the communication of corporate plans to individual offices should have taken account of that.

4. This unit has suggested these stages:

> Review – Objectives – External appraisal – Summary – Modified objectives – Corporate strategy – Internal activities – Evaluation ...

but provided that you have thought through, developed and can defend the logic of a similar list, there is no absolutely correct rigid ordering of stages in well-developed organisations.

Self-assessment questions

1. d. But the others, in ascending order, are closely influenced by it.

2. b.

3. d.

4. In corporate analysis an *opportunity* is not an opening the organisation can spot to better itself, but *something happening in the organisation's environment which is favourable to the organisation.*

5. A *threat* is not what someone is about to do to harm the organisation, but *something happening in the organisation's environment which is unfavourable to the organisation.*

6. A *strength* is not just a strong feature, but *something within the control of the organisation which gives it an advantage over competitors.*

7. A *weakness* is not just a weak feature, but *something within the control of the organisation which gives competitors an advantage over it.*

8. b. (Not planning, which is arranging to *deal* with them.)

9. All of these.

10. Any three from (and preferably all of!):
    - Is the strategy clear – in words and practice?
    - Does it exploit opportunities?
    - Is it consistent with competences and resources?
    - Is it internally consistent?
    - Is the level of associated risk acceptable?

Unit 4

Student activities

1. It is unlikely that you will have found businesses unrelated to the business of finance; and in a tightly competitive industry, most of your organisation's subsidiaries will probably be largely successful. Where the

profit is not outstanding, the association is probably preserved on the grounds of complete customer service.

4. It is probable that you were able to outline the success in terms of how your customers are now treated, most tangibly in new systems such as telephone response, queuing systems, better statement design, the rise in distance banking. Financial results or increased business figures are more difficult to demonstrate: but unless there is some increase in business or defence against competitors, what was the purpose of the programme in the first place?

Self-assessment questions

1. c.
2. 'Stick to the knitting'.
3. The Second Banking Co-ordinating Directive.
4. Consumer credit and charge cards.
5. IMRO   Investment Managers Regulatory Organisation

    LAUTRO Life Assurance and Unit Trust Regulatory Organisation

    SIB   Securities Investment Board
6. Their government, and other banks.
7. CAMEL stands for
   - Capital Adequacy;
   - Asset Quality;
   - Management Ability;
   - Earnings Level;
   - Liquidity Level.
8. Any three from those listed in paragraph 6.2.
9. d.
10. b.

Unit 5

Students activities

1. Do remember the technical definitions given above before you worry about your answer; and remember, that you are describing yourself as you see yourself. Ask yourself where others would put you. Where do your colleagues at work go?

2. You might have come up with a variety of phrases, which could remind you with some amusement or chagrin of your youth! But recall that we act and interact in all of these states in our mature life, based on how we were 'trained' as children.

3. This quiz is based on one designed by Richard Christie, a New York psychologist. The score reveals whether you sympathise with and motivate people through your own behaviour or whether you manipulate people using them for your own ends.

Add the numbers you have circled for A, B, C, D, E, F, G. For the other questions reverse the numbers you have circled; that is, if you have circled 5 score 1, if you have circled 1 score 5, etc. Add the total score: the average is 25. If you have scored more than this, then you are more manipulative than the norm, etc.

4. If you are understanding Maslow, then your answer will have suggested such things as *pay* to satisfy *physiological* needs; a *contract* for *security*: *working in groups* to satisfy the *social* needs; *responsibility* for *ego*; and a *satisfying job for self-actualisation.*

5. You should have noted in answer to the first question that Hygiene factors are those which, if operating, reduce dissatisfaction and negative feelings but do not make a positive contribution to well-being, such as good company policies and nice working conditions. As to motivators, if operating they do not remove dissatisfaction, but add positive satisfaction, such as real interest in the job, or learning on the job, or being recognised for achievement.

Rises in wages are a complex set of symbols as well as just the money. If it is an across-the-board rise, applicable to all, then it usually removes the dissatisfaction of falling behind inflation, and is a hygiene factor. If it is a merit rise, it is recognition for achievement, and a motivator.

Self-assessment questions

1. Introvert-extrovert, and stable-unstable

2. There is one in the text, in paragraph 2.1. You may have come across others in your studies. You would be well advised to learn one and be able to reproduce it.

3. d.

4. c.

5. a.

6. b.

7. Your diagram should have looked like this, with examples from your own experience included:

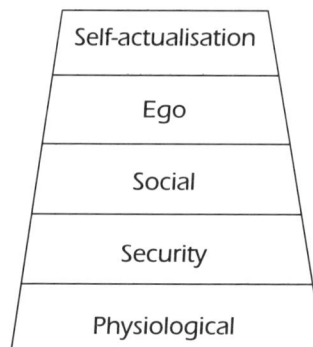

8. See Fig. 5.2 in paragraph 5.3.

9. The major problem with the expectancy model is its complexity, because of the number of variables, and because of the number of various 'real-life' elements which operate between the components of the model.

10. Alienated, Calculated, Moral.

Unit 6

Student activities

2. It is useful to plan answers to this kind of question in diagram form, eg:

	Advantage	Disadvantage
Organisation	No informal resistance when group is in favour of what is formally required	Informal resistance when group is not in favour of what is formally required
Individual	Protection when formal requirements infringe personal rights	difficulty when formal requirements counter loyalty to informal group norms

3. Unless your group is an improbable structure of eight people all of whom have different inclinations, you will find that some:

   ● Members will be taking more than one role; and

   ● Some roles may be missing.

   If Belbin is right, the group will work effectively in the ways implied by the presence of the role-taker, and ineffectively where the role is not taken.

4. First, it might just not have gone through the stages, or not in the order proclaimed. However, if it did then you might have observed such things as, at *form*, jockeying for position or interpersonal suspicion; at *storm* a loss of confidence in each other, or sarcasm behind people's backs, or a temporary withdrawal; at *norm* a possibly reluctant buckling down as deadlines approach; and at *perform* a powerful drive to get things done in time.

5. What you might have come up with cannot be foreseen. But for example, transfer of conflicting parties out of the situation might have occurred to you, or the brute force of authority: 'you will stop this or you will be punished', or banging heads together, or the like.

Self-assessment questions

1. b.

2. c.

3. d.

4. b.

5. The text suggests:

   ● Withdrawal of communication;

   ● Direct communication about norms;

   ● Social pressures as far as isolation.

6. They can, among other things:

   ● Have objectives and norms which are in conflict with the organisation;

   ● Provide resistance to change;

   ● Cause distress based on conflict within the individual;

   ● Provide a grapevine which can counter organisational communication.

7. The desire to join and remain a member of a group results from the individual's weighing up the benefits and the costs.

8. The stages are:
   - Forming;
   - Storming;
   - Norming;
   - Performing.

9. c.

10. b.

Unit 7

Student activities

3. Most credit scoring systems are carefully worked out in terms of the statistical likelihood that the 'right' answers will minimise loss by bad debt. Some of the 'right answers' seem a little odd, but they largely work well. They help the work of the lender in saving time and labour, speeding the decision process; improving it, and avoiding human error and bad intuitive judgement. Such systems, however, eliminate sensible human judgement, seem irritatingly mechanical to customers (especially if refused a loan!) and do not cover every lending situation.

4. You may have selected the system operated by your own bank, or one of which you are a customer, or just discovered the features of a system from advertising (and by the way, the customer advertising material would be the best source of information to perform this activity).

   The main features might be a:
   - Personal number;
   - Security code;
   - Choice of operator or push-button access;
   - Services including balance enquiry, funds transfer, standing orders, statement request, stopping cheques, reporting loss, paying bills, ordering chequebooks etc.
   - Long hours of availability, including weekends.

Self-assessment questions

1. Management Information System. There is a definition, by Kelly, in paragraph 1.1 of this unit.

2. You could have cited:
   - Timing;
   - Appropriateness/accessibility;
   - Accuracy;
   - Detail;
   - Frequency;
   - Relevance;
   - Intelligibility;

- Flexibility;
- User-friendliness.

3. Strategic, tactical/managerial, operational

4. Among others:
   - Relevant;
   - Measurable;
   - Specific;
   - Attainable.

5. Score-keeping, attention-directing, decision-making.

6. d.

7. A computer based record keeping system equivalent to a manual card-index system.

8. Electronic Funds Transfer at Point of Sale

9. Clearing House Automated Payment System

10. Security of information; but you might also have proposed fear of new technology.

Unit 8

Student activities

1. You may have seen an advertisement designed and placed by the department; you will have been recruited, interviewed, tested by them; they will have contributed to your induction; they are involved with wage payments, grievance, discipline; your job-description and changes in it are implemented by the department; in most cases training and development come under personnel/HRM functions; your career path is influenced, including transfer and promotion; there may be retirement preparation, and your pension is administered by them.

2. You may find that there is a *Recruitment* section; *Staffing* or *Operations*, which deals with making sure that all jobs are filled and operating, including *Job Analysis*; a *Training* section; *Salaries and Wages*, possibly including a *Pensions* section; an *Employee Relations* section; possibly other such groups. *Manpower* or *Human Resource Planning* may also come into this department, or not, as we shall see later in this Unit.

4. As with many other business ratios, figures are rarely good or bad in themselves, except in comparison with some other figure. Even if they can be described as 'extreme', that is comparing them with some idea of 'normal'. Labour is only unstable if the stability index in one area is greater than in another; absenteeism is only a problem if your section is 'better' or 'worse' than somewhere else, because *some* level of absenteeism is 'normal', and is to be expected because of sickness.

Self-assessment questions

1. All of these

2. c.

3. c.

4. It is what your Personnel Department say it is; but traditionally it has been 65 for men, 60 for women.

5. Because of equal opportunity and EU legislation, there is increasingly an approach towards equalisation, which may not yet have arrived in your organisation.

6. d.

7. c. This is a problem of *demand*.

8. c.

9. Numbers leaving in one year *divided by* number of employees at the start of the year *times* 100.

10. The exit interview.

Unit 9

Student activities

1. First, what is 'typical' depends on the level at which you were recruited: and the further up the hierarchy, the more flexible and variable the process. Then, the quality of the process depends on its design but also its performance: if you commented critically it could have been because the steps were not well carried out – a vague advertisement, an ambiguous application form, a poor interview. Bear in mind that you should be able to know what is good management, and observe where it occurs and where it falls short in practice!

3. (a) Good recruiters try to improve and update their form, and yours may be an excellent tool for its purpose. But because it may cover more than one starting function, there may be some irrelevant questions. Not everyone interprets words in the same way so there may be some questions which do not seem meaningful. And sometimes there are open questions on future ambitions or personal achievements which will be answered well only by people of special calibre.

   (b) As to the interview, while good recruiters are well trained, you may nevertheless have encountered an off-hand attitude, too many closed questions, irrelevant content, a failure to listen to the answers or spot a minor 'con-trick', an unprofessional close. Still, you were selected!

4. The *design* should have covered at least the majority of opportunities in which you would have to operate with the skill, with at least some of the more unusual possibilities. The *conduct* should have been by expert people who have communication and teaching skills, and paced so that you were able to learn step by step. The *timing* should have been reasonably convenient, when you needed the training, were at a stage when you could absorb it, and just before you were required to operate with it.

6. You will find that courses may not be a major component in terms of the percentage of time. You cannot learn to be a competent manager just by sitting in a classroom. It is like an apprenticeship: you learn by going all the way round Kolb's cycle, which you might now like to re-examine in the unit above, and compare with the activities in your organisation's Management Development Programme.

Self-assessment questions

1. d.

2. a.

3. c.

4. d.

5. c.

6. Rodger's seven points are:

   - Physical make-up;
   - Attainments;
   - General Intelligence;
   - Special Aptitudes;
   - Interests;
   - Disposition;
   - Circumstances.

7. Munro-Fraser's five points are:

   - Impact on people;
   - Qualifications;
   - Abilities;
   - Motivation;
   - Adjustment.

8. The framework is:

   - Objectives;
   - Introduction;
   - Investigation;
   - Listen;
   - Close.

9. Standard, reliable and valid, as defined in the unit.

10. Coaching, action learning, job rotation.

Unit 10

Student activities

1. Whether or not the changes are so labelled, jobs often change by job rotation, job enlargement or job enrichment. If well managed the changes will be:

   - Timed when on the one hand the jobholder is stagnating a little or on the other needs positive personal development;
   - Conducted with care, briefing and training, followed by monitoring and supervision;
   - Effective if they give the job a new lease of life or help the job-holder better fulfil the organisation's objectives.

3. If you work for a UK clearing bank, or another sophisticated financial

organisation, you will find that there is indeed overlap between grades, so that people at the top of a lower grade can be rewarded for working well even though not yet ready for promotion to a higher one.

4. Your definition is no doubt pretty accurate; but it should contain such elements as a:

   ● Basic rate of pay above which performance related pay is applied;

   ● Level of performance above which performance related pay is applied;

   ● Period over which the performance which is rewarded;

   ● Rules which define other conditions under which the extra pay is applied;

   ● Defined percentage of salary or sum for the performance related pay.

Self-assessment questions

1. c.

2. a.

3. a.

4. d.

5. a.

6. The Unit suggests these possible aims, to:

   ● Provide a rank-order of the jobs in the organisation;

   ● Ensure objectivity in judging the value of jobs;

   ● Provide a continuing basis for evaluating those jobs.

7. Job ranking, job classification, points rating and factor comparison.

8. At the most junior levels in an organisation, with 'birthday' raises.

9. Less opportunity for promotion, fewer levels of management, need to encourage individual productivity.

10. You could have cited:

    ● Rewards related to effort;

    ● Less need to promote;

    ● Can be integrated with objectives;

    ● Easy to calculate;

    ● Can be used for corrective incentive;

    ● Increased productivity can fund it.

Unit 11

Student activities

1. Most systems are reasonably sophisticated and serve all the purposes noted in the unit. This applies, however, only if the system is well-designed and it is applied well by the staff who use it. You may like to write a few notes in addition on how well or poorly your appraisal system is actually applied to you.

4. It is by taking such procedures carefully through imagined – or real – cases that you can memorise, relay and criticise them and their application.

In your case, did you honestly consider whether the procedures would be known, sensitively applied, steps omitted for convenience or from ignorance, and did you level criticism at the system or its application? If judiciously done and with good argument, you are entitled to do, and should have done so: congratulate yourself if you did!

5. Questions are:

    ● Selection procedure: how effective is it and should it be changed in the light of this problem?

    ● Do the interviewees need to change their technique to solve this problem?

    ● What is the position for the employee: should he have mentioned his condition or is it up to the employer to find out?

    ● What are the disciplinary rules for this situation?

    ● Should the medical conditions of employment be revised in the light of this experience?

    ● Does it matter when the organisation as gained a first-class employee?

    ● Implications for pension and sick pay.

    Courses of action:

    ● Dismiss the employee for lying;

    ● Take no action;

    ● Revise selection procedure.

6   It will come as no surprise if there are greater proportions of women in clerical positions than in managerial positions, for all the reasons discussed in the unit, and mainly because of family-based or historical male-attitude-based reasons. Please note that if your conclusions contained any reference to differing abilities in managerial terms, you would be mistaken, and you certainly would gain little credit for that in examinations.

Self-assessment questions

1. b.

2. c.

3. a.

4. They help in:

    ● Manpower planning;

    ● Career development;

    ● Succession plans;

    ● Training;

    ● Motivation.

5. They help in:

    ● Feedback on performance;

    ● Assessment of future potential;

    ● Assessing the need for training;

    ● Motivation.

6. Advisory Conciliation and Arbitration Service.

7. Any three from:

- Incapable of performing job, or not qualified;
- Misconduct;
- Redundancy;
- Continuing employment breaks the law;
- Other substantial, justified reason.

8. Any three from these, but get the dates right!

- Equal Pay Act, 1970;
- Sex Discrimination Act 1976;
- Equal Pay Amendment Act 1983;
- Employment Act 1989.

9. a.

10 The employer's responsibilities are to:

- Ensure the health, safety and welfare of all employees;
- Provide information, training and supervision;
- Issue a policy statement;
- Consult the trades unions;
- Establish safety committees.

Unit 12

Student activities

1. You may have noted the selection of people for jobs on the basis of their ability; people being trained progressively and steadily to the optimum of their ability; jobs being broken down into small parts; work-study or O&M; the pursuit of efficiency and productivity as a major aim, and the like.

3. If, for example, you work in a branch of a bank, you might have cited, as *input*, deposit funds; as *conversion*, the electronic recording of those funds; as *output*, the transfer to a head-office account; the *feedback* would be a computer message back from Head Office recording the transfer; environmental influences might be the *ethical* responsibility you have not to steal the customer's money or to give a lower rate than advertised, the *technology* of funds transfer, the *legal* obligation not to disclose details of the customer's accounts, and so on.

4. Your examples should be in the nature of the following:

- *Figurehead*: when representing the organisation at an annual dinner of a local charity.
- *Leader*: when addressing the staff about the need for more productivity next year.
- *Liaison*: when on a committee of local managers to discuss long-term plans.
- *Monitor*: when perusing the professional press for useful information.
- *Disseminator*: when telling a deputy about what was important in the press.

- *Spokesperson*: when writing to the press to correct false information.
- *Entrepreneur*: when taking the initiative in a selling scheme for a new product.
- *Disturbance Handler*: when settling a row between two unruly staff members.
- *Resource Allocator*: when deciding who will do what in a new project.
- *Negotiator*: when getting Head Office to allocate more funds for a promotion.

Self-assessment questions

1. b.
2. a.
3. c.
4. d.
5. d.
6. Elton Mayo, at the Western Electrical Company in Ohio.
7. Inputs, conversions, outputs, feedback, the environment.
8   The problems are:
    - Causality: does the structure affect performance or vice-versa?
    - Imprecise measurement of results;
    - Exceptions: monopolies, for example, can ignore environment;
    - Different contingencies unpredictably affect different organisations.
9. Mintzberg's roles are:
    - Interpersonal:
        o Figurehead
        o Leader
        o Liaison
    - Informational:
        o Monitor
        o Disseminator
        o Spokesperson
    - Decisional:
        o Entrepreneur
        o Disturbance handler
        o Resource allocator
        o Negotiator.
10. Demands, constraints, choices.

Unit 13

Student activities

1. You may have found that your leaders have a lot in common: a football captain and a party-leader can both have a magnetic air of authority; the

athletics coach you thought of could be as enterprising as the entrepreneur; the politician you named could be as intelligent as the managing director. On the other hand, one might be introvert, one extrovert; one could be bold, one cautious; one could be sunny in character, one morose. No research has really established what *kind* of a person a leader must be.

2. You might have been able to locate your manager, and if you responded well to the instruction 'critically evaluate' you will have looked at the advantages and the disadvantages of the style, to the organisation and to the staff. You should also have noted, if your manager is at least reasonably good at the job, that the style *does* alter when the circumstances demand. For example, even the most permissive manager should not call for participative discussion if a fire suddenly breaks out in the office!

3. What good management style 'depends on' is another way of asking what it is contingent on. In any such essay, therefore, you would lay out and explain Fiedler's model, or (or preferably *and*) Hersey and Blanchard's model, and explain that it could depend on leader-member relationship, power and task structure, or on the need for directive or supportive behaviour according to the readiness of the subordinate to be independent in the task.

4. ● Under *task* you could have written, among other such actions:
   ○ set clearly defined targets
   ○ set out a timetable
   ○ carefully and clearly brief the group
   ○ provide necessary resources
   ○ engage in timely controls;
   ● Under *team* you could have written:
   ○ have regular meetings
   ○ praise the achievements of the group
   ○ resolve conflict in the group
   ○ apply firm and fair discipline
   ○ pitch in and help occasionally;
   ● Under *individual* you could have written:
   ○ allocate tasks the individual will like
   ○ give training for the task
   ○ praise the individual for achievement
   ○ give personal responsibility for tasks
   ○ listen to grievances, suggestions, problems.

Self-assessment questions

1. d.

2. c.

3. a.

4. Authoritarian, democratic, *laissez-faire*.

5. Use of authority by manager, degree of freedom for subordinates.

6. Concern for people; concern for production.

7. Tells, sells, consults, joins.

8. Structure of task, postion of power, group-leader relations, LPC score.

9. Directing, supporting, coaching and delegating.

10. Task, team and individual.

Unit 14

Student activities

1. The message may have been well or badly:

   - *Conceived*, in that you may or may not have needed to have the information;

   - *Encoded* in that you may or may not have understood it;

   - *Sent* in that you may or may not have received it in time, for example;

   - *Received* in that you may or may not have had it circulated effectively;

   - *Decoded* in that you may or may not have understood it correctly;

   - *Feedback* is in fact unlikely: response to a circular is not usually easy.

2. *Attention* is not too difficult, since the staff are assembled to hear you and they are junior staff! Still, it is end of day, and you may want to make an early promise of ways of furthering their career and doing interesting work.

   Understanding can be checked by getting members of the audience to relay back to you some of the more complex points, and by asking for questions as you go as well as at the end.

   Acceptance is difficult at this stage, though calling for volunteers or giving responsibility for parts of the scheme will ensure that at least some are committed to the plans in advance.

   Action will result in any case, but it would be a good idea to plan something into the scheme which starts immediately the following day so that the scheme is under way; and immediate feedback to you should be part of the required action.

3. Your examples may have looked like these:

   You may, for example, have cited an *introvert* who may be left out of communications about charity events because they would be believed to be reluctant to appear in public.

   Because someone has a strong regional accent they might be assumed to be tough, when in fact they could be very sensitive, for example to criticism.

   A person who is technically expert and therefore excellent at their very specific job may have been assumed to be able to take management responsibility, or to be able to handle quite different skills: this might follow, but it might not.

   Branch/retail staff have ideas about how Head Office people are, and vice-versa: selling staff stereotype back-room people. This could have affected the way they talked to each other, at least initially, in your experience.

   Lots of examples on non-verbal communication: but the point is best illustrated by thinking of a possible contrast between talking to people on the telephone, where no non-verbal clues are available, and thereafter meeting them face-to-face.

4. All sorts of things contribute to poor meetings, but most of them will be explained by faults in not complying with all the suggestions in the section above. Check whether the problems in your meeting were covered.

Self-assessment questions

1. d.

2. a.

3. a.

4. Your diagram should have contained all of these:
   - Conception of message.
   - Encode.
   - Send via media, noise.
   - Receive.
   - Decode.
   - Feedback.

5. All members communicate with all others.

6. The four stages are:
   - Attention.
   - Understanding.
   - Acceptance.
   - Action.

7. Because the world is complex, and we have to classify information into handy compartments, at least as an initial way of coping with so much of it.

8. d.

9. c.

10. A chairperson should, among other things:
    - Prepare agenda.
    - Circulate minutes.
    - Arrange facilities.
    - Run the meeting.
    - Outline business.
    - Allow people to speak.
    - Control the time of speaking.
    - Summarise contributions.
    - Move the meeting on.
    - Establish final conclusions
    - Check the minutes.

Unit 15

Student activities

1. Notice in particular the second of the service quality definitions in the unit. If you look at your consideration of service quality, did it mention the concept of *exceeding* the customer's requirements?

2. If the system is really well designed, not only will they comply with the measuring techniques in the unit, but there will be numerical or tangible measures too: 'How many?', 'How much?' 'To what measurable extent?'.

4. In the 1990s major customer care or quality programmes significantly improved the customer experience. But vigilance and renewed enthusiasm is required, and you may have found that while most service quality remains high, and many improvements are irreversibly established, some may have slipped or may require a fresh injection of managerial energy.

Self-assessment questions

1. c.

2. Total Quality Management.

3. a b

4. b

5. A standard of quality which UK companies can comply with by a programme of standard improvements and by submitting to rigorous inspection.

6. Any part of the corporate body which receives a service from any other part of the corporate body.

7. Radically changing corporate structure, processes, products to meet customer needs and demands.

8. A group of people, usually from mixed hierarchical levels in a section of an organisation, formed to make suggestions as to improving service quality in their section.

Unit 16

Student activities

2. You will have analysed the risk in terms of the security of your present employment and the advantages of the new job.

   The risk can be quantified in terms of the difference in salary times the probability that you will get the new job, plus any probability that you might lose your own income if your employer gets wind of your wanting to leave.

   Objective data has to do with the nature of your present and the new job, the number of people likely to apply, the possibility of relocation and so on.

   The decision may affect others, such as members of your family, the need for training or education, changes in the effect on your lifestyle.

   All of this will take you back to adjust what you considered under 'security' and 'advantages' above.

3. Your decision, of course! But it could go:

- Quality requirement: YES The office must look good.
- Sufficient information: NO   You don't know what staff think.
- Problem structured: YES Just 'decorate the office'.
- Acceptance important: YES Otherwise you lower morale.
- Acceptance certain: NO   They might protest to Head Office.
- Goals shared: YES You all want to be comfortable at work.
- Conflict likely: YES Opinions will always vary.

The result of which is GII and a completely participative decision, which seems entirely reasonable! But you might have taken another route, because judgements differ.

4. Keep these notes handy as you read the rest of the unit, and adjust and develop them for possible future examination use as you go along.

Self-assessment questions

1. c.
2. d.
3. b.
4.
   - Personality
   - Division of labour
   - Consultation
   - Power
   - Organisational hierarchy
   - Risk
   - Training
   - Grapevine

5. The Unit suggests these forms of risk.
   - Country
   - Settlement
   - Product
   - Industry
   - Portfolio
   - Credit

6. Vroom & Yetton's five styles:
   - AI: make the decision yourself.
   - AII: obtain information, then make the decision yourself.
   - CI: see staff individually, hear ideas, make the decision yourself.
   - CII: get staff together, hear ideas, make the decision yourself.
   - GII: co-ordinate ideas, implement group decision

7. The problems might be that the decision maker:
   - Excessively avoids risk.
   - Hesitates until too late.
   - Makes hasty decision instead of taking available time.

8. c.
9. b.
10.
    - Breaks down programme into constituent parts.
    - Helps identify priorities.

- Represents a plan of action.
- Highlights difficulties if deviations from plan of action occur.

Unit 17

Student activities

1. In most organisations, the *challenge* of the job is only marginally under the employee's control, though you can ask for project work, especially if you suggest a realistic but challenging project for yourself.

   You can only be as good as you can be: realistically, to be *outstanding* depends on the 'competition', some born qualities, some luck, and the opportunity.

   You can actively *manage* your own career to the extent that you volunteer for tasks, jobs, moves, training and the like: and you can plan and time your anticipated items of advancement or moves.

   Choosing a *mentor* seems reasonable provided that your attentions are welcomed! But use of a mentor has to be either officially sanctioned, accepted by the mentor, or very discreet; and it must be well-judged not to be excessive.

   Taking *training* opportunities, as offered, is entirely within your control.

4. You might have chosen one of a number of techniques, many of them covered in the unit. But any technique should:
   - Save the time of the manager;
   - Not impinge negatively on innocent others;
   - Be under the control of the manager;
   - Be flexible enough to allow for enforced changes in plan.

Self-assessment questions

1. They are:
   - Challenging job;
   - Be outstanding;
   - Manage your career;
   - Seek out a mentor;
   - Take training opportunities.
2. c.
3. b.
4. c.
5. d.
6. In excess of 70–80 hours.
7. You could have named exercise, meditation, hobbies, diet.
8. b.
9. They are:
   - Deal with;
   - Delegate;

- Diarise;
- Dump.

10. The three features are:

- Integrate long term goals and short term priorities;
- Prioritise from vital to trivial;
- Establish record systems.

Unit 18

Student activities

2. If you are justifying the number you will have based your answer on the correct amount of complexity of the work and/or the relationships and the available time of the manager to supervise the work. If it is too large, similarly, the result will be poor or limited supervision and overload at managerial levels, and consequent problems of lack of (or poor) supervision among subordinates. If it could be expanded, then there are problems associated with managers not having enough to do in the line of supervision, and possibly overseeing in an excessively close manner.

4. Whatever your notes describe, it will have occurred to you that the structure which your organisation has adopted is partly because it sensitively reacts to the needs of its customers, and partly because organisational structure in large organisations is highly traditional and hard to change.

5. You should have written this mini-essay so that it might be expanded into an examination answer of, say, four handwritten sides. Note that to have done this activity properly calls for:

- A knowledge of established theoretical models;
- Prior observation and noting of local and personal phenomena;
- Reflection at a conceptual level;
- The ability to structure your thoughts.

Self-assessment questions

1. d.
2. b.
3. The number of subordinates reporting to one superior.
4. An organisation chart:

- Clarifies objectives;
- Provides flexibility for changes;
- Defines responsibility;
- Shows where delegation may take place.

5. These influence an organisation's structure:

- Nature;
- History;
- Size;
- Location;

- Philosophy;
- Skills;
- Technology.

6. On the principles of responsibility and authority.

7. Basic assumptions, norms and values, and artefacts.

8. Shared values.

9. Deal and Kennedy:
   - 'Macho';
   - 'Work hard, play hard';
   - 'Bet-your-company';
   - 'Process'.

10. Handy:
    - Power;
    - Role;
    - Task;
    - Person.

Unit 19

Student activities

1. You might, for example, have noted how a change in the *task* such as an increased emphasis on customer service will have changed the *technology* so that a telephone banking service could be introduced, which gave rise to the creation of a direct-banking division in the *structure*, requiring the training of current or the recruitment of new *people*. Or your change could have started at another point but had similar universal implications.

2. You might, for example, have considered expanding the staff rest area. The *problem* would be insufficient space for accommodating the staff comfortably. The *course of action* would encompass planning what space was available and the loss of such space for whatever is the present use; *diagnosis/analysis* would consider what the true benefits are of better staff rest-space; *alternatives* might be to improve the current staff area, or have rotas for its use; and *action* would be in obtaining finance, then clearing the new space, building work, purchasing new equipment etc.

3. Suppose, for example, you had selected to look at the introduction of a sales advisor in a management position. Was that person *trained*, or those who were selected to work with them? Were the jobs of those who had previously had selling responsibility *redesigned*? Was there any clear and deliberate *team development* in the way of meetings or team training? Were any *group problems* in terms of relationships between the new selling staff and other front-line colleagues addressed? Were there *meetings* to allow all to air views on progressing the change? And was any *restructuring* implemented to accommodate the new emphasis on selling?

4. Most manager do not possess only one kind of power, and they can operate with all five of French and Raven's suggested list:

- *Reward power* because they can control your merit rises or bonuses.
- *Coercive power* because they can apply the organisation's disciplinary code.
- *Legitimate power* simply because they are some grades higher than you.
- *Referent power* if they are role models and people you admire as managers.
- *Expert power* if they truly command a special knowledge of financial management.

Self-assessment questions

1. c.
2. d.
3. a.
4. d.
5. c.
6. Technology, people, structure, task.
7. The reasons given were:
   - Self-interest;
   - Contradictory assessments;
   - Misunderstanding;
   - Low tolerance to change;
   - Failure to see the success of change;
   - Failure to export the success to the resistors.
8. Charismatic, Traditional and Legal-Rational or Bureaucratic.
9. French and Raven list these:
   - Reward power;
   - Coercive power;
   - Referent power;
   - Legitimate power; and
   - Expert power.
10. Henry Mintzberg.

Unit 20

1. (a) A bank operates in a complex environment and is subject to a number of different influences. These can be summarised as
   - LEPEST & Co (legal, economic, political, ethical, social, technological and competitive).
   - All these factors had an influence on the Chancellor's action.
   - *Legal* – the banks were accused of price-fixing.
   - *Economic* – the country was in a recession and there were a lot of business failures.

- Small businesses had been encouraged by the government.
- They were also the group that suffered most in the recession.
- Small firms contrasted with the ability of the large to weather the recession.

Political

- The government was facing a general election in the next year.
- The banks provided a focus away from the government's economic policy.
- The government was seen to be taking action on behalf of small businesses.

Social and ethical

- The failure of small businesses would have an effect on the economy, leading to even more unemployment.
- The bank executives were seen to have large pay increases.
- The banks' discrimination against small businesses was seen to undermine society.

Technological

- Changes in the banks' systems made managers even more remote from their customers.
- Many tariffs were generated by IT systems.

Competition

- Few alternative sources of finance were open to small business.
- The difference between loan and equity-funded business was not appreciated.

(b) The banks defended themselves by showing:

- The cut in interest rates was usually passed on.
- Much of the higher tariff criticism was accounted for by the banks' offering interest on current accounts.
- The responsibility of the bank was seen primarily as belonging to shareholders rather than customers.
- The banks profits were reduced by the recession.
- The bank tries to act in the best interest of the customer, although this may be unpopular action at times.
- The banks did produce codes of practice and 'tariff guides'.

2. (a) A bank has an obligation to a number of different parties who have an interest in its activities.

   (i) *To the shareholders*

   - To provide a fair return on their investment and pay any monies owed.
   - To provide them with information about the activities of the organisation.
   - To comply with any relevant legislation.

   (ii) *To the employees*

   - To negotiate fairly.

- To provide employees with relevant information.
- To provide for career development and training wherever possible.
- To provide a fair reward.
- To comply with legislation relating to employees, e.g. Health and Safety at Work Act, Office Shops and Railway Premises Act. To follow disciplinary and grievance procedures.

(iii) *Customers*

- To provide value for money.
- To comply with relevant legislation.
- To provide information on services, charges, etc.

(iv) *The State*

- Account for taxes paid.
- Comply with relevant legislation.
- Take account of regulatory organisations.
- Responsibility to the community.

There can often be problems in deciding where the area of priority should be. This is sometimes expressed diagrammatically in the form of a continuum:

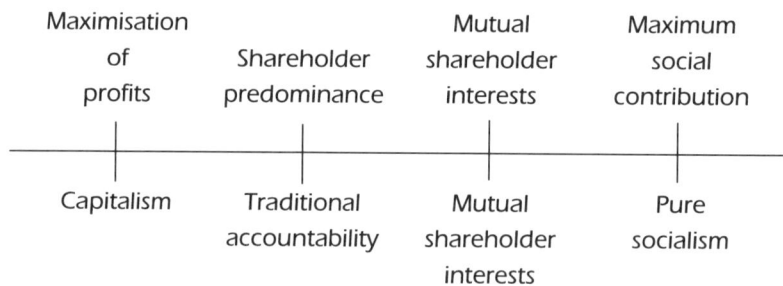

Maximisation of profits	Shareholder predominance	Mutual shareholder interests	Maximum social contribution
Capitalism	Traditional accountability	Mutual shareholder interests	Pure socialism

A business has to balance as fairly as possible the interests of the different groups, but conflicts can often arise.

Should salaries be increased at the expense of profits? Do you put employees or shareholders first?

(b) (i) *Shareholders and employees*

As indicated there is a conflict in deciding. The distribution of revenue, in salaries and conditions of employment versus investment and dividend.

Shareholders have consideration of higher dividends versus capital retention.

Employees want:

- Higher salaries;
- Investment in their working environment;
- Investment in human resources.

Both the interests of the groups could be served by:

- A drive for efficiency and concentration on results.

For employees

It is desirable to have a stable working environment and a commitment to long term employment, so the organisation should concentrate on:

- Keeping both sides informed of developments;
- Encouraging employee representation and participation as shareholders;
- Establishing fair negotiating systems;
- Using manpower planning;
- Establishing some means of rewarding through results.

(ii) *Employees and customers*

Customers want:

- Service;
- Flexibility of products and services;
- Better customer service areas in banks;
- Easy accessibility.

Employees want:

- Standardised procedures and products;
- Better working conditions (shorter hours, better premises).

Both the interests of the group could be served by:

- Specific training in customer services;
- Improved customer and staff areas;
- Good guidelines on product/service flexibility;
- Clear targets on quality of service;
- Flexibility in working hours and related rewards.

(iii) *State and shareholders*

The state is concerned with:

- Taxation levels;
- Legislative standards (either government bodies or self-regulating);
- A balance between control and the free market;
- A balance between competition and restrictions.

Shareholders want:

- Freedom from restrictions (minimum tax);
- Free markets;
- Restriction of foreign competition at home but free trade abroad;
- Profit maximisation.

Both the interests of the groups could be served by:

- Consultation between government and business;
- Commitment to the regulatory bodies;
- Compliance with legislation;
- Awareness of public opinion.

It is at times difficult for the banks to choose a path of action that will satisfy all interested parties, *but* the banks have over recent years managed quite successfully to achieve this objective. They now compete with the building societies on opening hours, but yet have retained the goodwill of staff.

Members of the banking group have written down/off Third World debt whilst retaining the goodwill of shareholders.

Note that the question asks you to consider only *two* of the three pairs. The three pairs are included here so that you can compare your answers with this suggested one.

3. The introductory sentence to this question gives some indication of how you should structure your answer, around the issues of strategy, structure, staff and systems.

    Strategy: Banks have had a choice of strategy:

    ● Operating globally;

    ● Remaining in traditional markets at home and abroad;

    ● Operating as a multinational (one central control);

    ● Operating as a conglomerate (multiple control bases);

    ● Operating as a niche player in the different countries;

    ● Or offering a more comprehensive service;

    ● Merger or acquisition of another institution;

    ● Or a joint venture with another institution.

    Structures: Banks have a choice of structures:

    ● Develop structures which reflect strategy;

    ● Enhance the chances of achieving objectives;

    ● Structure based on geography or product.

    Staff: Banks have a choice of staff:

    ● Using expatriate staff or local people;

    ● Remuneration and tax issues;

    ● Transferring culture and value systems.

    Systems

    ● Banks develop systems to reflect their structure.

    ● The systems have to reflect legal requirements.

    ● Systems to recruit, train and develop staff.

    ● Systems to deal with remuneration.

    ● Systems to provide communication.

    ● Systems to provide information.

4. Because of advances in information technology and communication, it is now frequently stated that banks are operating in a 'global village'. Banks operating in the international arena have new pressures and demands on their activities.

    The advantages banks possess for operating in the international arena:

    ● There is, as has been stated in the introduction, the importance of developing a global corporate strategy.

    ● The UK has a long tradition of international financial activity and export (although not necessarily in banking).

    ● London is a major financial centre.

- UK banks have started to operate on a global basis already.
- UK banks have a good reputation for stability and reliability.
- The banks have the new technology that makes international communications quick and effective.
- The banks possess trained and skilled staff with international experience.
- The banks can devote many resources to the exploration of new markets.

However, the banks have to acknowledge some weaknesses and problems.

The disadvantages:

- London faces severe competition from New York and Tokyo as a financial centre.
- Banks are very competitive nationally and internationally.
- Until recently banks have only focused on the domestic market: they can therefore lack the international viewpoint and experience.
- The large UK banks can sometimes be slow to innovate ideas and services.
- There has been poor business judgment in the international arena in the past and this might make them wary of doing too much too soon.
- Some countries are suspicious of foreign banks entering into their country, so expansion may be restricted. (Although Europe since 1992 no longer has any barriers to entry.)

It would seem that although the UK banks should be aware of possible problems and disadvantages, they are still in a strong position for expansion in the international arena. Before expansion, as part of the corporate planning exercise, a SWOT analysis (strengths, weaknesses, opportunities, threats) of the individual bank's position would need to be carried out.

5. (a) Growth in the service industries is normally built up by offering a good standard of attention and care to the customer. Customer care is therefore a fundamental concept in the bank's marketing philosophy.

   There are a number of steps that would be taken when initiating a customer care programme.

   (i) It would normally be developed as part of the bank's marketing strategy and therefore would involve some research into customer needs and the establishment of objectives.

   Politeness, efficiency, general attitudes of staff and appearance of staff can all convince the public that the bank can provide the standards the customer wants.

   There are other issues in the customer care programme, for example:

   - Opening hours;
   - Customer information that is easy to understand (including account information);
   - A faster service at peak times;
   - A quick resolution of problems;
   - The use of personal bankers in the banking hall to give some customer contact;

- Customer newsletters;
- Customers treated as if they matter (each letter or contact with a customer presents the opportunity for a good or bad impression).

(ii) A budget would need to be estimated for the proposed customer care programme.

(iii) Involve all staff in asking for ideas about aspects of customer care to introduce or concentrate on. The campaign will involve all levels of staff and it is therefore necessary to involve all staff in its conception as well as administration.

(iv) Draw up details of the campaign in the light of staff comments.

(v) Call meetings at appropriate times to discuss the campaign, allocate responsibilities, etc.

(vi) Train staff for the campaign, a possible technique is cascade training (training one person who can then train a group, each member of which can then train others, etc). As almost every member of staff is likely to be involved, an efficient and cost effective method of training will be needed.

Train staff in listening skills; advising, monitoring and assessing needs.

Staff also need to exercise sending and receiving skills with a good questioning ability, timing and pacing of speech, use of silence, personalising and verbal and nonverbal communication.

(vii) Ensure some evaluation of the programme will occur so its effectiveness in customer care can be assessed.

The importance of a high standard of customer care should be realised by the major banks, although it is not an easy concept to quantify. The banks have at the heart of their philosophy the idea that there is no point in emphasising the gain of new business, whilst losing existing accounts through poor service.

(b) There are a number of ways of ensuring that quality of service is maintained.

(i) In drawing up the campaign, set targets for staff to achieve. To encourage their achievement and maintain motivation, staff can be rewarded for high achievement. A points system could be used with gifts linked to the points achieved. Similarly, other rewards for successes can be given and achievement in the campaign can be built into the appraisal system.

(ii) Carry out market research to assess whether new quality of service is being maintained.

The market research could be divided into services, analysis and trends:

- Current account and money transmission analysis;
- Personal savings analysis;
- Consumer credit services analysis;
- mortgages and home improvement loans;
- Other personal market services.

As well as researching quality of service within service lines, research can also be carried out into market segment groups, e.g:

- Junior groups;
- School-leavers;
- Students;
- Women in work;
- Older/wealthier, etc.

(iii) 'Plant' an individual to test the quality of service received by a customer. It is a difficult technique to apply and can lead to a deterioration in employee relations. The agreement of unions or staff associations may be needed.

(iv) Ask the staff for feedback on how they perceive the programme to be developing and further action that could be taken.

6. This question subdivides into various issues: were the customer service programmes a failure? What circumstances do the banks operate in, and how do they compare with other sectors?

Were the customer service programmes a failure?

- The number of complaints was low (6,000 from a customer base of several million).
- Only 10% of these fell within the ombudsman's terms of reference.
- Many aspects of the bank/customer relationship were deemed to be satisfactory by the ombudsman.
- Banks' market share did not fall.

The circumstances in which the banks operate

- The UK is/was in recession.
- The banks are involved in many business failures.
- The banks got a bad press.
- This generated criticism.
- Customers are increasingly sophisticated and more willing to complain.
- The existence of the Ombudsman was seen by some as an opportunity to complain.
- The banks were seen by customers as acting together.
- There was a poor introduction and lack of reinforcement for the bank's customer service programmes.
- No attention was paid to the importance of the internal customer.
- Lack of commitment to the programme from non-customer contact staff.
- Lack of administrative support.
- The traditional banking culture did not encourage a retail customer service approach.
- Too little attention was paid to local initiatives – employees had no sense of ownership of the programme.

Comparison with other sectors

- The banks tried to portray themselves as retailers but the staff did not have the same experience.

- The banks' systems did not support this approach.

- Banks were not able to manage the customer, staff, products, and IT relationships.

- Banks not sure how best to market their products.

- Customers felt unable to move accounts – all they could do was complain.

7. This is an example of a textbook-type question. Examination of the allocation of marks reveals the number of points to be made in each section.

   (a) (i) A product structure divides the organisation into units where each is responsible for a part of a product or aspect of service of the business process.

   (ii) The product manager is responsible for all the activities which are required to produce and market a product.

   (iii) With this type of structure it is usual to find some functions remain centralised, e.g. corporate/strategic planning, personnel.

   (b) • The functional structure entails the grouping together into a unit or section of all those who share the same set of resources or expertise.

   - The divisional lines are likely to indicate those activities seen as crucial to the survival of the organisation.

   - The centralised functions are designed to co-ordinate the different divisions.

   - Clear promotion paths.

   - Allows for diverting of resources to areas which need them.

   (A maximum of four marks awarded.)

   (c) *The advantages of the product structure:*

   - Units can be run as profit centres because costs have to be recovered through successful sales of products.

   - Product units can be expanded or contracted without it affecting other sections.

   - The performance of the top management in the section can be assessed.

   - Provides a good training ground for general management, because product managers have to manage all activities.

   - Performance targets and reward systems easy to apply.

   - Co-ordination of services within unit is usually excellent.

   (A maximum of four points would be given.)

   The advantages of the functional structure:

   - Traditional and familiar structure;

   - High degree of specialisation;

   - Supervision easier because of concentration on a small aspect of business.

   (d) *Disadvantages of the product structure:*

   - Can encourage competition for resources.

- Does not allow for the development of functional specialisation at management level.
- Implementation of corporate strategy is difficult because of conflicting organisational and divisional goals.
- Creates a 'them and us' situation between centralised head office departments and product units.

Disadvantages of functional structure:

- Difficult to assess a department's performance.
- Change and innovation are difficult.
- Does not encourage the development of a general management stream.
- Slows down the introduction and processing of cross-functional issues.
- Conflict can arise between the different functional sections.

(e)
- An organisation which combines the benefits of both is a matrix structure.
- Managers are responsible for specific projects and have different functional specialists working for them on a particular programme.
- All members of the team have two superiors – their functional manager and the project manager.

8. (a)
- Culture is the atmosphere that distinguishes one organisation from another.
- It could be described as the way things are done.
- Culture is a representation of 'shared values', that is, the values people have in common.
- These are demonstrated in structure, systems, style and strategies.
- Selection seeks to identify applicants with similar values and attitudes.
- To maintain a culture the values must be obvious and exhibited.

(b) *Power culture:*

- Dominated by one individual who controls the system.
- Communication is through this central figure.
- Decision making is centralised.
- Little need for rules.
- Having the ear of the boss is important.
- Can try to compete for his attention.
- As the organisation grows it is more difficult to retain control.

People culture:

- People work as individuals.
- Use common services or resources.
- This allows for economies of scale.
- Common code of behaviour.
- No central control.

- Few rules and procedures.
- No need for individuals to conform.
- Little interaction between participants.

9. (a) Banks now need to manage costs because:
    - The recession has reduced profits;
    - They now pay interest on current accounts;
    - They compete with low cost operators;
    - Labour costs are high;
    - Not all the activities can be funded out of income.

    (b) The strategic initiatives banks have undertaken are:
    - IT as a way of cutting costs;
    - Restructuring to better control costs;
    - Moving labour to income generating roles;
    - Staff are using IT more;
    - Reducing staff numbers;
    - Reducing premises;
    - Using cheaper sites;
    - Reducing management levels;
    - Using performance-related pay so increases are partly funded out of profits.

    (c) • Forecasting expenditure.
    - Agreement of budgeted income.
    - Recording of budget.
    - Monitor expenditure.
    - Compare actual with budget.
    - Analysis of variance.
    - Corrective action.
    - Concentration on cost areas.

10. This is an example of a *World of Banking*-type question and refers to an article from *Banking World*. However, you may choose the areas to focus on in your answer. We suggest that you pick about eight areas; you then need to make three points in each area.

    (a) *Price competition:*
    - Because of deregulation there are now many organisations competing for the same market.
    - One feature which might give organisations a market lead is competitive pricing.
    - Technology can reduce processing costs and therefore ultimately the price of financial services offered to the customer.

    (b) *Segmentation:*
    - The banks are now moving towards an information data base rather than a transactional one.

- This allows information to be held about customers, e.g. age, sex, numbers and types of accounts held.

- This enables the bank to segment its customers in a number of ways and so sell relevant services to a target market. The previous type of marketing was a general mailshot. This should be more cost effective.

(c) *Oversupply:*

- Since deregulation there have been many more competitors in the financial services market. IT has meant much quicker processing time in launching new services.

- All companies understandably try to sell the most attractive profitable services.

- This could lead to an oversupply of financial services and saturation of the market with some companies failing.

(d) *Strategy:*

- IT now plays a crucial part in determining a bank's services, its quality of service, etc.

- Technology is of strategic importance to a bank and the future direction of IT must be linked to the bank's strategy.

- Investment in IT must be justified in terms of receiving an acceptable payback within a period and the investment being accommodated within the expenditure of the organisation.

(e) *People:*

- In the past, although IT has been introduced, the bank has continued to expand its services and so people have been deployed to other areas and no large-scale redundancies have occurred.

- In the future this may not be the case and some staff reductions may occur with the new systems introduced.

- However it may be that the demographic changes prevent redundancies. Technology may, in fact, help the banks to cope with what otherwise could have been a shortage of labour.

- Greater use of technology will mean staff have to be computer literate (word processing, spreadsheets, databases).

(f) *Investment:*

- Banks are large organisations and investment in IT has a lot to offer in terms of savings in processing time, quicker and better communications.

- The magnitude of the investment can however make it a risk-taking business for banks.

- Investment decisions can therefore be critical in determining the future success or otherwise of the bank.

(g) *Communications:*

- IT can prove a communications medium that is quick and efficient.

- This communication can be international as well as national.

- Banks will have to examine the feasibility of bank personal computers being linked into a national or local network to aid speedy communication between parties.

(h) *Income generation:*

- It will be expected to generate income as well as eliminate costs.

- This could be done by improving services to potential and actual customers.

- This can, at the moment, be seen in customer information systems which allow the marketing of products and services to be targeted and provide information for staff in contact with customers to establish their needs.

11. Organisational theory has played an important part in the development of business, influencing and in turn being influenced by its activities. Organisational theories can be divided into three different broad approaches. The Classical School to which FW Taylor belongs, the Human Relations School, that Mayo belongs to, and the Systems School.

   Taylor's writings were mainly concerned with organisational efficiency, and he was interested in trying to improve business productivity through a variety of means. He suggested the following broad principles:

   - Management should be concerned with planning, workers with doing.

   - People should be carefully selected to suit the job to which they are assigned.

   - People should be given a thorough training in order to aid their performance.

   - Each job should be broken down into its various components.

   - Employees should be rewarded according to their output and quality.

   Taylor was concerned with standardising and simplifying job method and first introduced the concept of work study and piece work. Much of Taylor's theory still applies today and his influence can be seen in banking in the work of highly routine tasks and the Organisation and Management (O & M) departments. The negative consequences of Taylor's work can be seen in dull monotonous work which results in low morale, higher labour turnover and absenteeism.

   Elton Mayo was initially interested in examining the effects of environmental conditions on productivity. However the results of his initial work (he found at the Hawthorne Plant in Ohio that the productivity of a small group at work increased whatever the environmental conditions) led him to conclude in his later studies that:

   - Man is an emotional animal: he has feelings as well as being logical and rational.

   - He will make a greater contribution at work if he understands the context of his job and knows of factors that affect him and his work. Employee communication is therefore important.

   - Managers must understand these needs and respond to them in their leadership style, interpersonal and communication skills.

   Mayo's contribution can also be seen as important today. In banking his influence is shown in the management development activities where communication, interpersonal skills and leadership training play a large part. His influence can also be seen in the procedure of selecting individuals for managerial positions.

The writers on managerial and organisational theory can be seen to have an influence on the activities of business today. Even though Taylor's and Mayo's work took place about 80 and 60 years ago respectively, the influence of their research and recommendations can still be observed.

12. (a) One key activity of a manager is forecasting. This involves a manager in:

- Examining the environment, so he can identify threats and opportunities.
- He can be pro-active (anticipate events), and this usually concerns opportunities, or he can be reactive (react to events), and this usually concerns threats.
- Forecasting looks to the future.

(b) Planning

- In a business as usual environment, managers should be following plans already established.
- It is important to consider plans when change is introduced.
- Planning involves establishing key tasks, success standards, short-term goals, actionable first steps and targets.
- Plans need to be monitored.

(c) Organise

- Need to match the resources available to the plan.
- Ensure financial, physical and human resources are available; that these are in the right place, at the right time and in the right number.
- Dependency on plan and monitoring.

(d) Monitor and control

- Check objectives achieved.
- Compare actual with plans.
- Analyse variances.
- Take appropriate action.
- Eliminate variance.
- Adjust plan so reflects achievable goals.
- Use of exception reporting, etc.

13. (a) The advantages of delegation are:

- More opportunities for delegatee.
- Greater motivation for delegatee.
- Allows greater trust between delegator and delegatee.
- Allows new experiences for delegatee.
- Greater flexibility in work allocation.
- Gives more time to delegator.
- More cost effective.

(b) Why managers are reluctant to delegate:

- Does not trust subordinate to do work.
- Subordinate not trained to do work.
- No time available for training or briefing.
- Worry that subordinate may do the job better.
- Subordinate unwilling/unable to take on more work.
- Subordinate unable to delegate any of his work.
- Job is rigidly defined so no scope for delegation.
- Delegation is not encouraged by the organisation.
- Senior management do not delegate.
- Guidelines by organisations mean certain jobs cannot be delegated.
- Customers (external and internal) will only deal with senior managers.

(c) Points to consider when delegating work:

- What are the benefits of the delegation?
- Can the subordinate cope with the delegated work?
- Is any training needed and how long will it take?
- What and how much monitoring is needed?
- Who needs to be told that the delegate is now completing the work?

14. (a) Martin has to make sure the department performs well in the future. The problems for Martin are:

- Trevor's sickness record.
- Trevor's search for a *new* job.
- The poor relationship between Trevor and Rebecca.
- Rebecca's poor organisation of her work.
- Rebecca's lack of team spirit.
- Rebecca's failure to adopt a 'managerial' role.
- Rebecca probably does not understand the concept of the role of the manager.
- The inflexibility of the section.
- The section's relationship with other departments.

(b) The obvious route for Martin to follow would be to dismiss Rebecca but this may be difficult because of the culture of the company.

- He needs to investigate Trevor's sickness record.
- He needs to investigate the section's image.
- He needs to instigate a disciplinary procedure with Rebecca so he can give her feedback about the section's targets.
- Agree new targets with Rebecca.
- Give training to Rebecca.
- Arrange to transfer Trevor.
- Monitor the section's progress.

15. (a) Analysis of the situation as *person accountable for the work of the project*:

- The project may be too long.
- Time is seen by the team as unimportant.
- Quality is seen by the team as important.
- Time delays are big and unacceptable.
- The project is over budget but this may be acceptable.
- Project is not controlled by senior management.
- A change of project is undesirable.

As the leader of the project team:

- The effort of the team is in the wrong direction.
- The emphasis is on the team rather than the project (Adair).
- Laura's behaviour is unacceptable.

(b) David should manage the situation by focusing on the task and individual rather than the group, but this may be unpopular.

- Consider the length of the project – it may be better to divide it in two and have shorter projects.
- Set targets for the team to achieve.
- Set standards of performance.
- Renegotiate budget.
- Use more resources.
- Set up control mechanisms.
- New project director.
- See Laura about lateness and her excuses.
- Take whatever action is needed.
- Stop the extended lunch break on Fridays.
- Ensure the priority is time, not quality.
- Achieve this through directive management.

16. Effective communication is a key activity in a successful organisation. The communication process incorporates many barriers and obstacles to effective communication and every employee should have some awareness of these difficulties.

(You could include Fig. 14.1 at this point.)

The Sender

There are certain key activities the sender can be involved in to ensure his message is clearly conveyed.

Aim. The communicator must have a clear idea of the information he wants to convey, by having clear objectives himself. It then becomes much easier for the receiver(s) to understand.

Preparation. The sender must think through the problem or idea he wants conveyed. The more he understands it, and the attitude of others toward it, the clearer his own communication is likely to be. He should also think about any additional information needed from other sources and any training needed in how to communicate.

Environment. The sender should consider the environment in which he is making the communication, particularly if it is to be a presentation: timing, what should be in writing (e.g. tables of figures, summary of main points), and the layout of the room. The traditional methods of communication in the organisation may also have an influence, because these have an effect on the attitudes of the receiver(s).

Presentation. At this stage the sender must anticipate the reaction of others, the barriers that may exist to stop effective communication and how to break them down. He must consider how to establish and maintain interest. He must also consider the media of communication, the use of tone of voice, expression and body language; and even style of presentation (tells, sells, consults). The sender must also be prepared to listen, not only to the verbal reaction of the receiver, but also to watch for signals from body language, gestures, etc. The sender can, through this, get useful ideas as well as showing a willingness to understand others.

Feedback. The sender could gain feedback from the communication thus enabling him to find out where it has succeeded and failed so he can improve next time.

The Receiver

The communication process is an interactive one. If the sender observes good practices he can reduce barriers and noise, but the receiver can also take steps to encourage a good communication process.

The receiver must:

- Be aware of possible barriers in his own attitudes and prejudices;
- Pay full attention to the communication;
- Respond positively to the sender, make contact, look interested, etc.;
- Respond in a neutral manner to the message and avoid excessive emotion;
- Give helpful feedback to clarify understanding and summarise the message.

The communication process contains many difficulties. Action by both the sender and receiver can aid the process and help remove some of the barriers.

17. Effective meetings do not just happen. There is a certain amount of work needed in their preparation and conduct that can add considerably to their usefulness as discussion and decision making tools.

    Preparation

    Selection of personnel. The chairperson, secretary and participants should be selected so it can be ensured all the skills, knowledge and roles needed to take a decision are present.

    Notice of meeting. All participants should be notified in good time of the time, location, objectives and agenda for the meeting. If relevant, the participants should also be sent minutes of the previous meeting so they are reminded of discussions and previous decisions taken.

    Preparation by and role of the chairperson. The chairperson should ensure he/she is aware of the objectives of the meeting and that participants have had the opportunity to prepare themselves. He/she should also be clear as to the leadership style to adopt, his/her rights (say to a casting vote) and the general regulations governing the meeting (quorum, etc.).

The meeting. The chairperson should state the objective of the meeting and ensure the participants understand it.

The chairperson should act as a guide, encouraging participants to present their views. He/she should encourage appropriate contributions, discourage the inappropriate, and curtail the lengthy ones. The chairperson should work through each item on the agenda, ensuring it is discussed and summarising the points as a consensus is reached, or draw attention to disagreements for further discussion.

The participants should express themselves clearly, listen to contributions by others, add to contributions by others, ensuring they are positive and lead towards the achievement of objectives. The participants should also raise queries if any points are made they do not understand.

The secretary to the meeting has a responsibility to record contributions or conclusions (if these are reached), and to draw up and send out the minutes ensuring that action recommended at the meeting is taken.

If each of the parties in a meeting follows the guidelines as to duties, then it is likely to be a more effective meeting with the decisions reached through relevant, adequate discussion.

18. Decision making is a key activity in organisational life and is carried out at every level: strategic, managerial and operational. Different types of decisions, require different amounts of information (external and internal), involve others to varying degrees and are decisions affecting different future periods.

    (a) ● Administrative decisions concern the regulation of the organisation and affect the timetable or routine of the business. These decisions can generally be dealt with by applying already established rules, procedures and systems.

    ● Operational decisions are concerned with making sure the daily business operations proceed smoothly. They arise in an unpredictable fashion and respond to changes in normal working patterns; for example when an output target is not met.

    Administrative decisions are concerned with applying rules already established, whereas operational decisions (because they respond to newly created situations) are one-off decisions. They often arise without warning and to make an operational decision requires skill in analysing, judging and innovating.

    Administrative decisions just involve applying rules. It would therefore seem the most difficult decisions are operational ones.

    (b) There are a number of possible structures available for decision making but most seem to involve very similar stages namely:

    ● Problem awareness;

    ● Define and gather more information;

    ● Specify;

    ● Diagnosis;

    ● Develop alternative courses of action;

- Establish criteria for appraisal;
- Appraisal;
- Choose;
- Evaluation.

(c) There are three common faults in decision making:

- The decision maker is risk aversive: he makes the decision that is the easy option and largely trouble-free, thus avoiding organisational and personal risks. However this is not always the *best* decision.

- The decision maker hesitates about the decision and the optimum time for making it is gone. Opportunities can be missed.

- The decision maker hurries the decision. He does not wait for all the relevant information and does not attempt to share the decision with his subordinates. The decision is not necessarily the best one.

(d) • A manager should share a decision with his subordinates when the commitment of subordinates to a decision is essential for its success. By sharing a decision the manager is far more likely to gain commitment, although it may not be the decision he personally would prefer. The decision could be delegated altogether, but whether the manager retains the decision or not depends on how important it is to him personally.

- A manager should refer a decision upwards when:
  - it affects other departments;
  - it has an effect on the boss's responsibilities;
  - it requires information which can only be supplied by the boss;
  - it has implications for the section's budget;
  - the boss is likely to feel he should be involved.

One model which is useful in deciding whether decisions should be shared or not is the Vroom and Yetton model of decision making, which tries to classify decision making and hence determine which decision making style is most appropriate.

19. (a) *The features which distinguish project management are:*

- A project is for a fixed time;
- A project involves a team;
- A project has a budget;
- A project utilises different skills;
- A project has objectives;
- The project members have two bosses.

(b) *Clear aims:*

- Aims are needed because projects introduce change;
- The aims detail what is expected of the project;
- Difficult for aims to be clarified at the start of the project;
- Aims may change as the project develops.

Sponsor:

- The project needs a sponsor who has influence in the organisation;
- The sponsor secures resources;
- The sponsor deals with political issues that may arise;
- The sponsor should be committed to the project.

Management structure:

- Project teams have their own structures;
- For large projects there may be a director;
- Who will allocate resources and oversee progress;
- Project managers are responsible for day-to-day operations.

Owner:

- The owner will benefit from the work of the project;
- The owner has a vested interest in the project's success;
- The owner has an interest in the project as it is running, because the owner will be most affected by an alteration in its aims.

Project team:

- The team should be chosen for their expertise;
- It helps if they work well together;
- Or time can be spent on team building;
- Important that issues relating to the matrix structure are dealt with.

Communication systems:

- Clear lines of communication are needed between project members;
- And the project and the owner;
- And the project and other areas of business affected by it.

(c) *Process of planning:*

- Give objectives;
- Estimate budget;
- Plan and secure resources;
- Define key results and tasks;
- Define standards;
- Allocate resources;
- Monitor;
- Compare actual and estimated results;
- Revise plan.

20. (a) *Factors to consider when choosing a career generally:*

- Important to make the right choice.
- The decision could be postponed.
- If it is postponed it is important to preserve flexibility.
- Katherine could address issues relating to work – does she want to work for an organisation or herself?

- If she wants to work for an organisation – what type?
- Seek advice from a career specialist.
- Try and find jobs that might suit her personality, etc.

(b) *Factors concerning a career in the banking industry:*

- Banks now recruit fewer people.
- Careers no longer fit a traditional pattern.
- It may take longer to be promoted.
- People may move horizontally not vertically.
- May work in a variety of areas.
- May enter banks at a number of levels.
- Staff specialise within banks.

(c) *The level at which Katherine should enter banking:*

- The bank has three main entry points – 16, 18 and 21 year olds.
- Employees can move between career streams although this is not usual.
- The entrant needs to choose the entry point with care as banks have many applicants for each level.
- Someone selected at a lower level may not be of a high enough quality to be considered at a higher level.

(d) *The subjects she should study:*

- May help to study commercial subjects.
- May help to have a foreign language.
- Needs to be computer literate.
- Have keyboard skills and word processing.

(e) *Other activities:*

- Be involved in Chamber of Commerce.
- Join debating society.
- Gain vacation work in a business.

21. (a) The problems with Julie's time management.

Paper in 'in-tray':

- Cannot deal effectively with paper;
- Inability to delegate;
- Inability to prioritise.

Time on telephone:

- Confusion about role;
- Inability to manage incoming calls;
- Inability to differentiate urgent and important.

14-page report:

- Brief unclear;
- Lack of assertiveness;
- Unclear about job components.

Two late appraisals:

- Inability to plan;
- Inability to work to deadlines.

Illness/lack of holiday:

- No balance of work and home life.

No idea how much work will arrive on her desk:

- No forward planning;
- Inability to schedule time.

(b) *Suggestions*

- Study job description.
- Consider core elements of her job.
- Assess work according to importance and urgency.
- Schedule time to deal with incoming items.
- Divert incoming calls to secretary.
- Deal with e-mail in bulk.
- Use 4Ds for paper:
  - deal with it;
  - dump it;
  - delegate it; or
  - diarise it.
- Do not accept work unless there is time to deal with it.
- Plan in deadline events.
- Establish balance between home and work.
- Complete time management training.
- Allow time for oneself (appointment with self) to organise work.

22. This is a textbook-type question and the marks are not divided in any way. It is likely that naming a factor minimising the risk of suffering from stress would be worth one mark and to elaborate by giving a description would be worth another two marks.

Individuals can take steps to minimise their suffering from stress:

(a) Relaxation – make an attempt to reduce stress by releasing tension. Concentrate on breathing. This has the effect of relaxing muscles and is calming to the body.

(b) Control and manage your environment maintaining a proper balance between work and leisure. Ensure that the individual plays a number of different roles and thus has different interests (but not too many).

(c) As part of this ensure care is taken of one's health and diet by eating less fats, starch and sugar, more fibre and keeping a sensible body weight.

(d) Again, avoid overdependence on drugs, tobacco or alcohol to relieve tension. Caffeine (as found in coffee) can be addictive.

(e) Ensure that one is fit by taking regular exercise. This is a means of relaxation, so reducing stress.

(f) Awareness of factors that induce stress – being aware of your attitudes or situations that create stress for you. The technique used is termed perceptual adaptation – interpreting situations in a positive way and so reducing stress.

(g) Manage one's time and work effectively. Be realistic about what can be achieved, be assertive and allow adequate time so things are not rushed.

Mention should be made of time management techniques:

- Better bandit control;
- Time with oneself;
- Deal with things once;
- Establish priorities;
- Manage by walking about, etc.

(h) Ensure that you have support to help you cope with situations. This support can be derived from another individual or group inside or outside work.

23. Demographic changes have received much attention over recent years. One of the most significant changes for banks is the drop in the number of school leavers available for work. By careful manpower planning and action, the problem of shortfall in recruitment can be resolved.

(a) To enhance the banks' chances of recruiting school leavers, they can:

- increase marketing expenditure aimed at school-leavers, e.g. more talks, brochures, adverts;
- focus advertising at school-leavers;
- encourage links with schools in the number of services the banks offer and give support to schools with placements;
- have a more attractive remuneration and career package for recruits, with some discretion given to the banks to respond to local competition with rates of pay, etc.

(b) Other actions the banks can take to fulfil manpower needs are:

- Reduce manpower needs. Introduce more technology to take over basic jobs. Streamline operations so not as much manpower is needed.
- Get a clear manpower plan with budget, and focus more sharply on the type of recruit needed.
- Reduce turnover by an attractive reward package, redeployment, better selection systems and late retirement packages, career break schemes and turning from full time to part-time staff.
- Focus on recruiting from different areas, i.e. minority groups, EU countries, women returning to work. Use part-time and job share staff.

The bank, in order to meet its manpower requirements, must make itself as attractive an employer as possible to potential as well as existing employees.

24. This is an example of a question addressing a topical issue: reduction in staff numbers.

    Again each point made is allocated a mark, so 15 points are needed in (a) and 10 in (b) for full marks.

    (a) When formulating plans for a reduction in workforce the factors that should be considered are:

    - The corporate strategy.
    - What developments are likely to affect this.
    - The manpower plan.
    - Sources of supply for future employees.
    - Workforce requirements in terms of age, numbers, skills, location.
    - Profile of current workforce in above terms.
    - Demographic trends.
    - Wastage trends for workforce.
    - Criteria for selection for redundancy.
    - Should recruitment be maintained.
    - Public image of company.
    - Redeployment and retraining rather than redundancy.
    - Policy for redundancy – voluntary or compulsory?
    - Communication to employees and unions.
    - Provision of counselling and support.
    - Costs.
    - Effect on morale of remaining staff.
    - Consequences for workload.

    (b) A manager should consider the following if someone is leaving:

    - Reasons for leaving (exit interview).
    - 'Demob' happiness.
    - Succession arrangements.
    - Recruitment of replacement.
    - Celebration of work done by employee.
    - Redefinition of role and jobs.
    - Reformation of team.
    - Continuing with customers and work.
    - Exit management paperwork (inform personnel, etc).
    - Leave the employee with a positive impression of the department.
    - Security.
    - Morale of remaining team.

25. (a) What the bank should do to ensure a pool of individuals to fill senior posts:

    - Ensure manpower planning is sound, so the bank recruits the right number of people eventually to fill these management posts.

- The bank must start with a good quality recruitment programme to ensure it gets the best candidates available.

- It should have a sound training and management development policy, so people are being given the skills and knowledge necessary to fill the senior posts. This must be backed up by a good appraisal system so people know their strengths and weaknesses.

- Encourage staff to develop themselves by sitting relevant professional examinations and offering opportunities at work for development.

- Ensure that individuals are offered career development and promotion opportunities to advance to the top jobs and match the vacancies with suitable candidates.

- Follow up initial manpower planning with succession planning so the top jobs can be filled from internal promotions.

- Offer rewards to the successful staff that will encourage them to stay with the organisation.

- For existing senior managers, encourage those still developing. A good coaching policy should be encouraged as well as on-the-job training.

(b) The individual, in order to enhance his chances of advancing to senior managerial posts, should:

- Be aware of strengths and areas that need developing, and be prepared to work at these to overcome difficulties.

- Have clear career goals and be flexible in pursuing them, so the individual can respond to changes in his job and career.

- Plan career moves and specify goals to achieve.

- Take training and job opportunities as well as reacting positively to appraisal comments.

- Learn about the organisation and its politics.

- Be prepared to study and try to balance work and life goals so the two are consistent.

- Raise himself by doing consistently high quality work and activities that get one noticed.

- Help the boss achieve his goals and find a good mentor to learn from: avoid working for poor bosses if possible.

- Develop the skills of good management. This includes:
  - technical skill;
  - interpersonal skill; and
  - cognitive ability;

  using Mintzberg analysis of roles: the
  - decisional;
  - interpersonal; and
  - informational role.

26. (a) *Three objectives for recruitment:*
    - Recruit best person;
    - Ensure all treated fairly;
    - Ensure good image of company.

    (b) *Key features of framework:*
    - Job analysis;
    - Man specification;
    - Job description;
    - Job advert;
    - Application form;
    - Short-listing;
    - Selection;
    - Decision;
    - Notification.

    (c) *Advert depends on your personal knowledge but should include:*
    - Job title;
    - Organisation's name and business;
    - Job location;
    - Nature of job;
    - Who you report to;
    - Qualifications and experience needed;
    - Age range;
    - Salary range;
    - Rewards and benefits;
    - Promotion possibilities;
    - How to apply;
    - Closing date.

27. (a) *Process of Selection*

    If the process for the selection and recruitment of staff is to be as effective as possible, it needs to follow several predetermined steps.

    (i) Prepare a job analysis. This will allow a job description and personnel or man specification to be drawn up. These are most effective if based on a standard format. The Rodger seven-point plan includes:
    - Physique;
    - Attainments;
    - Intelligence;
    - Aptitudes;
    - Interests;
    - Disposition;
    - Personal circumstances.

    The Munro-Fraser five-point plan includes:
    - First impressions;

- Qualifications;
- Innate ability;
- Motivation;
- Personal adjustment.

(ii) Advertise the job using the job description as the basis, in relevant journals, magazines and newspapers. It should be clear and specific about requirements.

(iii) Design an application form, so the candidate is only asked about relevant information.

(iv) Receive the application forms and carry out an application sift with the user department involved. Use a short-list, if only one set of interviews is to be held.

(v) Take up references, if this is part of the company procedure.

(vi) Interview candidates.

(vii) Apply tests: personality, IQ, ability, etc.

(viii) Carry out final selection of candidates: ensuring they fit in with current staff as well as meet the job and personnel specifications.

(b) *The Interview*

The interview is obviously a critical step in the selection process. Care has to be taken to arrange a suitable room with no interruptions. The interviewer should ensure:

(i) Adequate preparation.

(ii) The right questions are asked: open-ended not close-ended, so more than just a yes or no response from the interviewee is elicited.

(iii) The subject matter for questions is correct. It usually covers the points on Rodger's or Munro-Fraser's scale:

- Dates of starting and finishing each period of employment, education and training undertaken;
- Family background including marital status, children, etc;
- Health record and state of health (there may also be a medical examination);
- Interest and leisure;
- Information on experience of work and handling cash, etc, in position of trust;
- Any other areas that need investigation from the application form.

(iv) The pattern of the interview should be explained with the procedure for offer of a job and rejection.

(v) If there is a need for tests, these should be arranged as part of the selection process.

(vi) The interviewee should be told about the company, job, salary and prospects. The interviewer may involve the supervisor.

(vii) The interviewer should be aware that this is a public relations exercise for the company and the motivation of the candidate can be raised by answering questions frankly when raised at the interview.

(viii) The interviewer should be aware of the problems associated with interviews:

- Personal bias;
- Halo effect;
- Stereotypes, etc, when assessing the candidate and filling in the rating form.

28. There are a number of factors which could explain the varying rates of turnover amongst clerical staff.

   (a) The difference in organisation:

   - Size: one organisation could be larger and less personal;
   - Structure: there could be difficulties in communication;
   - Supervision: the quality as well as amount of supervision may vary;
   - Nature of work: there could be a large scope for variety and development;
   - Interest of work: the work could be more varied in a branch;
   - Opportunities for reward, promotion, personal ambition, training.

   (b) The difference in employees:

   - Selection procedure: there could be better selection procedures in the branch;
   - Age: there might be younger employees at head office who are more likely to leave;
   - Qualification: head office staff might be better qualified and more able to leave;
   - Ability: head office staff are more likely to move on.

   (c) The difference in environment:

   - Travel time and cost: in the branch there may be locally employed people who have minimum travel costs and find the job very convenient;
   - Physical conditions of work might be more attractive in the suburb: the head office might be located in a noisy, dirty part of town, with difficult parking and no convenient public transport available.

   Provide a questionnaire for staff: explore altering environmental factors, e.g. travel allowance, new office layout, flexitime.

   Consider altering organisation issues, e.g. job rotation, enrichment, rewards and structure of departments.

   If the bank wishes to lower the turnover rate at head office, they must initially establish the causes. They could do this by providing an exit questionnaire and perhaps interviews for staff who are leaving, asking them about various factors: travel time, location, etc.

   In response to the questionnaire the bank may wish to make alterations in selection procedure, working conditions, flexitime, office layout, travel allowance, job rotation and enrichment, and reward systems.

29. (a) Steve has problems with motivation and organisational systems.

 (i) *Motivation*

 ● Pauline has put in effort.

 ● She expects the appraisal/reward system to measure effort.

 ● Steve needs to contain costs. If Steve does not reward Pauline, she may become demotivated and withdraw effort.

 ● Steve also needs to see the effect of what he does on Pauline.

 ● Difficult to recognise Pauline's effort without overrating her.

 (ii) *Organisational systems*

 ● Four systems overlap: job evaluation, appraisal, remuneration and budgets.

 ● Pauline is now doing a different job and it needs re-evaluating.

 ● Appraisal and reward should be different systems.

 ● Steve could use the appraisal to reward Pauline, but this would mean her rating is not really appropriate.

 ● Re-evaluation of her job would take time and is outside Steve's control.

 (b) You can argue in favour of overrating Pauline or rating her accurately and risking a loss of motivation, but you must be clear as to the path of action and why.

30 (a) *Issues:*

 ● Only Keith's views available – find out Gill's.

 ● Was Keith the right man?

 ● Why didn't he fit into the department?

 Induction: not carried out well.

 Training: error oriented.

 Development: appraisal not utilised.

 Operation of departments: not co-ordinated and not paying attention to social aspects of work of department.

 Management style: by Gill is authoritarian.

 (b) *Proposed course of action:*

 ● Need for caution.

 ● Gill's views not known.

 ● Keith's views not known to Gill.

 ● Need to improve for Ian.

 ● Coach Gill.

 Therefore:

 ● Ask for induction plan for Ian.

 ● Ask for Ian's job description.

 ● Discuss why Ian was selected.

 ● Management problems that may result.

 ● Monitoring mechanism.

 ● Resolve to talk to Gill about management style.

31 This question, although largely a scenario based one, still requires text-book knowledge to answer part (a), allocated 10 marks. You are expected to give the theoretical aspects of planning a training programme – that is, the stages to be covered in such a plan.

(a) (i) Training has as its objective to improve the performance of an employee at a given job.

(ii) The employee should be shown the context of his work in terms of the organisational and departmental needs.

(iii) The first stage in planning a training programme is to use a job analysis to decide the skills, knowledge and attitudes required by a particular job.

(iv) The second stage is to assess the skills, knowledge and attitudes possessed by the trainee.

(v) The difference between these two is termed the training gap and the programme should concentrate on reducing or eliminating the gap.

(vi) Plan the training in terms of a time schedule, detailing the skills and knowledge to be gained.

(vii) Consider the most suitable method for carrying out the training.

(viii) Secure the resources needed to carry out the training.

(ix) Carry out training with monitoring and evaluation.

(x) Get feedback from the employee on training.

(b) (i) *Training available*

There is no-one in the section, apart from his predecessor that Bruce can learn from – this creates problems and suggests an early training course, followed by a two-week session observing and being instructed by his predecessor might be one solution. However two weeks is a short time! The alternative is to observe for four weeks, but the course providing a theoretical framework for the job would not take place for five months.

The other factor the manager should consider is the effectiveness of Fiona as a trainer.

(ii) *Learning style*

From the information given it seems Bruce is a reflector (Honey & Mumford) – he learns best from observing others and considering his own experiences.

He does not respond to a 'throw him in at the deep end' approach and would do best to undertake considered learning at his own speed.

(iii) *Other considerations*

Bruce should be given targets in the job and his own learning to aim for.

Bruce should be carefully monitored and evaluated. He should be set tasks to achieve. Bruce should be encouraged to acknowledge his own learning styles and plan his own training and increased knowledge of the job.

32. Job Evaluation

Job evaluation can be defined as an attempt to provide a fair pay structure by comparing jobs or their parts and the relationship between them.

(a) *Advantages of Job Evaluation*

- Job evaluation tries to impose a system which attempts to be fair in assigning values to jobs.

- It provides a standardised system for salary structure.

- Because job evaluation concentrates on aspects of jobs, it can be used across different jobs, highlighting common tasks.

- It can take into account any job changes, even altering grades if necessary.

- Employees can understand the system easily, and problems of gradings and salary can be explained clearly.

- It can be used to reward factors important to the organisation.

- It gives employees a clear understanding of job design.

Drawbacks of Job Evaluation

- All types of job evaluation systems involve some subjectivity in judging the worth of different aspects.

- It is expensive to introduce initially and can become very rigid over a period of time, not responding to changes in market demand. If one category of staff becomes more marketable then this category has to be altered to account for this.

- The job evaluation system must therefore be continually monitored as changes occur in the job and the factors involved.

- The system indicates the relationship of one job to another but does not assign a monetary value to it.

(b) *Two Types of Job Evaluation System*

One is quantitative: for example, the HAY/MSL System uses a point scoring system giving numerical value to components of jobs and then weighting them. Once a final score is arrived at the jobs are then ranked. The factors used in the HAY/MSL system are things like job knowledge, skills, responsibility. It is useful when a wide variety of jobs has to be evaluated.

The second is non-quantitative: something like a benchmark system which ranks all jobs on the basis of the job description. It is normally used in small organisations to determine a hierarchy of jobs which are comparable in task, e.g. all those in personnel department.

This system is easy to use.

(c) *Steps an Organisation Takes in Implementation*

- Choose the most appropriate job evaluation system.

- Discuss the system, why it has been chosen and its operation, with staff.

- Include the right to appeal.

- Provide for changes in evaluation if job content changes.

- Ensure all staff are represented in the administration of the system.

- Monitor the system and make sure it is working.

Job evaluation is an effective means of assigning values to jobs, *but* people are very sensitive about the worth of their jobs and any system must be introduced and administered with care.

33. Two supervisors are appraised, both get reasonable results, but manage in different ways. Jim emphasises training in different tasks, so his staff are well-trained and he suffers from higher labour turnover because they move on to other parts of the organisation. Charles trains people well in just two tasks at most. He is respected and fair but staff leave for other careers and he has a high sickness rate with good output figures.

- Charles is rated more highly because the bank is probably looking at short-term productivity measures.

- However, the bank should consider the longer-term factors: for trained people to leave the bank costs money, because there has been substantial investment in training now wasted.

- Jim has trained his staff in many jobs. This gives employees flexibility and is to the bank's advantage in filling vacancies and covering for absence.

- High rates of sickness also cost the bank money but often are not taken into account like labour turnover.

- Charles being rated more highly, is being encouraged as a supervisor to follow the shorter-term goals and emphasise productivity at the expense of longer-term benefits, like trained staff.

The appraisal system should perhaps be altered to try and examine several aspects of a manager's role: his interpersonal relations as well as productivity, motivation of staff, etc.

- It seems that Jim's employees are being promoted frequently because of their skills across several jobs, yet no account is taken of this in the appraisal form for Jim and Charles. It would seem there is a conflict of objectives. The supervisors are not being encouraged to carry out work (extensive training of staff), which is essential for the long term health of the organisation.

- The appraisal form does not examine the managerial styles of supervisors. Charles is tending to act in an authoritarian manner, closely supervising employees, limiting their work and responsibility. He acts as a strict disciplinarian, who expects high productivity from his staff. Jim acts in a more liberal and democratic way, training staff intensively and introducing variety of work. Although in control of the department, he does manage it in a more casual way than Charles, which encourages motivation from his staff.

34. *Problem*

It appears that the group is not working effectively as a team:

- Poor productivity;
- Targets missed;
- Absenteeism higher;
- Interpersonal conflict;

- Lack of co-operation;
- Apathetic and at times hostile.

Recommendation

Adair provides a useful framework for encouraging effective group working by a leader. He suggests the leader should be concerned with three factors: the task, the group needs, the individual needs.

(a) *Task*

The leader should make all members aware of the aim of the section and discuss it with them. Standards of achievement should be set. Information should be provided on progress towards these standards at regular intervals. The leader should ask for ideas about improving performance and draw on the needs and abilities available to enable him to do so.

(b) *Group needs*

The leader should encourage the co-operation of the group by holding regular meetings to discuss progress and ask for ideas in solving problems. He should encourage social activities by the group thus encouraging group feelings and the desire to help one another. Encourage activities and ideas to aid the development of the team.

(c) *Individual needs*

Define and clarify roles and interdependencies. Meet and discuss work progress, setting individual goals for the section. Review progress of each. Identify areas for improvement, and coach or offer training. Encourage and reward good performance and reprimand bad. Encourage individual initiative to achieve group tasks.

Indications you are succeeding:

- Targets achieved;
- Reduced overtime;
- Reduction in sickness, labour turnover, absenteeism;
- Discussion of problems open and frank;
- Co-operation between members;
- Plenty of good ideas;
- Lively meetings with contributions by all;
- Enthusiasm and energy.

35. As a newly appointed supervisor, you have entered into a situation where certain things are fixed. These things are static, and are termed by Adair the 'givens' of the situation.

- The nature of the group you are supervising, i.e. the people given to you in the group.
- The task the group has been given to complete the targets and goals that have been set to achieve.
- The broad environment in which the group operates: the organisational climate and culture (although you can have an influence on the atmosphere in which the group works). The room or rooms in which the team works, although there could be some alterations in layout introduced.

These factors, because they are given and cannot be altered to any great extent, are not really things that would play a part in *you* getting your section to work effectively as a team, although they will obviously have an influence on the way you behave and alter other factors.

There are, in addition, certain factors which you can directly alter and adjust to influence work:

- Leadership style: although you cannot change the members of your team, you can influence their behaviour, motivation and work, with your leadership style. By offering advice and support to members, helping them build on their strengths and identifying and improving weaknesses, the skill of the team can be improved. The leader can also give individual attention, again motivating others with feedback on progress.

- The processes and procedures used by the group: you, as leader, can have some influence over the standards of work and set targets for each individual within the team. They can then be evaluated on their performance, thus increasing the motivation experienced by the group. Each member of the group needs to be encouraged to co-ordinate his work with other members and be helped in seeing the task of the group and his particular contribution as a worthwhile and essential part of organisational procedures.

- The way in which the manager operates – his enthusiasm, interest and openness – will influence the productivity of the group and the degree of satisfaction experienced by members.

- Relationship with other sections: the manager is responsible for relationships with other departments and sections. He should encourage good liaison with other teams and make resources available when and where they are needed by his group.

Index